RED-HEADED REBEL

SUSAN L. MITCHELL
Poet and Mystic of the Irish Cultural Renaissance

Susan Mitchell by JB Yeats, 1899

Red-Headed Rebel

SUSAN L. MITCHELL
Poet and Mystic of the Irish Cultural Renaissance

HILARY PYLE

The Woodfield Press

This book was typeset in Ireland by
Gough Typesetting Services for
THE WOODFIELD PRESS
17 Jamestown Square, Inchicore, Dublin 8.

© The Woodfield Press and the author 1998

The catalogue record for this title
is available from the British Library.

ISBN 0-9528453-7-7

Printed in Ireland
by Genprint Limited

For
Colm, Sorcha, Dúinseach and Manus

Here's to their sense of humour
and their love of Ireland

Contents

Part Two: SUSAN – 'A KIND OF RENAISSANCE' [1899–1926]

    The Irish Homestead   75

12. 'Down by Sligo'
    A Western Inspiration   92

13. 'Persons are my medium'
    A Shy Verbal Cartoonist   104

14. 'Art, the most strait-laced lover'
    The Living Chalice and *Aids to the Immortality of Certain*
        Persons in Ireland   118

15. 'By high ideals fired'
    A Dublin Full of Tensions   129

16. 'My distinguished sinfulness'
    Franchise and Frankincense   142

17. 'He still prances naked . . . before a prudish world'
    George Moore as an Over Ripe Gooseberry   155

18. 'With patriotic glow'
    The Dublin Insurrection   167

19. 'The first faint hopes of Ireland's future'
    The First Irish Convention   178

20. 'The first fruits of the gun'
    Peace *Morya*   189

21 'Everything good & bad has boiled up'
    Living through Civil War   206

22. 'Death my gentle nurse'
    Susan's Last Days   218

    Susan Mitchell's Writings   227

    References   230

    Sources of Chapter Titles and Illustrations   233

    Index to Persons and Places   235

List of Illustrations

Foreword

The enormous interest in Susan Langstaff Mitchell, still remembered by friends and relatives who knew her in Dublin in the nineteen-twenties, was a constant stimulus when writing this book. Kitsy Mitchell, her niece, and Michael McGuinness and George Mitchell, her great-nephews, provided the family papers, memoir and letters from which her life has been traced. For personal memories, I have relied particularly on three people, who sadly have not lived to see the completed book: her nephew, Michael Hermann Franklin, Fitzroy Pyle, a cousin, and Elizabeth Fitzpatrick, whose mother, Mabel Purser, was a close friend of the poet. Elizabeth Fitzpatrick read the manuscript, suggested changes, and made other pertinent comments, for which I am most grateful. All of her advice was illuminating.

Other members of the family who helped with reminiscences and illustrative material were the writer's nieces, the late Dora McGuinness and the late Stella Latham. Niall Moore of Cork did some essential photography, and Marie McFeely was really helpful in finding appropriate portraits and other illustrations, as was Liz Forster.

Among many who were generous with assistance and information, I would like to mention especially the late Shane Flynn of Carrick-on-Shannon; Eddie Fraser of Sligo; Pádraig O Snodaigh; Leslie Matson; Bud Burke; Joe McGovern; the Knight of Glin; Dr. P. Kelly; the late Colonel James Doyle; Pamela Latham; Norah Good; Bill McCormack; Susan Parkes; Muriel Gahan; and the late Liam Miller. Professor William Murphy provided transcripts of letters from John Butler Yeats and Lily Yeats, and a most welcome enthusiasm for the subject. Sadbh Coffey and Dr. Michael Solomons also contributed letters. I am grateful also to Trevor West, biographer of Horace Plunkett, for much encouragement and an abundant supply of references; to Dean Browne, Canon D. L. Keegan, and the Reverend Philip Knowles for assistance with tracing births, marriages and deaths of the Cullen and Mitchell families; and to Sorcha and Duinseach Carey for their humorous and constant support in many ways, not least in the tortuous matter of making an index.

I thank also the librarians and staff of the following, where relevant papers and memorabilia are, for their expert assistance: the National Library of Ireland; the National Gallery of Ireland; the Hugh Lane Municipal Gallery of Modern Art, Dublin; Trinity College, Dublin; University Colleges, Dublin and Cork;

the City Library, Cork; Offaly County Library; Sligo County Library and Museum; the Representative Body of the Church of Ireland; Armagh Museum; the Public Record Office; the Plunkett Foundation for Co-Operative Studies, Oxford; the War Office, London; the Houghton Library, Harvard University; and the Archives of the Allied Irish Banks Ltd. Finally I owe my gratitude to the board and staff of the Tyrone Guthrie Centre, Annaghmakerrig, for a halcyon haven in which to finish the writing at ease: and to Maurice Carey for his interest and support and patience at all times, even when reading proofs. Helen Harnett has been very sympathetic as an editor, and once again it has been a joy to work with Terri McDonnell.

The chapter titles are from the poems and prose of Susan L. Mitchell; and the portrait of her house, 'Halcyon', by Mike Carroll, is illustrated by kind permission of Margaret Gunn.

Chronology

1866   Born 5 December in the Provincial Bank House, Main Street, Carrick-on-Shannon, Co. Leitrim, fifth of seven children of Michael Thomas Mitchell and Kate Cullen.

1873   Death of Michael Mitchell. Adopted by three paternal aunts in Dublin. Rest of family moves to Sligo, two adopted by maternal aunt. Susan educated at Morehampton House School. Takes Trinity College Women's Examination with honours.

1884   Moves with aunts to Birr, Co. Offaly. Reacts against unionism of Mitchell family, and gradually drawn to Parnellism.

1897   Lives briefly in Sligo after death of last aunt, Jane, and teaches in her sisters' infant school. Death of fiancé, Douglas Crook. First sign of tuberculosis. To London for medical treatment and editorial training. Lives with the Yeats family as companion to Lily Yeats for two years.

1899   Portrait painted by JB Yeats. Returns to Sligo. Urges mother Kate to write her memoirs.

1900   To Dublin as sub-editor on the *Irish Homestead*, published by the Irish Agricultural Organisation Society (IAOS).

1902   Meets George Russell (Æ). Joins Dublin Hermetic Society. Poetry published for the first time in *A Celtic Christmas*. Begins performing satires and political parodies at parties.

1903   Clinic at Yverdon, Switzerland.

1904   Susan's poems included in Æ's *New Songs*.

1905   Æ appointed editor of the *Irish Homestead*.

1907   Death of brother Gilly. Kate and sister Jinny leave Sligo to live with Susan in Dublin at 16 Frankfort Avenue.

1908   *Irish Homestead* moves from Lincoln Place to new office in Plunkett House, Merrion Square. John Butler Yeats leaves Dublin for New York, and corresponds regularly with Susan. *Aids to the Immortality of*

          Certain Persons in Ireland published by New Nation Press, *The Living Chalice* by Candle Press.

1909   Publicly criticises WB Yeats's theatrical policy in article in *Sinn Féin*.

1910   Founder member of the United Irishwomen, later renamed the Irish Countrywomen's Association (ICA).

1911   Death of sister Bidz. Adopts and educates her Brabazon nieces.

1912   Article on co-operation in South African paper, *The State*. Joins the Irishwomen's Franchise League. Publishes *Frankincense and Myrrh*.

1913   Death of mother, Kate Cullen. Supports the General Strike.

1914   Critical of Church of Ireland attitude to the War. Later acclaimed leader of progressive views in Cumann Gaedhealach na hEaglaise (Irish Guild of the Church), and elected Chairman. Grace Gifford's cartoon of Susan published.

1916   Easter Rising. Looks after Constance Markievicz's affairs while the Countess is in jail. Publishes *George Moore* (Maunsel Press, *Irishmen of Today*), which is received enthusiastically.

1917   Lampoons first Irish Convention, set up by Æ and Lloyd George.

1919   Contributes to the first *Irish Statesman*, founded by Plunkett as voice of the Irish Dominion League. Delivers public lecture on JB Yeats.

1921   Satirises plans of Lloyd George and Carson for partition. Sympathy for Sinn Féin. Break up of home at 25 South Leinster Road, as nieces emigrate. Reviewing for *Freeman's Journal*. Major operation.

1922   Criticises Republican outrages strongly. Financial crisis in the *Irish Homestead* is overcome by readers. Attends opening of Free State Dáil.

1923   Plunkett's home, Kilteragh, burned in Troubles. Sub-editor to revived *Irish Statesman*, writing articles and reviews. Moves to final home, Halcyon, in Rathgar Avenue, where her *At Homes* become famous. Contributes to W.G. Fitzgerald's *The Voice of Ireland*.

1924-5 Becomes ill while in Portrush on holiday. Reviewing novels and plays in *Irish Statesman*.

1926   Operation on eye. Dies 4 March. Buried at Mount Jerome Cemetery, Dublin.

Introduction

'My Wild Will Spreads Its Wings'

Armagh Notebook

While Susan L. Mitchell had been a household word at home for as long as I can remember, and as a student I often perused a studio portrait photograph of her which I had been given, her life (apart from her poetry) started for me in the shape of a couple of large cardboard boxes, stuffed with letters and papers, that landed on me by chance some years ago. Layered among the tattered envelopes were old faded snapshots, a small circular watercolour in which I recognised the initials of the artist Pamela Colman Smith, and two worn hair brushes. There were some small books of poetry, a lock of red hair wrapped carefully in tissue, a torn page outlining some mysteries of Masonic procedure, a kid glove and an ivory notebook, where names pencilled over a century ago can be read faintly.

A wad of mouse-eared paper covered with pencil manuscript lay against some carbon typescripts. At the bottom of the first box was a crumpled violet tinted silk cloth, announcing in black capitals a melodrama performed in Carrick-on-Shannon one hundred and forty years ago. In the other, wedged beneath the flap, was a handsome framed photograph of three sisters, caught together unexpectedly in a garden in the past, unfolding their personalities slowly in expressions which I learned gradually were true to themselves.

Add to these the sequence of memoirs of the last century, recorded by Susan's mother, Kate Cullen, some scribbled in a black covered exercise book, others typed no doubt by Susan Mitchell in the *Irish Homestead* office where she worked, to be circulated among the family. Here was a further dimension.

The boxes were full of such memorabilia as their niece had gathered together hurriedly about the time of the funeral in 1961 of Susan's youngest sister, Victoria Diana, then over ninety, in Sligo. Nancy (who had also been christened with the family name Susan) intended that they would form a biography. She was convinced that one day I would write it. Many years later, when Nancy died, the papers came to me through the poet's great-nephew.

Susan Mitchell had been born into a Protestant ascendancy, which endured a rude jolt and a step downwards in their own estimation about the middle of the last century. Her hopes and sensibilities were atune to the class in which she had been nurtured, and, while she embarked on a professional life with inspiration and purpose, it was always with the notion that she worked only because she had to. Not that she objected to her lot. She thrived as a writer and as the satirical commentator of her generation, and still carried out her responsibilities to the less fortunate in society. But she was always conscious that the principal literary geniuses of the time, like her, had almost all originated in a caste society elected at birth.

So what had started out as a projected biography of the poet, Susan Langstaff Mitchell, quickly became a wider undertaking, tracing the descent and the life of the poet's landed ancestors. This was published last year by the Woodfield Press as *The Sligo Leitrim World of Kate Cullen*. Susan Mitchell was fascinated by her forbears and their family connections. She depended on her Protestant planter roots for her literary energy; and was eager to graft these roots on to the native culture, bypassing religious divisions. In the liberal society in which she found herself, that claimed a common national inheritance and had one common aim, her creative gift had found a lasting voice.

She persuaded her mother Kate to write down all she could remember of her family and her personal experiences in the memoir, which, with the papers, letters and other memorabilia, forms the biographical background to the book.

Like the Yeats family it took just two generations of vital colourful personalities to span a whole century. Susan Mitchell's mother, Katharine Theresa Cullen (later Kate Mitchell), was born in Co. Leitrim in 1832, the youngest of a family of ten fathered by Lieutenant-Colonel John James Cullen, descendant of a Scottish general who had been rewarded with land at Manorhamilton by Cromwell. Her first ten years were spent in Skreeney, the great house of Manorhamilton, where the Lieutenant-Colonel looked after his deceased brother's son's estate. Her grandfather had not only been heir to Skreeney, but was rector of the parish of Manorhamilton too. The family portraits hanging in the diningroom were constant reminders of the ancestors whose eccentric characters left their mark on the impressionable child.

Her own generation and the extended family had idiosyncrasies also, which she noted with enjoyment during lengthy visits to her married sisters in Donegal, Sligo and Carrick-on-Shannon. The security of her sheltered upbringing, in a privileged environment with butler and liveried servants, was shattered when her father died and Skreeney reverted to her bizarre cousin, Carney Cullen, who with his family was worthy of inclusion in an Edgeworth tale. Kate went to live in Dublin, where she attended a privileged school, and continued to visit her relatives in the West. She was first engaged to a military officer working on famine relief, later to the governor of Portlaoise Prison, and finally settled down to a more conventional life as wife of the first bank manager in Carrick-on-Shannon, in County Leitrim, where her daughter Susan was born. Michael Mitchell's premature death brought about the separation of her family, some adopted by close relatives, while she went with the remainder to seek a living by various means in Sligo.

While raised in Dublin, away from her family, Susan was eventually to rediscover her essential blood bond, especially with her mother, Kate Cullen, whose striking red hair and warm captivating personality she shared. Kate came to spend her declining years in Dublin when Susan was enjoying a kind of notoriety as a mystic-cum-satirist. Despite her advanced age, Kate played her familiar role as hostess to her daughter's literary circle.

But Susan was daughter also to the equally attractive Michael Mitchell. Because of her exceptional qualities, she had been brought up as a member of her father's close-knit unionist family, given an excellent education in Dublin, and brought to the Mitchell stronghold in Birr, Co Offaly, where they reigned as Crown Solicitors for three generations.

The first part of this story is about the early period of Susan's life, when she compared herself with a cork on a wave. She was a gentlewoman, unmarried and without profession or aim, walled into a confining society. But she was a beauty, confident in her personality and strongminded, with a capacity for deep affection that she longed to express. Her sense of humour led her at least to study the wealth of character about her, her strong mystic sense developed the poet in her. While typical of her privileged class, she rebelled quietly against the rigid ruled establishment in which she had been raised, laying the ground for her later vocation as literary and social critic.

Life changed for her dramatically in her 33rd year. The collapse of her adopted home, the end of an unsuitable relationship, and a life threatening illness, sent her to London, where she became a life long friend of JB Yeats and his daughter Lily and gained entrance to the Irish literary world.

Part II tells of her personal renaissance on her return to Dublin, now living at the centre of the most exciting cultural quake since before the Act of Union. She was literally in the middle of the movement for Home Rule, intimately involved with Plunkett's co-operative journal, *The Irish Homestead*. Her remarkable personality unfolded in an individual fashion. She was now self-consciously a modern woman. She was a minor, but original and extremely popular, author, playing on her different instinctual strings so as to enhance the Irish Literary Revival in memorable musical phrases. Painters loved to paint her. Conversationalists listened eagerly to her lampoons sung in a rich contralto voice to traditional Irish lyrics. An ardent republican, she was equally confirmed in her pacifism. All Dublin was entranced with her during her short lifetime, and remembered her for her warmth and unusual beauty.

Susan's own letters and manuscripts have assisted in fleshing out events - her life as it was expected to be and her life as it became. Her contribution to the Irish cultural renaissance as a poet and satirical bard has always been acknowledged. Now through her own previously unpublished commentary and through excerpts from her poetry, her personality is allowed to speak more roundly on its behalf.

PART ONE

Susan – 'A Cork on a Wave' (1866–1899)

Mitchell Family Tree

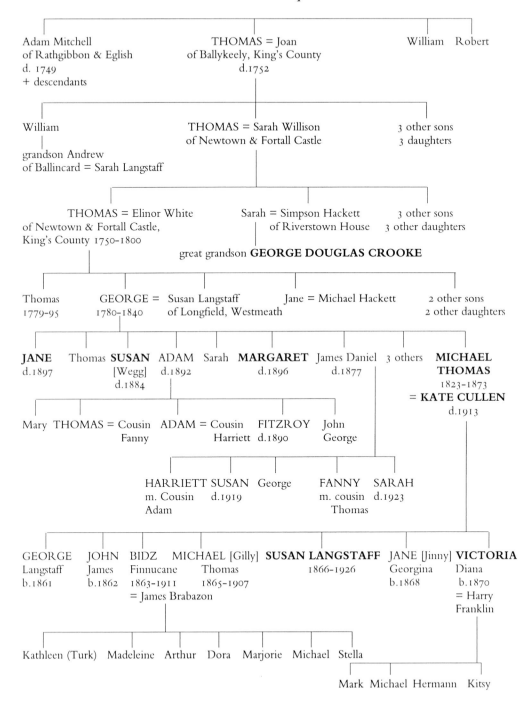

Adam Mitchell
of Rathgibbon & Eglish
d. 1749
+ descendants

THOMAS = Joan
of Ballykeely, King's County
d.1752

William   Robert

William

grandson Andrew
of Ballincard = Sarah Langstaff

THOMAS = Sarah Willison
of Newtown & Fortall Castle

3 other sons
3 daughters

THOMAS = Elinor White
of Newtown & Fortall Castle,
King's County 1750-1800

Sarah = Simpson Hackett
of Riverstown House

3 other sons
3 other daughters

great grandson **GEORGE DOUGLAS CROOKE**

Thomas
1779-95

GEORGE =
1780-1840

Susan Langstaff
of Longfield, Westmeath

Jane = Michael Hackett

2 other sons
2 other daughters

JANE
d.1897

Thomas

SUSAN
[Wegg]
d.1884

ADAM
d.1892

Sarah

MARGARET
d.1896

James Daniel
d.1877

3 others

**MICHAEL
THOMAS**
1823-1873
= **KATE CULLEN**
d.1913

Mary

THOMAS = Cousin
Fanny

ADAM = Cousin
Harriett

FITZROY
d.1890

John
George

HARRIETT
m. Cousin
Adam

SUSAN
d.1919

George

FANNY
m. cousin
Thomas

SARAH
d.1923

GEORGE
Langstaff
b.1861

JOHN
James
b.1862

BIDZ
Finnucane
1863-1911
= James Brabazon

MICHAEL [Gilly]
Thomas
1865-1907

SUSAN LANGSTAFF
1866-1926

JANE [Jinny]
Georgina
b.1868

VICTORIA
Diana
b.1870
= Harry
Franklin

Kathleen (Turk)   Madeleine   Arthur   Dora   Marjorie   Michael   Stella

Mark   Michael   Hermann   Kitsy

ONE

'No Bigger than a Bulrush I'

CHILDHOOD IN CARRICK-ON-SHANNON

Susan Mitchell valued her origins in the West of Ireland. Though she was to spend only the first seven years of her life in Carrick-on-Shannon, the fact of her birth there was an enormous influence on her. She was the fifth child of Michael and Kate Mitchell, born on December 5, 1866. Her birthplace was the bank house of the Provincial Bank of Ireland in Carrick-on-Shannon, County Leitrim, where her father was manager; the time ten days before her mother's thirty-fourth birthday. Dr. Alan Swayne, one of a family of apothecaries who had been for a long time in the town, was in attendance. Whether it was a difficult birth is untold. But her mother's pains were rewarded with an answer to her fervent prayer. This child, among seven that were given to her, was richly endowed with the merry wit she desired for them all.

The child was named Susan Langstaff after her father's mother, a Quaker in her eighties with Westmeath origins, who would live for ten more years. Michael Mitchell was quite sentimental about his old mother in Birr. 'I feel wonderfully softened and subdued whenever I get a letter from her, it makes me run back through all my career. My life past all comes before me. . . .'

There were to be two more children in the family of red heads, Jane Georgina, born on January 25, 1868 (named after her mother's two favourite sisters), and Victoria Diana (given the names of another sister, Diana de l'Herrault, and her husband Victor), who was born on January 16, 1870. These two sisters were to become Susan's closest confidantes when they were of mature years.

Kate Mitchell, descended from the Cullens, an old County Leitrim family, fed her daughter's mind with stories and descriptions of her family home Skreeney, near Manorhamilton.[1] A great-grandfather was rector and landlord there during the '98 Insurrection; and she talked about his son, the distinguished Lieutenant-Colonel Cullen, who was her father, and of her mother who had recently died, who came from an old Gaelic family in County Clare, the Finucanes.

Kate Cullen (that was) made sure that her children were educated as she

---

1. See H. Pyle, *The Sligo-Leitrim World of Kate Cullen, 1832–1913: A 19th century Memoir Revealed* (1997).

herself had been – and probably Michael's family – without discrimination between girls and boys. Their first tutor was a man known as 'Professor Donnelly',
a spoiled priest, who had taught the Peytons and half of the families in the
neighbourhood. He was a good classical scholar. 'My idea of him', wrote Susan
later, 'was that he wore a frock coat & a tall hat & recited poetry beautifully,
that he was a person of importance, but I have no recollection of any facts he
imparted to me.'

He was impressed by Susan, even at this early age of four or five years. Kate
remembered coming into the room and seeing the child sitting beside the professor on the table, 'and he pointing her out to me with the words, "This is a
splendid article".'

Professor Donnelly was an idiosyncratic man. He wore a large blue cloak
and tall hat, and spent a good deal of his time chopping tobacco, which he
rubbed and roasted, and kept loose in his pocket for chewing. His reciting
poetry, Kate thought, implanted in Susan her love of the art. But he indulged
his drinking habits to such an extent that Michael decided he was a bad example, and dismissed him. The last they heard of him was that he was seen begging
at Strokestown railway station.

He was succeeded by a clever young national school teacher named George
Loten, son of the head constable. The children all called him 'The Boy'. 'My
only memory of him is the ignominy he put on me', recalled Susan, 'making
me inscribe pot hooks & hangers in my copy book when every one knew that
a girl going on for six had been writing long words for a considerable period.'
But her mother Kate remembered differently.

> I fancy he had not the classical scholarship of the Professor, nor his poeti-
> cal imagination, but he gave a good English education, and in my children
> he had good material to work on.

> I never prayed for them that they should be rich or handsome, but I did
> pray that they might not be "thick"; and that they should have a sense of
> humour. This prayer I believe was granted, for there was not one of
> them who did not know how to laugh. For I myself enjoyed nothing
> more than a good laugh, and could never give much welcome for those
> who were totally destitute of humour.

Michael Mitchell her husband – middle-aged, rotund, bewhiskered, benign and
hyper-sensitive – contributed to the fostering of this sense of humour. He was
deeply spiritual, and had a genuine love of ritual, unlike his low church wife,
who was drawn to the Congregational Church with its simpler form of worship. He was held in high regard by fellow members of the Masonic Order in
Carrick-on-Shannon: and his years as Prince Mason, and Master of Lodge 854
went down in history as the great years of that lodge. He was received into the

Michael Mitchell, c.1870.

Order of Knights of the Eagle & Pelican in Chapter no. 5 in Dublin: and, on May 7, 1872, received a certificate naming him Knight of the Sun (Chevalier du Soleil) of the 28th Degree.

Such honours, and the celebrations acompanying them, meant a great deal to his standing in society. But they were important to him personally. The mysteries of freemasonry for him were intimately associated with his religious faith. He was actively involved with the local church, helping to effect a smooth changeover in Kiltoghert Parish at the traumatic time of the Disestablishment of the Church of Ireland; and he was registered as a member of its new vestry in 1870.

His relish for the good things on earth, however, was taking its toll as his last child Victoria was born, and his health beginning to decay. On June 30, 1871, he told his wife Kitzy that he hoped that Dr. Little would next week 'be better able to judge of the Claret Regimen.' 'Non professional!! I think myself it will do!' He evidently kept a tantalus, or had a trusty cupboard. 'I hope I am right in my idea.' 'I have not yet relaxed', he added, 'the keys are not on the bunch in case.'

He wrote in good spirits, despite a tendency to be depressed. Typically, he was more concerned for Kate's cold while she was on holiday than he was for his own debilitation. 'Shake off the cold at once, it is a nasty neighbour, but I hope you will not increase it. Mind this.' He liked nicknames, mentioned a servant he called 'the Needle': and he quipped about her brother Jemmy, who, he said, had returned to Carrick 'from foreign service' at Athlone.

Writing the following year when she was on holiday again in Sligo – it was their son John James's tenth birthday – he told her he had sent four good trout to her by train. He wanted good likenesses of George and Bidz to put in the brooch his sister Jane had sent her. 'Nelson could take them in Brooch size, and one at each side of the Brooch would answer rightly.'

> I went to church today with Johnny Gilly and Sue: they behaved very well and Susan waited to walk home with me. . . . I dine with the children, or rather they dine with me in the parlour at four o'Clock.

He was a caring father and subscribed to *Little Folks* and other infant periodicals for Johnny and Gilly (young Michael). He had recently been finding he had a rapport with six-year-old Susan, who was a pretty child and noticeably intelligent. He probably talked already of sending her to the Masonic School in Dublin. His eldest son George was certain of a good education. George now lived with Aunt and Uncle Shepperd in Sligo, where he attended the Elphin Diocesan School, a school with a century's reputation, standing above the town.

The Reverend Shepperd wasn't indulgent to his nephew. When it had been decided that he should go to the Diocesan School, he wrote to ten-year-old George,

> First . . . I expect you will every evening when you come from school at once set about your lessons and get them off hand without being either watched or forced. You are no longer a child. You know well what you ought to do. Ever remember that the sole purpose of your residence in Sligo is your education. That you may be fitted to occupy a respectable position in your future life as well as to have all the enjoyment a cultivated mind bestows. If this is not attained, your coming here is a mistake and a failure. . . .

> Second, I expect you will be at all times respectful and obedient to your aunt. Under no circumstances will I allow or excuse anything else, you know her unceasing . . . kindness and you profess to love her. I expect you to show this by deeds as well as professions, I hope I need only mention this.

Michael would have chosen the same disciplinary note for the children at home. Whether young George applied himself as scrupulously to his books as his uncle desired, time does not record. He was only an average scholar, according to his midsummer report of 1872, very good at geography and spelling. His conduct was 'fairly satisfactory', and his progress 'tolerably satisfactory' (the grade above 'deficient'!).

Bidz, Johnny and Gilly were being educated at home in Carrick, Johnny and Bidz winning prizes at Sunday School. Johnny, who was imaginative, made a tiny book about this time for Jinny and 'Baby' – it would be many years before Victoria Diana cast off this pet name, or her other nickname 'Tory'. Within its miniature pages, measuring 1 5/8 inches by 7/8 of an inch, the booklet has brief stories and instruction, with illustrations of animals, buildings etc, as well as a steam engine, all drawn in pencil and lightly coloured.

Susan's memory of her childhood in Carrick-on-Shannon was hazy, but nearly forty years later she looked back with nostalgia to those days in the bank house above the river, to the fun and mischief she enjoyed with her copper-headed brothers and sisters.

> O brothers, sisters, come with me.
> The old house still stands there, you see,
> My little red-haired Tories, come,
> For none can shut the door of home.
> We're safe before the sun goes down,
> And sleep is sweet in Carrick town.

> O hide me, Carrick, shut me in.
> Here in your little streets begin
> Again for me the young surprise
> Of life, give back the eager eyes,
> The bounding hearts, the hands that clung,
> The songs our comrade voices sung.

She did keep an early memory of the awesome journey by rail to Sligo, to see Aunt and Uncle Shepperd in the Manse. She was a tiny child. She could not have been more than four or five, too young to be told beforehand.

> I can still recall a wonderful morning when tidings of great astonishment were brought to the bedside of a very small girl in the nursery, who had fallen asleep the night before, all unknowing the distinction that awaited her. The great ones who inhabited a vague region beyond the gate at the head of the staircase were about to travel to what I believed to be a mighty city – indeed the terminus or place where the world terminated – and on me the honour had devolved of accompanying them thither.

> Nothing of that journey do I remember at all except my anticipation of it, and that at the railway station of our departure I should see Paddy Burns, the awful, yet indulgent figure that presided, unofficially, at the birth of trains. He wore a big brown coat tied round him with sugans, a

tall hat shading from brown to green, a big brown beard grew on his
face, and in his hand he carried a great bell that clanged when a train
appeared or disappeared. All his colour was the rich brown of a sod of
turf, and I admired him very much, though inferior children feared
him. . . .

Beyond Paddy, I remember of that visit to my sea town nothing but
breakfast next day in the brightest room I ever remember having breakfast in. . . . Beautiful was morning in that room, and beautiful was that
house then and afterwards to one family of children, and lovely is it still
to me in memory – a house where children, even the bad ones, were not
only tolerated but encouraged; where praise and coaxing tones and currant cake perpetually awaited them; where no one could forfeit heaven
for any misdemeanour, for was not the little church next door, with its
atmosphere so familiar, and yet so dignified, a safe haven for hope for
every small delinquent.

The house and the little church next door – Sligo Manse and Congregational
Church – are still in Stephen Street, but have more recently become the Yeats
Museum and Sligo County Library.

Dr. Little's 'claret regimen' was of little avail; and Michael Mitchell died
on October 7, 1873. He was fifty, over-weight as was the Mitchell tendency,
and still good-looking. For some time he had been in a delicate state: and he
had had to resign his post as Bank Manager a month before to spend his remaining weeks being nursed tenderly by Kate, and their faithful servant, Mary
Cleary.

Dr. Bradshaw, a military doctor who would attend Douglas Hyde's brother
in his illness, was with him when he died: and certified that the cause of death
was nephritis, or kidney disease, from which he had been suffering for two
years. The Masons buried him with full honours in Kiltoghert graveyard beside
the parish church: and later raised the memorial to him in the sanctuary, beside
the organ.

His family in Birr mourned him. As was the custom, his sisters – Margaret
and Jane Mitchell, and Susan Wegg – did not attend the rituals, but stayed at
home with their mother, while Adam, Tom and James went to their brother's
funeral. Adam and Tom arrived back in Parsonstown at two in the morning,
and Margaret, and Susan Wegg, waited up for them. 'We did not tell our
Mother, as she would not have slept.'

Susan's mother, Kate, now found herself not only a widow, but bereft of a
home, and in severe financial straits. Just before Christmas, the Secretary of the
Provincial Bank of Ireland wrote to her from the head office in London, sending a draft for £400 on the Sligo branch – a munificent donation towards her
own maintenance for life and towards the education of her family of seven

children! With this, her husband's insurance money, and the support she knew she could count on from her own family, the Cullens, as well as from the Mitchells, she would have to survive.

For Susan herself, 'no bigger than a bulrush' at this date, the breaking up of their home would mean a parting from the brothers and sisters who had shared with her the surprise and laughter of youth. The move might be for her own good, but it would be linked inextricably in her mind, as her poem 'Carrick' relates, with Death's certain tread. Already at a tender age her inner resources were to be tried as to their depth; and a solitary childhood was to nourish her capacity for vision.

TWO

'The Walled Garden of the Ascendancy'

GROWING UP IN DUBLIN

K ate Mitchell wrote in the concluding pages of her memoir, 'I left Carrick on the death of my dear husband and went to live in Sligo, in order to place the boys in schools suited to their years.' George had been living with the Shepperds at Sligo Manse for three years, attending the Diocesan School: and the Shepperds readily adopted ten-year-old Bidz – who had spent much of her time in Sligo anyway, and who came to regard Aunt Shepperd as a second mother.

Kate, who was forty, and whose energy and assertive spirit were unaffected by fading hair, went first to lodgings in Sligo where Michael had once stayed, at 1, George's Street. When these lodgings proved unagreeable, she took a house on the Mall. Her family which had dwindled to five, now shrank to four because it seemed best to accept the offer of the Dublin aunts to adopt Susan.

Aunt Wegg, Michael Mitchell's married sister, whose only child had died in infancy, had been widowed three years previously. Since the death of her husband, she had shared the house at 21 Wellington Road, Dublin, with her two unmarried sisters, Jane and Margaret, who were gentle but distinctive personalities, quick to make the affectionate child feel at home. Susan must have gone to live with them in the spring of 1874. On April 13, Aunt Wegg wrote to Kate in her spidery script,

> Dear Sue is getting on very well. I never saw a better child, just like what dear Michael was at her age. I am glad you told me about her bowels. I intended each time to ask if she was strong, & forgot, but every day since Wednesday they have been moved.
>
> I give her Honey at breakfast & it does her good & she likes it. Every one is in love with her & anxious to have her in their class at Sunday School. She went to School today to a Miss Templeton on Waterloo Road, a nice Christian person.

Susan at seven-and-a-half had already developed a natural self-composure. Her aunts glowed at her singing of hymns; as an adult she was to have a low melodious singing voice like her mother. She profited from the company of Aunt Wegg. Aunt Wegg was a compulsive reader of history and literature, and kept a commonplace book with lists of the volumes in Colonel Wegg's extensive library, together with interesting local anecdotes she gathered, pious verses, and useful recipes. Her delight in street ballads had its influence on her niece, who later used their rattling rhythms for her comic satire.

The house next door to Aunt Wegg, 19 Wellington Road, shortly became the home of the Purser family. As they sprang up the flight of steps to their hall door, they would see the young girl with flaming hair, sitting singing on the top step of no. 21. Sarah Purser, still in her twenties, whom Susan later called 'the wittiest woman in Dublin', was an artist, a painter of portraits. In later years, Susan would dance with the youngest of her brothers, Louis Claude, a distinguished scholar.

Susan always had a warm feeling for the Pursers.

> It was my good fortune to live during an impressionable period of my life next door to a family whose influence on the intelligence of this city has been far reaching though never noisy. I mean the Pursers & I omit no member of the family that gathered under their roof. To one little being the advent of that gifted family brought a great Liberation.

> Intellectual ideas began to agitate the rare field & refined atmosphere of Wellington Road. In books they were borne across the railings that divided no. 19 from no. 21. In flesh & blood they walked up the front path beside the privet hedge & into the door of 19, watched by a pair of young observant eyes, wondering & worshipful.

Among those who walked up that path she saw 'one masculine figure, tall, with head thrown back, waving beard, a gait expressive of a mind brave and untrammelled.' This was 'an impression rather than a memory' of the man who later became her close friend, the artist, John Butler Yeats.

That she longed, even in childhood, to be associated with the gifted Pursers she admitted elsewhere when she told how she sat on the stairs at the top of the house 'singing away' her soul. 'I felt I had no talents to equal me to such people, but I had a singing voice and through it I would claim my right to be among them'.

Susan attended a select school run by Miss Abbot in Morehampton Road. Girls of Anglo-Irish families in the provinces as well as the daughters of Dublin's professional classes tended to go to Morehampton House. The school may have been privileged, but the education as Susan experienced it, despite the Montessorians 'and all their tribe', was designed to 'wall out' ideas, she later said.

John Butler Yeats, c.1875

Susan particularly regretted that Protestant education was based on a British curriculum: and this became a persistent sore in her mind.

> An Irish girl . . . is given only the barest outline of the history of her own country & always in a subservient & secondary place to the histories of other countries, so that an enchanting subject like history is divested of all personal charm & distinction & becomes as great a bore as all the other subjects of the school curriculum. At the most enquiring & receptive age, when the strings of being are most sensitive, a heavy hand is laid on the wires & all their melody is muted.

A deliberate distancing from the local milieu was what she most abhorred; the lack of nourishment allowed to a girl's mind between ten and sixteen, 'while things edible & succulent for youth spring all about the children's feet in the intellectual & political movements in their own land.' There was 'no ghost of a hint' of her country '& my part in it', its literature '& my share in it'. All this came out at a much later date, when she was lecturing in Dublin about John Butler Yeats and her first memories of him (the script of the lecture now preserved in Sligo Museum).

She did remember one teacher with gratitude, who brought Keats to life for Susan. 'From such a one, I apprehended also that a universe of ideas may lie behind an algebraic formula or a historical or geographic fact.

> True, she was a headmistress & she took classes, but her gift to her pupils
> was her own rich personality. She was whimsical, irritable, full of hu-
> mour & humours, & best of all she had flexible eyebrows. Often she was
> ignorant & said so − but she made the most listless feel that poets &
> writers were not just created to enable examination papers to be set to
> humiliate schoolgirls but that their thoughts were meant for the enrich-
> ing of life & that riches lay around us & within reach of us & of her. She
> impressed us with the feeling of heirship & claimed no rights of primo-
> geniture in inheritance. We were her coheirs and her coequals. She was
> not what is commonly a teacher [so much] as a fellow worshipper with
> us in a temp[le].

As a school girl, Susan still had occasional contact with Sligo: and she left a
warm description of a youthful journey there, five years after her first memorable trip when she lived in Carrick-on-Shannon. This time she moved from one
side of Ireland to the other. She must have been about ten, and already aware of
a native pride stirring within her.

> All across Ireland I went, a momentous journey, my face leaning to the
> open window of the train to catch the first breath of native air. For,
> happy as I was in the big city east of Ireland, the Connaught woman's
> passion for the home country had never died in me. It was with a swelling
> of the heart I saw Ireland unfold before me, recognising as I was borne
> swiftly westward certain clumps of trees, certain stretches of land that I
> knew to be forerunners of where Shannon himself began his dominion.
> Then the King river revealed himself a moment to his small subject, and
> she bowed herself before his sceptres, the brown-headed rushes. . .
>
> I found myself at home with Ben Bulben and Knocknarea; right in the
> midst of the bountiful unfolding of hill upon hill, and where, from a
> rocky foreground of brown and grey, the eye might travel, wondering,
> to the regions beyond, where, parapet above parapet, the blue walls of
> distant hills ascended skywards. . .
>
> The stately terminus . . . still awed me, and unimpaired in its wild savour
> was the slap of the sea wind, and the tarry smell of ship's wood that
> assailed me when I emerged from the train.

Distanced by memory, she could still picture the quays, the masts and figure-
heads of foreign vessels, a Norwegian name on a salty prow, the peculiar rolling
gait of two Chinese sailors as they paced in leisureliness on the quay, the activity surrounding a Greek ship unloading a cargo of corn. Her mother had talked
of walking here in the eighteen forties chaperoned by her liveried servant.

Sketch of Sarah Purser by JB Yeats, early 1880s

Susan thirty years later, unencumbered by such formality, found the waterside of the sea town irresistible.

But the great lure, her imagination looking back on the past realised, had been 'the homely sun of the hearthstone' rising from a huddle of houses.

> One picture in my heart. A door in a friendly street flies open to my knock, I am blown, the tarry sea wind clinging to me, into a hall warm with light. Round me, in a welcoming chorus, ring the singing voices of childhood. The kind, protecting caves that made the heaven of infancy beam on me, the hands of young comrades hold me. I am needed, expected, loved . . .

Dear as they were, her fond aunts in Dublin could not replace the Carrick-on-Shannon family. Susan knew she was apart, and understood what loneliness was, from an early age.

At the same time she appreciated that a Dublin upbringing had its advantages. She could walk with her aunts in Herbert Park, or along the grassy banks of the Dodder: in Spring about the suburban roads of Ballsbridge, with their blossoming trees. Trinity College alumni, Professors George Salmon and John Kells Ingram, like the Pursers, lived in what was an urban haven for professionals of every kind. Her school, for all its limitations, provided an excellent classical education, which allowed her to pass the University of Dublin Junior Examinations for Women with first class honours.

In later years she did not set so much store by this courtesy academic distinction for women as by the cultural and political climate she had been unconsciously imbibing, and of whose importance she was at last aware:

> A cork on a wave, a feather blown in air had as much sense of aim or direction or value to itself, as I let loose from school at a period when a remarkable intellectual change was taking place in the very city where I lived. Yet did I snuff up something strange in the air as I emerged as the wild ass snuffeth up the air of the wilderness.

THREE

'The Wisdom of the Town'

THE BIRR SCANDAL

When Aunt Wegg died in 1884, Susan and the two remaining aunts, Margaret and Jane, moved to Birr to be near the rest of the Mitchell family. Birr, or Parsonstown, as it was then known in elegant society – taking the name Parsons from the Earls of Rosse, who were resident landlords – is sixty miles from Dublin, right in the middle of Ireland. Susan's first Christmas card to her mother, at Wine Street in Sligo, is addressed from 'The Square, Parsonstown': but thereafter she was to follow non-Unionist practice, calling the town by its original name, Birr, from the River Birr on which it is situated.

The town, as Lewis described it in his topographical dictionary of 1836, was 'pleasantly situated, well built and inhabited by some wealthy and many respectable families'; and in the 1880s it still flourished with the dominant Protestant prosperity built up by the Earls of Rosse since the beginning of the century, the present Earl being a wise and intellectual figurehead of the settled enclave.

In Duke, or Cumberland, Square – which Susan referred to regularly as 'The Square' – where she and the Misses Mitchell made their new home, the main business of the town took place beneath a statue of the infamous Duke of Cumberland on a Doric pillar, erected after his victory at Culloden. Here were a watchmaker, a stationer, a draper's, a wine and spirit merchant, a medical hall, and Dooly's Hotel: while the proprietor of the *King's County Chronicle* – Susan would call it *The Birr Chronicle* – had his house in one corner.

A short distance away, in Oxmantown Mall, running between St. Brendan's Church and the Castle, was the family home, Walcot. Margaret, Jane and Susan Wegg had grown up at Walcot with Susan's father Michael, and the present head of the family, Adam: so Susan now had first-hand acquaintance with the Mitchell side of her ancestry. Adam had gathered his unmarried nieces, Susan and Sara, daughters of James Daniel the bank manager, who had died a few years before, into the family home. Their sisters, Fanny and Harriett, had married Adam's sons, Thomas and Adam, so family ties were close.

Walcot, at the fashionable end of the town, near the Castle gate, was a pretty two storey building, long and low, with a porch decorated with relief heads, and set in 2 acres of land. In front, the walled garden centred on a circular terrazza, with garden seats and urns, and beyond were orchard and vegetable gardens, and a tree house for children. Over the encompassing garden wall, the elegant Mall was planted with beech and chestnut trees. The side facing Walcot was benign with the facades of Georgian houses of varying sizes, with wide doorways and steps fringed by iron railings.

In John's Place, which lay to the other side of the Square, lived Adam's eldest son and heir, Thomas, in equally agreeable surroundings. The wide street, bordered by trees and Georgian houses, with the ample door frame and low fanlights typical of the town, had a statue of the previous Earl, in his chancellor's robes, and with his famous telescope. The architectural ease of Birr must have appealed instantly to Susan, coming from the spacious streets of Dublin.

She had yet to get to know her cousins. Even more pressing, she must get to know her own family. The presence of her brother Johnny in the Birr bank hurried it. They had an instant and warm rapport. He introduced her to the other young bank clerks. Her intimate friendship with Johnny lasted till the end of her days.

It took slightly longer to get to know her sisters. That first Christmas card from Birr of 1885 is signed formally, 'Susan Mitchell'. A letter of the following year in December, to Jeanie and Tory ('My dearest Two'), is anything but formal, and must reflect a happy summer spent at Sligo. She made frantic apologies for not replying to their long letters which she had received in Kingstown (now reverted to its original name Dun Laoghaire).

> I was staying at the St. George's, & the Legges, after my aunts went back to Birr, & I was so fearfully occupied going about & seeing people & things, that the time slipped by very fast I need hardly tell you.

Back at Birr, she had been 'running here & there getting winter clothes, etc. made', as well as receiving a lot of letters: and, like many a maiden relative, she was drawn in to minister to the needs of others. Cousin Tom was away from home while Fanny was bringing another son into the world. Cousin Sara of Walcot, Fanny's youngest sister, was away too, so Susan – who hadn't 'the remotest notion of housekeeping' – was staying in John's Place, looking after children and servants. At 2.30 on Wednesday morning, she had had to go off by moonlight to fetch the nurse for Fanny, who was very ill, though 'she is going on beautifully now, & the baby is an immense boy.'

Fanny had had six boys, one of whom died in infancy. 'We are coming to an end of the family names, so there must be innovations!', Susan wrote. She told them about Harriett and Cousin Adam, who was a doctor in Borris, and their three children.

> I hope you are enjoying the family history, but you really should be

acquainted with the extensive cousinhood. – I expect I shall have a fine description to give you of the Christmas gathering this year at the family mansion of Walcot!

Having brought Fanny's three eldest boys home to the Square with her, Susan set them down to letter-writing, and took the opportunity of observing them closely. 'Tommy the youngest is not 4 yet, such a pretty little fellow with red hair & brown eyes,' she told her sisters. 'Adam & Jim aged respectively 8 & 6. Adam is a clever chap enough. Jim is rather slow. Tommy is bright & cute.'

In April, she had been eager to hear what was Jinny's first impression of Dublin – bombarding her with questions. Jinny had gone there to sit the same exam that Bidz and Susan had taken, the Trinity Junior Examination for Women.

> So you have come up [to] the big City. – What do you think of as much as you have seen of it. – How did you get on at the Broadstone, who met you & how did my Aunt & Cousins receive you. I am sure they will be very kind to you, for they are awfully good-natured . . . Did you go to Baggot St. Church on Sunday. Did you see where we used to sit. Isn't it an ugly Church? – I suppose Milly St. G will go to see you as soon as she knows you are in town. Be sure & talk up to her like a brick – & don't be too shy.

She stopped the letter for a short time, because Johnny and Aunt Jane were 'clamouring for prayers'. Back to the pen, she was once more tumbling over herself with questions and instructions.

> Be sure & tell me all your impressions of Dublin. How long will you be staying. I hope you will get on at the Exams. Did Sara or Susan bring you down to Trinity? . . . Isn't Baggot St. awfully noisy. Have you been down town in the tram . . . Be very attentive to my Aunt Margaret, for really she is very jolly. Don't think me impertinent please. How I wish I could give you a hug – you dear little bit of demureness.

In with the disjointed, excited sentences, she inserted an offering from an ad-mirer, no doubt to bring Jinny luck. 'I enclose a geranium Douglas Crooke gave me. I hope you will appreciate it! & that it wont green all the letter!'.

Johnny sniffed an affair in the wind: and told his mother that Susan was 'more than ever absorbed with the Crookes': though 'Master Douglas' was away when he wrote. He himself was engaged upon 'that important work the Balance book' – a very 'solemn' undertaking – and had looked after the bank premises while the Manager was away. He was concerned about his mother and sisters during the political riots in Sligo; and was glad that none of them had been hurt. 'I was sorry that such a thing should have occurred if it were only for the town's sake.'

A photograph of Susan about this time shows her as a very lovely girl, and her letters have a natural preoccupation with dress, not lacking a touch of vanity.

Susan Mitchell in 1888

> I am getting a navy blue dress with hat, pointed turban, trimmed with those wings Mamma gave me when I was in Sligo. . . are they wild duck or what? They are awfully fashionable. – I have had my brown dress altered & turned, & have a brown felt hat trimmed with plush to wear with it. Then I have a black chip hat trimmed with cock's feathers & velvet. I also have a new jacket of slightly curly cloth, London make, it fits me awfully well. I have quite a respectable figure in it. I wear my hair rolled at the back now, instead of plaited. It has a terrible effect & shows off the color!

To illustrate, she drew her hair (a deep Titian red) rolled in a wide, circular coil at the back of her head.

She found notions for details of bonnets, trimmings, and fabrics in the *Ladies Pictorial*, a practical paper with firm views about the abuse of fashion.

> The wasp-like waist, which makes a woman's figure look like two distinct things badly put together, cannot be a desirable substitute for the graceful, gliding unity of outlines which nature gives her. . . The deformed, ill-used foot, arrested in its process of development by the fashionable tight boots on stilts, is destructive of everything like ease, suppleness and capability of rapid or graceful movement.

In 1887, an English girl at a French school, obtained a prize for the smallest waist, which, with intense suffering, she had reduced to 13 inches; and the general ambition of the madly fashion conscious at the time, according to the *King's County Chronicle*, was a waist measurement of 15 or 16 inches.

Susan could not aspire to such perfection, knowing that with the Mitchell physique she could only hope for a tolerably 'respectable' figure. But the main direction of the *Ladies Pictorial* – aimed at women of 'the better classes' – affected her future attitudes in journalism: for, apart from 'Household hints' and notes on how to deal with servants, and reproductions of sentimental paintings, the editor held a strong position on the franchise.

At the time, Susan herself had no noticeable interest in women's rights. She was feeling her way in an ultra-Protestant community, analysing her own position – asking herself if she had any place in it: and she was the horrified but fascinated observer of a nasty incident in Birr, where she saw at first hand the evils of sectarianism, and her Uncle Adam and Cousin Tom playing central roles.

Adam Mitchell as a young man

From the beginning she had been critical of her Mitchell cousins, coming as she did from the more finished society of the capital city. But for Uncle Adam she had little but admiration and respect, even though she might shrink from his rigid Protestant bias. Adam was both father and son to the legal profession in Birr, appointed one of the first Parsonstown Commissioners in 1852, a post which he held for the remainder of his career. He was an important person in the local community: and for Susan he resurrected the ghost of sociable hospitality and boyish gaiety that had vanished with her father, Michael.

He was widely loved. But he was deeply Protestant, and opposed to anything that remotely resembled ritualism, or which leaned even slightly away from orthodoxy. There was a real fear at the time that the Irish Church would develop the high church practices that were growing in the Church of England. The atmosphere was still sensitive a decade after the rumblings and erruptions of conservatives about the revision of the Prayer Book that followed on Disestablishment. Now Parsonstown, in Adam's view, was in danger of turning Papish, and in no other place than St. Brendan's.

Ten years before, the sixty-year-old church had been given a chancel, designed by Thomas Drew who included an east window and some carved stonework in his plans. The parishioners had accepted it; they only queried 'a small ornament . . . upon the east gable . . . which, upon close examination, was considered to resemble a cross'. The Select Vestry made no objections – that the Earl was to pay for the stained glass window in the new chancel was their major concern. They approved the drawing of the chancel stonecarving, one man alone remarking casually that all three apices in the design appeared like crosses.

By July 1886, when Messrs Sharpe of Dublin had completed the work, the trouble commenced. The stonework was no more than a simple side lining to the chancel, beginning at the chancel steps, and including six small panels, and a centrepiece above the altar with four more panels. These four ornamental panels, described by the conservatives as a 'reredos', had representations of the symbols of the four evangelists, each holding a scroll with some text from scripture. Supporting the panels was a ledge – which they called a 're-table' – projecting about four inches, which could be used as an altar with crucifix, flowers and other ritualistic objects, the conservatives claimed. To add to their disquiet, there was above the panels, with a Latin inscription, a dove flanked by two cherubs.

There was a sudden escalation of emotions. Various members of the parish protested that the Romish spirit was infecting St. Brendan's – this though they had never objected to emblems on the font, or to ornaments on the ceiling. The Select Vestry split into two groups: and

St. Brendan's Church, Birr, drawn by M. Good, 1974

Adam Mitchell chaired a meeting of the dissidents. An official vestry meeting lasted from eight in the evening until midnight, and, after meeting next morning at ten, came no nearer to reaching some compromise solution. There was such intense acrimony between the opposing parties that the Earl of Rosse and others resigned from the Vestry.

The Bishop was brought in. In his letter, read to the Vestry on October 18, he pointed out that there were similar ornamentations in other Church of Ireland churches, which hadn't even the smallest ritualistic tendencies, and that to order the entire removal of the controversial carvings might lead to complications elsewhere. He himself felt no objections (he had in fact been Rector of the parish when the original plans had been adopted): but he suggested that the offending figures could be replaced by some simple floral design (the Vestry decided on vines), that the ledge should be sloped so that nothing could be placed on it, and that the finials above the panels should be changed 'so as to take away the smallest appearance of Crosses.' He suggested that a motto be engraved upon the stone above the Table, perhaps the words 'Till I Come': but he was cautious – only asked them to consider the proposal.

Most of the Vestry complied with the compromise, and the resignations were withdrawn – except those of Thomas Mitchell and Richard Clancy, who had wished the Bishop to propose that the 'reredos' be totally removed. It didn't make matters any easier, when one Sunday a poor woman came to church, and began to say her rosary near a vestryman who had particularly objected to the carvings. Who had put her up to it? The local nationalist paper rejoiced in the opportunity to point a finger at tensions in the Protestant community.

The Earl of Rosse was dismayed by the controversy. He decided not to put in the east window, fearing for its safety: and he put aside his plans for a new Orange Hall. Matters had reached a point of uneasy deadlock when, on Sunday night, January 23, 1887, Susan wrote – 'absolutely bursting with news' – to Johnny, who been transferred to the bank in Limerick.

> Some time on Saturday night or Sunday morning Birr church was broken into & the reredos covered with tar! The words "broken into" must be taken in a qualified manner, the Church being during some part of the night or morning left open while Woods was arranging the fires. It is surmised that the perpetrators slipped in – & bided their time, carrying on their evil work during the hours of darkness, & getting quietly off by the vestry door, which was I believe found open. Woods discovered the outrage about 7.30 Sunday morning & immediately Clergy Constable Magistrate Sub-Inspector proceeded to the scene of action.

> When I went up to Sunday school, Miss Brown informed me of the occurrence, which was not however generally known till after morning service. Ah! then what indignation, what head-shakings, what surmisings, what suspicions. The structure had been covered with a sheet so that people didn't all guess what it meant.

> Dr. Berry very nearly wept during the service, & in his sermon made remote hints – as to the Devil having been busy amongst us. There are many suspicions, everyone is talking, of course Tom Mitchell's opposition to the erection has caused him to be fixed on as one offender. Honestly the man did not do it, being at home all the evening & night – as to his connivance in the matter, of course, I cannot know. – But I believe he was as much astonished as any one else at the occurrence, though he behaved sillily in that he was sniggering & laughing instead of expressing honest indignation. He came to church this evening, which everyone remarked. It is a very rotten business.

The reredos was not completely covered with tar, but was daubed and streaked in various places, with special attention to the four panels with the evangelists, and to the dove and cherubim. The altar cloth was stained, there was a large pool of tar on the ground: and, as a final insult, the tar pot was placed on one of the gables of the reredos. Susan commented in her letter that the penalty for sacrilege was seven years penal servitude. A reward of £50 was offered for identifying the culprits, and the Vestry, with a deeply distressed Uncle Adam, met all afternoon. The practical Earl had spent the day applying chemicals to the panels, trying to extract the tar: for the Caen stone was so porous that any delay was a danger.

Susan noticed the bank clerks 'grinning in knots all over the Square' that Sunday: and her cousin, Fitzroy Mitchell, more civilised than the rest of the cousins she always felt, and of whom she was very fond, came in to tea, with Mr. Anderson,

> both boiling over with indignation, specially the former, who speaks in a rational & very gentlemanlike way about it. Mr. A. imagined he had the whole matter as it were in a nutshell, but I snuffed him & his opinions calmly out, until he humbly came to see he knew nothing at all about it.

The following morning she wrote Johnny a running commentary of events, as she saw them taking place beneath her window.

> Constables are tearing about the Square. Likewise Sub-Insp. likewise

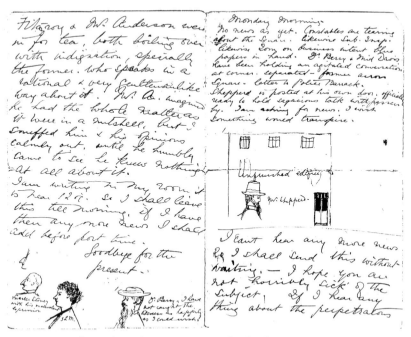

Susan's letter about the Birr outrage to her brother, 23 January 1887

Tom on business intent blue papers in hand. Dr. Berry & Micl Davis have been holding an agitated conversation at corner. Separated – former across Square. Latter to Police Barrack.

Shepperd is posted at his own door, officially ready to hold sagacious talk with passers by. I am asking for news. I wish something would transpire.

Nothing did ever transpire, though there was one clue in an old tin pan, with a paper of Davis & Son wrapped round it, which had been left at the scene of the travesty. At a special meeting the following Wednesday when the verger was questioned he said stubbornly that if he knew who had committed the desecration he would not divulge the name. The Vestry dismissed him instantly.

Susan sent a card to Johnny a short time afterwards to say – 'It has not by any means died out yet. The subject I mean – not the tar. The latter is scarcely perceptible, owing to a preparation of yellow ochre & something else.' She was writing from a tea party in her house, 'all sitting round saying nothing': and she had just been singing herself hoarse to entertain them.

FOUR

'I Damn Respectability'

THE GRAND OPENING OF THE OXMANTOWN HALL

It was some time before Birr recovered from the reredos outrage, but the amiable Earl didn't dwell on the matter for long. Before a month had passed, he had relented and agreed to proceed with the plan for the Oxmantown Hall (the hall called after his son, Lord Oxmantown), arranging for a Bazaar to be held in the Castle stables in aid of the building fund. A few years more, and he renewed his offer of an east window, altering the original design, which included the crucifixion, and substituting more acceptable scriptural scenes.

The Fourth Earl of Rosse, besides being a stout supporter of St. Brendan's, was a gifted mathematician and astronomer, who had used his father's celebrated telescope for his researches into the radiation of heat from the moon. During his time, he was President of the Royal Irish Academy, Chancellor of Dublin University, and President of the Royal Dublin Society. Susan couldn't help admiring such a man, and so she helped readily at the Bazaar. Each person was admitted to the Stables on presentation of a silver token valued at twelve pence. The Countess brightened up the stable landing with a flower stall, covered with ferns and flowers in fancy wicker baskets, and a special display of fir cones. The wreaths of primroses were a reminder that it was Primrose Day.

Mrs Hackett, aunt of Susan's friends the Crookes, helped at the Indian work stall; Lady Rosse presided at the handwork stall, where there were photographs of the demesne taken by the Earl. The Rector's wife, Mrs. Berry, produced embroidered pincushions, and panels painted by herself: and for the children there was a small theatre with marionettes, and a lantern show put on by Lord Rosse.

Susan, by 1887, had settled well into Birr, the centre of Ireland, aptly described by Petty two centuries before as 'umbilicus Hiberniae'. She arrived at the Bazaar in the company of Mrs. Crooke and her daughter Jeanie, who, with the local singer, Mrs. Henry Frend, were her constant companions at concerts and dances.

Mrs. Crooke's husband, the Reverend Milward Crooke, would shortly retire from his post as Chaplain-General to her Majesty's Forces in Ireland at Cork, after a long period in the Curragh. His wife's relatives, the Colonel Robert Hacketts, lived scarcely half a mile from Birr, at Riverstown House: so it was natural for Mrs. Crooke and her family to make their home there: and since Susan claimed a loose relationship with the Hacketts through her Mitchell cousins, it was natural for her to visit Riverstown, and introduce the Crookes to Birr.

Riverstown House, a charming 18th century building on the bank of the Little Brosna river, was approached from Birr by a winding road over an old bridge with triangular recesses to protect pedestrians taken unawares by vehicular traffic. The whole ethos was poetic. Swans covered the water's surface, or lay in the road, rising lazily as a carriage lurched slowly round the corner, or padding over to the garden gate for food. The path up to the hall door, through the small walled garden, was lined with roses and old-fashioned flowers.

Susan was already teased by her sisters about Riverstown, and the second son of the house. 'The Riverstown car is not at the door!!', she insisted in one letter: and told them that every one was in a fuss there as the Chaplain-General was coming home for a few days. 'Of course they are in a state of high excitation. Tomorrow is Jeannie's birthday – but I won't be out, as the Guest will be arriving by the 5 o'c train, & I would have no comfort.'

> I am presenting Jeannie, you may be interested to know, with a book of selections from R. B. Browning in the hopes that she may be able to unravel his mysterious English, for I have tried to do so in vain.

And she went on,

> You will laugh at the little details I tell you, but every single thing I shall tell you, whether you resent the infliction or not. It will feel more like as if I were with you. Indeed I feel now as if there were only a part of myself left, when I walk about without my two dear supporters. The Crookes tell me that the reason I am so fond of my family is because I have been away from them so long. But however that may be – I never can think there is anyone like my own. I think with love and longing of Mamma & her three young savages all sitting up in the room preparing for bed.

Nostalgic though she might be, she could still make fun, wherever she was. In the same undated letter she enclosed a photograph she had been given by a friend, Jack Byrne.

> He gave me my choice, & I took this head & shoulders' one, as in the other he appears to be seated on a window sill in a melancholy attitude in a large check suit! He is just the same as ever, except that he makes a practice of having a fatigue coat, which he imagines enhances his beauty. It has shoulder straps, tell Gilly, with two stars having a shamrock in the middle one.

The minor flirtation amused her: but the aunts did not approve of the young man. 'I shall have to suppress this photo of Mr. Byrne. My aunts are angry at my taking it. I suppose it isn't strictly correct to take promiscuous people's photos. Is it like the old Pater? . . . His moustaches look like linseed poultice on brown paper. Picture to yourselves that his hair is dark blue – with a mixture of slate color.'

Aunt Margaret wrote vexedly to Susan's mother Kate, in Sligo, 'This is such an age of unrest, that I at least feel my whole time occupied doing nothing. How the majority of the people here love running about after so called pleasure, I know not, one cannot think of any thing. . . . Susan is gone to Riverstown, I asked if she had any commands, she said her love. I have little, if any of her company, but old people now, know nothing'.

Yet Susan was teaching assistant to her aunt in Sunday School. Susan, despite her aunt's fussing, was serious at twenty-two. When she was not assisting with charities, she pursued her interest in music. She also looked forward to the satirical ballads Percy French would perform at his concert, on his coming tour round Ireland. But she could stand apart, taking a broad amused view of life, while Jinny – with first class honours in the Trinity diploma, and eager to be independent – had started to teach in the Misses Blyth's Academy. 'Jenny is a brave good little girl to do something for herself', sighed Aunt Margaret, comparing her mentally with Susan. 'I hope she will get on.'

The brother next above Susan in the family scale, Michael, or Gilly, even as a school boy took an interest in the national situation, and made a point of wearing the shamrock on St. Patrick's Day. He read about the investigations into the Phoenix Park murders, the car driver who gave information, and the trial and sentencing of Joe Brady for Mr. Burke's murder: and he noted down the arrest of seventeen men on a charge of conspiracy to murder government officials. He watched the gunboat which drew up to Sligo Quay: and he was at the station before the local elections, when the 'very large' military force came in. He was treasurer of the YMCA when a heated debate on 'Has Ireland been properly treated by Ireland' had to be adjourned. After further debate the decision was in the negative.

Gilly was sceptical of the military presence in Sligo. He saw the militia called up for training on May 27, 1889,

> & marched to Point to be under Canvas on Greenlands. Some of them rather drunk. Met some going down about 6 pm with an officer & Sergt. Thorpe, rather drunk looking.

When they returned to barracks a few weeks later, he laughed at 'Col. Wood-Martin swelling about Town on horseback'. Wood-Martin on another occasion had a quarrel with Captain Gethin over Lady Gore, and had his head cut while Gethin's umbrella was broken. The incident was discussed all over town.

Gilly (right) with a friend, posing in uniform of Scots Highlanders

In his diary he also noted the more sombre aspects of life. Mrs. Sands, wife of Sergeant Sands died of typhoid fever in March 1899, her husband the next day: and both were buried as quickly as possible, the sergeant with full military honours.

Sligo had continual political dramas and tension, unlike establishment Birr. Gilly left a YMCA meeting, in May 1889, to join the end of a rally welcoming McHugh home from Derry Gaol. There was a torchlight procession, with bands and illuminations, which escorted McHugh to the Market Cross in the town

centre, where there were heady speeches from a wagonette. Kate might de-
mur, but the young Mitchells were excited by the prevailing growth of
nationalism.

In King's County, Unionism continued to flourish. Uncle Adam represented one of its more colourful aspects, with his Mitchell ring engraved with
the Archangel Michael vanquishing the Arch-Enemy of Adam's children from
the Field of Paradise. His 'juvenile hair . . . imparting dignity to the rosy genial
features', fun and frolic bursting out of every pore of his ample proportions, he
presided at a fund-raising auction for the new Oxmantown Protestant Hall, and
himself came third in the subscription list, placed next to the Earl and the Lord
Bishop, and before the Parsonstown Loyal Orange Lodge. (Susan's Aunt Jane
was among those who gave the more humble contributions.) The hall, built
from local limestone, took about eight months to erect, with Mr. Fuller from
Dublin as architect. It was opened grandly on January 15, 1889. Everyone admired the fashionable half-timbering, Elizabethan style, and the brick lining to
the side windows.

Inside, it was capacious, with a sloped stage, and many windows and tinted
glass. It was heated with hot water pipes, and lit with four gasoliers hanging
from the ceiling. The painted spandrils, and the decoration in terracotta and
wedgewood blue, were thought 'delicious': and the place was packed for the
opening.

Despite the rain, Susan arrived, through flooding, with Cousin Thomas
and his party. Jeanie Crooke came with her family, to reserved seats priced at 3
shillings. Others were content to cram in standing, even at 1 shilling: and as
many were turned away. By 8.15, the hall was completely filled. The Earl and
Countess brought a glittering party of friends, who were staying at the Castle:
and one of them starred in the evening's comedy, *Cool as a Cucumber*. There
was also *Barbara* – a play to touch the emotions, about a woman's sacrifice. It
was 'pathetic and pretty'. Mrs. Frend sang some solos, including 'Maud', and a
duet with the Countess.

The hall rapidly became a centre of activity for Protestant Birr. The next
year, when St. Brendan's was damaged by a freak thunderstorm in June, one
pinnacle knocked down, the tower stripped of its mortar and the bell twisted
out of shape, it was a welcome refuge for divine service each Sunday, while the
church was being repaired.

Susan made no comment, good or bad, on the grand opening. Her letters
show that she was becoming contemptuous of 'respectable society' as she knew
it. Her fastidious, demanding soul was making her analyse and measure up
without compromise even those nearest to her. Uncle Jemmy, for instance,
staying with Aunt Shepperd in January 1889, to wind up Aunt St. Leger's affairs. In June he and his daughter Dido arrived in Sligo, 'without ever telling or
writing', and walked in on good-natured Gilly, alone in the house while Mamma
was on holiday. 'Dido slept here with Baby & others at Aunt Shepperds – great

arrangement', he observed in his diary.

Susan was very critical of her uncle and aunt. 'I agree with you Baby about Uncle Jemmy', she wrote to Victoria,

> he can say awful things, things no man should say before a woman, but he is an eccentric character, & perhaps does not realize the effect of his tongue. The one thing I can't endure is coarse conversation, it fills me with disgust. It is too much the fashion, I grieve to say. I never willingly listen to it, & would under no circumstances encourage it. Aunt St. Leger was an example. My cousin, Tom, uses shocking language, & is very coarse. Indeed it is a Walcot trait, Mary [Tom's elder sister] not being exempt, & the Baggot Street people are the same. As to the stories I have heard him & Aunt Sydney tell about Aunt Diana, I should never for an instant believe them. As you say they are servant tales, for the most part, & the rest inventions and exaggerations.

Analysing character was a habit with Susan. She was also interested in the current enthusiasm for Buddhism. Gilly heard Mr. Watters talk about 'Buddhism & Christianity' at the Sligo YMCA ('not many there'). Susan went to hear the Rector talk about the same subject in Oxmantown Hall. Thomas Sterling Berry had given the Donnellan Lectures in Trinity in 1889 on the subject of Christianity and Buddhism, and had published the lectures in book form. 'He is supposed to be great on this subject', Susan wrote to her sisters.

> I am sure it will be confusing and my intellect is not wildly active now. Do you know anything about Buddhism or take any interest in it? Dr. Berry will be great on the subject of Buddha or Gautama's hatred and contempt for women. "Ster dear" is always glad of a jocular cut at our sex. He is not a bad sort of man, clever & full of attainments, but with a touch of commonness that spoils him to one, though many people might not notice it. He is not a deep scholar, I think, rather a wide & very accurate one.

Susan would cross swords with Dr. Berry on a very different matter years later; but whether or not he belittled women at the lecture, she was later deeply interested in eastern mysticism, and a leading member of the Dublin Hermetic Society. According to his book *Christianity and Buddhism* (published 1890), Dr. Berry was broad in his views, looking for cogent parallels between Christianity and Buddhism, but coming down firmly on the side of Christianity.

Susan about this time was engaged in less orthodox pondering on differences between the religious sects in her own country: and, in after life, in her book on George Moore, wondered if any one realised 'the social aloofness of the two religions' in her youth. 'In the West of Ireland, a Catholic nurse might indeed hold a Protestant infant in her arms at the Protestant baptismal font, and hear our heresies unhindered, but a Protestant vestry could prevent the burial of a Catholic wife in the same grave as her Protestant husband, lest it might mar the perfection of a Protestant resurrection. The tables have turned on us now . . . but are the barriers breaking down?'

She refused to have anything more to do with the Oxmantown Hall, already known as the Orange, or Protestant Hall.

> There is to be a great Bazaar at the Castle in May to clear off the debt... The Frends, Mary especially, are madly working for it. I sometimes put in a stitch to help her, but utterly decline to help on my own account. The Girls Friendly Summer fete is to be held in May. Hope I shan't be here for either event.

She remained aloof, her nationalist soul stretching and yawning, a tiny unhappiness rearing which she could not at the time explain, except as a rebellion against the 'respectability' to which for the moment she was doomed.

A view of Birr, Co. Offaly

FIVE

'The Heart's Low Door'

AN UNSUITABLE ENGAGEMENT

Susan could damn 'respectable' society, because she knew respectable society was only too ready to damn her. She had fallen in love: but with a man who was totally unsuitable in society's view. That meant her family's view too – except for her sisters. She wrote to them in March 1890 in nervous excitement.

'My darling Jenny & Baby', she began.

> I am glad you like Douglas' photo. Not that the fat boy's face would give you any idea of him. He is thin, & of course much older looking now. I will send you a proper photo of him when I get it, as I want you to admire him. I am going to tell you a profound secret, indeed I should have told it to Mamma, it would be more respectful, but I did not want to frighten her with a letter. You will tell her.

> I am engaged to Douglas Crooke, but nobody is to know about it as yet. You see he is only a Sergeant, and of course cannot marry until he gets promotion.

George Douglas Crooke came from a good background, being the second son of the Chaplain-General, Milward Crooke. Milward Crooke, ordained in Dublin before serving in the Crimean War, had distinguished himself during the Siege of Sebastopol, and had been awarded the Crimean and the Turkish medals. The family were treated to long monologues about this period of his life – 'The old man continues to live in the past', Susan commented. Mrs. Crooke came from a military family. Her eldest brother, Simpson Hackett of Moorpark, was a Major-General, and currently Governor of Cyprus. Three other uncles were Lieutenant-Colonels, Colonel Robert Hackett of Riverstown having lost his sight in the Battle of Kambula in the Zulu War.

But the problem was that Douglas himself was not distinguished. He was a mere sergeant, and perhaps reacted against the overwhelmingly glorious presence of his father and uncles. After the Crimea, Milward Crooke had continued to serve as an Army Chaplain, at Portsmouth, in Birr, and in Templemore, where Douglas was born, in July 1865. Later, based at the Curragh, Milward became Chaplain to the Lord Lieutenant, and Principal Chaplain to Her Majesty's Forces in Ireland.

In some ways it seems strange that Susan, with her extreme intelligence and growing nationalism, should be attracted to a man who was so totally unintellectual and with such a bristling British Army background. But she was a strong character, and in her ardour felt that Douglas, who was easygoing and unambitious, might be encouraged to find some nonmartial career, the bank perhaps. Her own grandfather had been a Lieutenant-Colonel in the Leitrim Militia, and Douglas probably talked about his grandfather, who had been one of the curates in Manorhamilton about the time Mamma had been born there. As a further link in the genealogical reference, it would have pleased Susan that Milward Crooke had been curate in Carrick-on-Shannon, her own birthplace, before he went to the Crimea.

The main thing was that Douglas was a kind and attractive young man, and she was in love. 'He is such a fine fellow, not clever but a good honesthearted man', wrote Susan. Where he excelled was in sport. He was captain of the football team, which played at his uncle's demesne, Moorpark. He was gentlemanly in all athletic contests, yet 'able to keep the athletic spirit at white-heat'. 'With features ever "beaming" with happiness, he was a pleasure for all to see'.

Susan was fond of his family. Mrs. Crooke's warm welcome, Jeanie who was her own age, and like another sister, and the magnetic hospitality of Riverstown, where she spent so much of her time in Birr – all helped to compensate for the emotional gap in her adolescence. Uncle Adam, whom she admired, was a firm friend of Douglas's father. They had a similar Protestant zeal and British bias. Adam, as Chairman of the Commissioners, had received from the military authorities, on behalf of the town of Birr, a Russian gun captured in the Crimean War, and had it placed in the enclosure in John's Mall. This would provide a topic for the two veterans during their evening conversations.

Though Douglas found it hard to live up to such a warlike family, he seems to have accepted that he would make a career in the army. When he was twenty-one, his father obtained a commission for him in the 3rd Battalion of the Leinster Regiment in the King's County Militia: but he failed to reach the required standard, and worked his way up from a private in the Seaforth Highlanders to the rank of sergeant. At the time of his engagement (he was nearly twenty-five), he was stationed in the Beggar's Bush Barracks, in Dublin. 'He had six weeks furlough, & went back on Friday last', Susan told her sisters. 'I have known him for 4 years now, so he is no new acquaintance.'

Uncle Adam may have been relied on to regard the young couple favourably: but Susan's aunts behaved quite differently.

Of course my Aunts were angry at first, & said it was madness, but when he came & spoke to them in the most manly way & said he would work & make a home for me, of course they couldn't hold out. Mrs. Crooke said she would stand by both of us – but that it might be years of waiting. But what do we care for that. He hopes for his commission in 6 months, & then he will try for some staff thing or something. I am afraid I don't understand these matters. But this is to be a profound secret . . . Bidz may be told but it must not go beyond our family, as things are so much in the future as yet.

Now my darling children, having made my announcement, which I have done very awkwardly & confusedly, I'm afraid, I want to tell you that I am very happy. Douglas & I have always been fond of each other. I wish you knew him . . . I am afraid Mamma will be disgusted after her advice to me to marry a man of 40. Douglas is not quite 25.

Douglas was going back to Dublin. He would give the news to her eldest brother, George Mitchell, and she 'commanded him not to let George breathe it, as he can't keep a secret.' He had been introduced to Jinny through a photograph, and thought 'Jenny's photo the image of George & is interested to hear Baby is like me.'

Douglas was very musical: and kept urging her to sing for him.

You had just to go on, one after another. He goes to all the things in Dublin, & has heard plenty of good music there as well as in Edinburgh & Glasgow. . ... He says my way of sitting at the piano, putting my fingers on the keys, raising my eyes, & all my little tricks are just like George. Douglas has a capital ear. Can whistle any tune, corrects my general impressions very often. He has a decent voice, but refuses to sing. He dances nicely, we had great dancing on Tuesday last. A friend of his, another Sergeant was staying at Riverstown, such an ugly fellow – but gentlemanly. It was amusing to see the way Douglas hunted him about, making him dance when he had scarcely finished his tea, they appear very fond of each other.

And she emphasised to her sisters that, though Douglas was in the ranks, 'he is exclusive & refined in his tastes & no one could say the associations have done him harm. He is very gentlemanly & quiet. I am sure you would like him.'

Though her letter is bursting with affection and excitement, nowhere else does Susan refer to Douglas Crooke, other than in passing. Victoria wrote from the Mall to Johnny telling him elatedly that it was 'of course a profound secret, not to be breathed'. But Douglas, 'commanded' to meet Jinny at the train in Dublin as she passed through en route for Frankfurt in August, never turned up. Jinny suggested to Susan that he might have been on guard, 'or something'. The following year, writing from Germany, she complained to Susan, 'You never mention Douglas. Why? I hope he is quite well: I suppose you saw him in Dublin'.

There is no clue as to how long the engagement lasted. Certainly both Douglas (whom she now referred to as 'G. Crooke', using the initial of his first name 'George') and Susan were torn within themselves: and may have found the engagement harder to sustain than they had at first believed possible. Susan was eager for Douglas to get some kind of office appointment. In February 1892, she wrote to her brother Johnnny to say that 'G. has been stuck for the Line his 3rd chance, but I believe he can go in again as a University student or something – & no doubt he will be made do so though his soul hankers after brewing.'

In May 1892, Douglas was gazetted as a second lieutenant to the Suffolk Regiment. At his own request, he was immediately sent on foreign service to the 2nd battalion, in Secunderabad, in India, and after two more years he was promoted to be a lieutenant. His military blood was asserting itself. He proved to be capable and efficient, and was soon assigned to the Adjutancy of the Bangalore Rifle Volunteers. Like his father as a young man, he headed to where the action was: and was one of the first to volunteer for the front in the Indian Border Campaign.

Susan at home, and devoting her life over the next few years to very proper activities, could only hope and be resigned. In a copy of Whittier's poems, three years after his departure, she marked a few lines of 'The Ranger', a tale of waiting love which was rewarded.

> . . .far away,
> Turns my heart, *for ever trying*
> Some new hope for each new day.
> Ah my heart, my heart is breaking
> For the dear one far away.

And the final couplet –

> Life is sweeter, love is dearer
> For the trial and delay!

In March 1890, however, in the first flush of her engagement, happy and confident, she wrote her tremendously long engagement letter late at night, sitting on a stool wrapped up in shawls and petticoats at the fire, too happy to go to bed. She planned in future to retire early, 'to get that beauty sleep I have lacked these years, because of course I must preserve my beauty (?) for the sake of Douglas. I expect it will be worn out in a short enough time now. Still as the

Mitchells are wonderful people for keeping young looking, I won't give up hope'.

She was concerned about Jinny's proposed trip to Germany, about the lack of a salary, and who Jinny would be travelling with. She was glad to get greetings from Mary, or 'Pinkie', Blyth, at whose school Jinny was teaching. 'I like her, the poor wretch, though she was innocent enough to be shocked at my broad views.' She was getting interested in her Langstaff relatives in Athlone; and she explained about 'midget' photos – ancestors of the modern polyphoto, and the latest vogue. In her warmhearted way, she praised up her aunts.

> Aunt Margaret at her best now doesn't look sometimes much over 50, and Aunt Jane certainly looks years younger than 83. They are as well preserved and as pretty a pair of women as you could see. I am very proud of them on Sundays, in their best clothes, & they dress most becomingly, lots of black lace. They have both such complexions and Aunt Margaret a set of teeth white and even, such as very few young people possess nowadays.

Her spirit of independence still asserted itself. She was writing on St. Patrick's Day. 'I hope you had your shamrock today. I got mine from Riverstown & wore it in triumph.' And the cousins still came in for tough criticism. Dr. Adam, her favourite after Fitzroy, was over from Borris, staying at Walcot, with a 'common' Queen's County friend, a horsetrainer.

> Adam isn't a bad fellow . . . less of a bigot than the others, but he has lowered himself to the level of his associates over in Borris. He could have known the nicest people, for his manner is good enough, but either he or his wife have sunk into the society of farming people & general cads, & as a consequence Adam has sadly deteriorated.

Her letter reads like a passage from Jane Austen. Harriett, Adam's wife, and another Mitchell cousin, she dismisses in one sentence. 'As to Harrie, she was always common'. Susan was a snob about manners and behaviour: but the standard by which she criticised was based on an high estimate of the quality of life: and Harrie's commonness in her judgement was partly due to her emptyheadedness.

She felt she was edging into respectability again. 'Went to the 8 o'clock Holy Communion on Sunday morning. It is such a nice quiet service, makes one feel so much better . . . We only have the early celebration once a month, the other is at the 11.30 service, & is not half as nice, the long service before making it very wearisome..'

Just as a postscript she gave a hint of her ambitions as a writer. 'That dish of rhyming was done by me in a moment of frenzy. I have forgotten it now. I cannot write a line of verse now. My talents have departed, supposing I ever had any. I wish I had Mrs. Henry Woods' facility of writing tales. I would soon amass a fortune.'

Early drawings with captions by Susan Mitchell, portrait of her sister Victoria on right

SIX

'The Young Surprise of Life'

JINNY, GERMANY AND THE YEATSES

S usan at twenty-four, with all her criticism of others, was quick to admit her own shortcomings: one being her hot temper. In the summer of 1890, she wrote from Sligo to Johnny . 'I have been 2 months already, it is great fun being here. Baby and I fight on every occasion.'

Susan's youngest sister, Victoria Diana – now and again she used her second name 'Diana' in preference to the imperial 'Victoria' – was a warm, confident, articulate character, not so imaginative, or self-questioning, as Susan, nor so intellectual. She accepted the low church inspiration of her mother and aunt without question, was in regular attendance at Band of Hope meetings in Sligo, and developed her rich contralto voice, becoming well known as a soloist at the feis competitions and concerts in Sligo and Dublin. 'Baby has a very pretty face & a very hot temper', Susan commented to Johnny. 'Jenny is much improved, has a lovely complexion & most dignified manners. . . They are certainly an unusually nice pair of girls': and she was able to be objective, for she saw them roughly once a year. She lodged in Sligo first at a boarding house, 'the fabric', and then stayed with her eldest sister Bidz.

Jenny, or Jeanie (always pronounced 'Jinny'), whose name was Jane Georgina, was a quiet, stalwart person, who sensed her own inadequacy in the company of her three handsome and gifted sisters. She was smaller than they, not pretty, but an alert personality – according to John Butler Yeats's pencil portrait in Sligo Museum. She was lovable by all accounts, slightly puritanical in outlook, and with mild energetic ambitions which never got her very far. Though hardworking, she was destined always to play second fiddle – to Mamma in Sligo, to Susan in later years in Dublin, and after that to Diana and her brilliant family. Jinny adored Susan who was outgoing and loved company. Jinny enjoyed the company from a distance.

She longed to be accomplished. 'Do you think it wd be any use for me to take lessons in singing or playing?' she wrote to Diana once. 'You will say "such cheek! a person without an idea of music", but of late I have become imbued with a thirst for knowledge, and I want to learn everything in the world – but . . . at present I have no money to assist my ambitious flights – besides there's the "want" – the awful, indefinable thing that haunts us everywhere.'

Sketch of Jinny Mitchell by JB Yeats, 1892

'Little Jinny' may have lamented her lack of talents, but she was the most enterprising of the sisters, unlike Susan, who at this period seemed to let life carry her along. When she was twenty, she went to Donegal as governess to the Crawford family. After they moved to London, she returned to teach in the Blyths' school in the Mall. But she wanted to go abroad: and found a position in Frankfurt, giving part-time lessons in English, while she herself took lessons in German. She set out on a pittance, received no salary, and found it nearly impossible to get tuitions to improve her penniless state. Worst of all, she found the inactivity preyed on her. She wanted to be stimulated, surprised. 'I am sick of hanging about, and longing to exercise my latent strength before I get too old & "rust out".

Still, she stayed away for a year and a half; and even tried to persuade the lackadaisical Susan to come out to a similar position. 'The Germans would delight in you. They would admire you extremely I am sure – and your talent for "public lecturing" would come in handy'.

Jinny had first set out in the August of 1890, to be welcomed in Dublin, on the first stage of her journey, by George, who found her 'a very nice little room', went out and 'purchased a seed-cake, pears & apples, and presented me with a bottle of "White Rosé" – regretting that his funds were low, or he would have given me more!' A cloak that had been ordered at Elvery's was about two inches too long: but George 'displayed quite an unexpected talent for dress-making – talked of gores & such like and was far more particular than I about the sitting of it. You shd. have seen me standing on a table, and George going round me with pins, making the hem even!'

George would have accompanied her to London, he said, if he had had enough money: but Jinny had an unexpected stroke of luck. At the North Wall, Lily Yeats was being seen off by her cousin Ellie, and she observed George and Jinny – 'a brave little figure' – boarding the boat also. George, thinking Ellie, whom he knew, was travelling, came over to ask her to befriend Jinny: and so Jinny was introduced to Lily, and the Mitchells to the Yeatses (Jack alone they had known as a boy in Sligo). Lily was just a few months older than Susan.

The two girls travelled to London together, and Jinny stayed with the Yeats family on her way back through London in 1892. Lily confessed later to having a great admiration for Jinny, 'she was brave & true all her days'. 'As we come from the same country & place & county we may drop the Miss,' she wrote to Jinny in Frankfurt. Lolly, she said, had returned from the seaside look-ing brown, and was going about on a tricycle they had been asked to look after for a friend, and which they had to 'warehouse' in their hall.

She herself had gone back to work with May Morris.

> There are 5 other girls as well as myself – they are all nice ladies & we are all good friends together – & the house we work in is by the Thames. The garden runs down to the riverside – the river itself is thick with dirt but in London you put up with a good deal in the way of dirt.

Lily apologised for her handwriting. 'My family say it is impossible but I dont on principle believe all the statements of my family.' Lily, too, had had to learn to protect her individuality among high-powered relatives.

Jinny wasn't long in settling into the Schultz's academy, at Halbe Stadt 7, Frankfurt: but regretted that she hadn't enough to do, or the wherewithall to spread herself. The demonstrativeness of the Germans astounded her.

> These people are always kissing and hugging each other – "they are so gushing", Mademoiselle says: – and indeed they carry it to a pitch of distraction. You can understand one liking to kiss somebody that was very nice or pretty or interesting; but here they all go about embracing each other indiscriminately – old and young – gentle and simple; and one is rather startled to see one stout old lady conversing with another, and

suddenly flying at her and giving a resounding kiss, for which you can see no reason whatever. Certainly I should be more sparing of my kisses.

For Gilly she described the regiment stationed in the town, and their manoeuvres – 'the town is alive with soldiers'. Their uniform was dark blue with a deep crimson collar, the cavalry having only a piping of crimson. The brass helmets with spikes, gathered together in formation, could be 'weird and terrifying'.

She visited Saxony at Christmas, and Beckermuhl, near Sorau, the following Easter, more as a holiday governess than as a guest: and, in the summer of 1891, she went to Berlin, where it was very hot, and there was a terrific thunderstorm: 'Lucky for Susan that she doesn't live in Germany', she commented. The skin was coming off her hands with the baking sun – 'my fingers look as if they were covered with white lace.'

In the autumn of 1891, she moved to Austria, as governess to the Holzers, in their hotel at Franzenbad, near Bohmen. She found it lonely in winter, for there were not many people about; but she wrote enthusiastically of a day trip over the border to Waldsassen to see the baroque church designed by Dientzenhofer.

Being abroad made Jinny more conscious of her Irishness, and appreciative when her German acquaintances noticed the differences between the English and the Irish. Though she had little interest in politics as such, she was infected by the current desire for national independence, and intrigued that the whole family were won over by Parnell's radical Fenianism. 'He certainly is a wonderful man – I wonder how the elections will go off.'

Emotions in Sligo had reached a pitch in February 1891, during the canvassing for the North Sligo election, when parties were equally balanced in the county, and victory depended on the results of the borough vote. Despite the priests' general opposition to Parnell, five from the county came out openly in his support. The opposing side, the Home Rulers, were the inciters of violence, chasing and stoning the supporters of Parnell, intimidating and terrorising them. Roughs and Belfast nationalists down for the occasion joined in the street skirmishes with the police: and this, coupled with the bad weather, and the fact that the Unionists abstained from voting, meant that the poll was low.

'You seem to be quite enthusiastic about Parnell', Jinny wrote in April: still finding it hard to believe that the divorce case had not shaken the Mitchells' faith in the leader. 'How exciting it must be to be in Sligo now, even tho' there are no rows! Are they going to have the election over again?' She herself had got a thrill from seeing the word 'Sligo' in German characters in the local paper, considering no one there had ever heard of the place until she came. And, when he died so suddenly in October, she thanked Diana for the three newspapers with accounts of 'poor Parnell's funeral'.

She was always eager for news from home. Frankfurt had diversions of a different kind. She described going with one of the Frauleins and Mademoiselle to hear music being played in honour of 'the old General'.

> When we got near the Lindens, we could hear the strains of music: and could see the crowd assembled, the band in the middle, lighted up by lamps and torches. In getting through the crowd we tried to pass through inside the ring of soldiers which was formed to keep off the people when we were severely ordered out of the ring by two soldiers, who quite frightened us with their helmets and rifles – and the fierce expression of their faces. They might have run us through had we gone on – as a sentry did not long ago (some place in Germany) to a man who persisted in passing him when he ordered him not to, when the sentry despatched him on the spot.
>
> Yes, the "fiery Hun" is, I think, a ferocious animal when his blood is up, and the military laws are very strict. However, we did not suffer any injury, but got through safely. We went to Fr. Grasso's house. She came out and the three of us paraded the streets for about an hour. Oh Baby! if you had heard the band! and had seen them! It was most exciting. There seemed to be hundreds of soldiers – You could see the helmets lighted up by the lamps and torches in the middle – and round them were crowds of people. They played lovely things – and then ended up with several volleys (I don't know what else to call them – but it just expresses it) of drum music, which had a most weird and exciting effect.
>
> Then they marched through the streets, on their way to the barracks. We went another way, and waited near the barracks till they appeared again, followed by the crowd. They then played what they call a "prayer" before retiring for the night. This was the tune which we sing to "Rock of Ages": it sounded beautifully in the night air.

She had become quite 'gay', attending supper and coffee parties. 'These German Coffees are amusing', she wrote to Diana,

> you go and bring your work, then everybody gathers round a table and drinks coffee, and then the talking begins – oh! if you only heard them once – how they shout and get into a state of excitement, and how each one seems to try to talk louder than the other – till you find yourself half bewildered with the noise, and you wonder – cold Northern that you are – how people can get so excited with so apparently little cause.

Despite the fact that the place was 'deadly' lonely with wintertime, she liked Austria, and she determined to stay through till spring, amusing herself by observing the differences between the Austrians and the Germans. The air, of

Sketch of Lolly Yeats by her father JB Yeats, October 1898

course, was very pure, and she did not feel choked with dust as she was in Germany. With Frau Holzer she visited the churchyard.

Yesterday if was the "Todtenfest" (Feast of the Dead). . . and the whole population visited the churchyard carrying huge wreaths to decorate the graves. Today it had quite a gay appearance, but most of the wreaths were made with paper flowers, and had a very gaudy effect. Then there was a procession from the village close by, accompanied by the band of the "Veterans" (dressed in black coats trimmed with crimson cord, and black hats with yellow cords & bunches of cocks' feathers). There were two priests in "full canonicals" & little choristers, and they chanted as they went along, while the people shouted the Paternoster and "Heilige Marie" with all their might, beginning one in a hurry as soon as the other was done. It was a strange sight, and I could not help thinking of the "vain repetitions".

In February 1892, Jinny was on her way home again, greatly stimulated by her experience, though no better able to concentrate her thoughts to express her creative instincts. Thomas Cook & Son arranged an itinerary for her back through Nuremberg, Heidelburg, Carlsruhe, Strasburg, Paris, Calais, and Dover, to London, to stay with the Yeats family, where John Butler Yeats took her portrait in pencil. She made a sympathetic friend in Lolly, Lily Yeats's younger sister.

Lolly wrote to Jinny towards the end of the year to say how her father had taken to Jinny. She added that Mrs. Yeats, who had never recovered from her stroke, now stayed in her bedroom all the time, '& sits & looks out of the window most of the day . . . the fewer people she sees, the better she is.'

Lolly herself had her immense painting class, with about forty-five girls, at Nottinghill Training College, which she found exhausting, but satisfying. She preferred the students to school children, who were 'such little demons'. Lily had been exhibiting at the Arts & Crafts exhibition in the New Gallery in Regent Street. Her embroidered curtain had been much admired. Oscar Wilde, Mrs. Alma Tadema, '& people of that kind', had been at the opening. Lily was also 'busy trying to make the poet's study into a bedroom for herself. She is making curtains of blue & white morris cretonne, she is going to line them with butchers blue & she has got matting for the floor'.

'I am most excited to know what was "the most awkward thing" that occurred,' Lolly asked Jinny – 'bad enough to put you in a temper. I am sorry I wasn't present at Susan & Victoria's battle royal. What was the subject of the dispute: Miss Lyard's good looks perhaps . . .'

SEVEN

'Brother Protestants'

CINDERELLA AT BIRR CASTLE

While Jinny was in Frankfurt, a violent thunderstorm in Protestant Birr caused much damage, and the Reverend Dr. Berry, walking past Miss Horan's confectionary shop in Cumberland Street, narrowly escaped being hit by a flying chimney pot. Susan, fortunately (for she hated thunder storms) had been in Dublin, staying with her aunt's friends the Miss Legges, going to the theatre. The Unionist attitude of the Legges grated on her. 'I don't wonder that you were mad', wrote Jinny. 'I should have been. It is mean of people to run down their own country, and there is no country like Ireland anywhere'. From afar she extolled 'the aristocratic bearing and delicate refined features which distinguish the Irish gentry', and Irish wit and Irish beauty.

Jimmy Brabazon had been appointed Sub-Agent of the Bank of Ireland in Cavan, where he and Bidz occupied a handsome Georgian house, originally the Presbyterian manse, at 6 Farnham Street, a broad and gracious thoroughfare. Bidz's view of the place was muted when she wrote to Aunt Shepperd, shortly after their arrival. 'The town is not a bad one: a few good shops, but not nearly such a town as Sligo. It seems rather sleepy &, until we know some people, decidedly uninteresting. One advantage, the meat is cheaper . . . splendid steak at 8d per lb!' The house they found 'very satisfactory'.

The Brabazons now had three children. Madeleine, aged three, was 'so wise', 'looking very well & her appetite grand, but . . . she has the cough again.' Tory was one of the first visitors at the Manse, and earned praises for her singing at a local concert. Susan approved of what the Cavan paper said – 'discriminating, just the right things were said. I was not quite so pleased at the remarks about that expensive looking mass Mrs. Stradone, however'. The Flamingo was 'a truly generous bird – & I wish his concert had gained more money . . .'.

Victoria's penchant for nicknames, relished by Susan, was paired by an enjoyment in men of the cloth. Susie had seen the Darling, with whom Baby had been boating in Sligo, in one of the lake parties.

You may tell Auntie that her opinion of Charlie Darling will not be raised when I say I strongly suspect him of trying to cut me the other day. I was wandering about Monkstown on Monday, looking up the Groves – when I saw a neatly dressed cleric in a tall hat coming up the other side of the street – a sudden inspiration told me it must be the Darling – but though I looked over – the curate walked on, turning neither to the right hand or to the left. Now I cannot swear it was the late Sligo man but it was awfully like him at first glance – I did not give a second, so I may have been wrong – Charlie Darling's outward man being very similar to that of the ordinary young Clerk in Holy Orders.

While her letters are full of spicy commentary, Susie confessed to her sisters that, as the old ladies were chatting, she sat 'up in a dream', coming to with a start when Sligo, and some familiar names, were mentioned. 'Now you are laughing at my taste for genealogy'. When George visited her, they had not had much time to talk of 'family affairs, or the excitement & strong language of Captain Cullen' – their Uncle Jemmy.

However, I gave an outline of his remarks – & we both laughed over the same – & arrived at the same conclusion about the brave Captain namely that he is harmless & scarcely acountable – being simply a puppet in the able hands of the more or less malevolent Kidney [his wife Sydney] – so Auntie needn't vex herself over his stupid remarks – as the poor little man is not at all worth fighting with.

In this letter of Autumn 1890, Susan first intimates the breakdown of health, which by the end of the decade was a permanent trial, to bedevil the remainder of her life. Aunt Margaret and she had gone to a meeting at the Mariner's Church, were late and had to take a back seat – fortunately, because she had become faint, and had had to come home. A good morning in bed had helped, though she was still 'not up to much'.

'You would scarcely recognise the needlewoman in the bookworm that I have become,' she told Tory. *Daniel Deronda*, George Eliot's last novel, she had just borrowed from Mrs. Hackett, '& I am reading hard at this wonderful work – which for close & true delineation of character surpasses any book I ever read.'

She was already thinking of her return to Birr, and how she had promised to be involved in the working Guild – 'I forget the terms I agreed to.' She hoped to be back for the 'great' Masonic Concert. One Birr event more to her taste, in November 1891, was the Reverend Robert Boyd, speaking in the Methodist Church, on 'Women: Ancient and Modern'. The 'new woman' was the rage in the newspapers. Already universities were beginning to open their doors to women: and delegates were going from Dublin and Belfast to meetings of the National Conference of Womens' Suffrage Societies in England.

Susan, living the sheltered life of a gentlewoman in provincial Ireland, listened and was aware, but still confined herself to singing, social visiting, reading and writing a little, while she absorbed what she heard and read. There

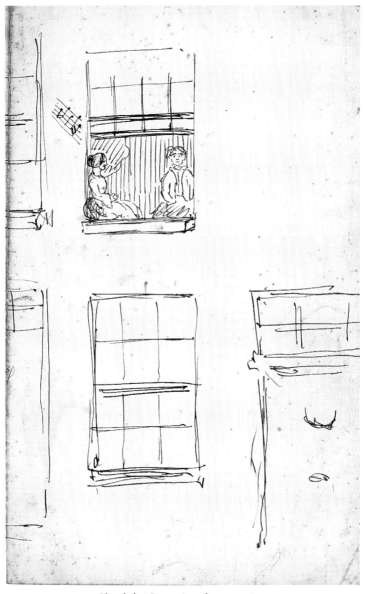

Sketch by Susan in a letter, c.1890

were tragedies near at hand. Bidz lost her two younger children in January of 1892, the wise and rosy Madeleine, and baby Arthur, who was less than a year old, victims of typhoid. The following month, Aunt Shepperd, Bidz's god-mother and adoptive parent, to whom she was closer than anyone, died of influenza. 'Such awful things have happened since I saw you', Susan wrote to Johnny in 'dismal' Kilrush. 'It has been a miserable winter. I think Sligo can never be the same again – now dear Auntie has died – Bidz has had a sad time of it.'

She did not dwell on the tragedies – 'the facts are miserable enough' – but was looking forward to Jinny's return from Germany. Uncle Adam had re-signed as Solicitor to the Grand Jury, and Tom had succeeded him. 'Tom is becoming quite rational & responsible over it', Susan remarked sarcastically. 'He was actually heard to speak in a genial way about priests the other day.'

She regretted that the Rector was leaving Birr, and thought they would never get a parson as nice as he was: 'but I fancy he is rather glad to be in civilised regions again' (no doubt she was thinking of his clash with her cousins over the reredos in St. Brendan's). Dr. Berry was making a clean sweep and taking the curate with him: and she feared that he would be succeeded by 'a "psalm singing divil" – as Dr. Stoney prognosticated to the Rector the other day.'

Another bit of news was the rumour that Dr. Woods was thinking of re-signing – and inevitably the family saw an opening for Adam, so that he could return to Birr. Dr. Woods had 'got a great fall off his tricycle the other day – hurt his shoulder & got a severe shaking . . . Adam & his wife came over just to see how the land lay – but this is strictly private – & probably the old veteran has no idea of resigning at all.' She and her aunts had thankfully escaped the influ-enza, though the winter was by no means over yet, and, she told her brother, she could scent snow in the air.

There was to be a great Sergeants' Ball in the Oxmantown Hall, with all the rank and fashion of the neighbourhood going, 'not the Crookes', nor Susan. However Susan left a colourful account of a Birr's most spectacular event of 1892, the Fancy Dress Ball at the Castle in April. It says much for her objectiv-ity, and her innate love of writing, that her bubbling description of the evening comes in a letter where she related at length to her sisters, and with genuine sorrow, the circumstances of her Uncle's death. After that she launched straight into a mischievous account of the Ball, with herself as centrepiece, dressed as an eighteenth century shepherdess. In her opinion, 'the best done fancy dress was the Greek of Lady West Ridgeway – straight white draperies & gold bands – lovely'.

For the night, she herself was Cinderella, said by everyone to be 'gor-geously handsome'.

My eyebrows were a little darkened because of the powdered hair – but

I didn't touch my eyes. I did my hair myself – turned back over a pad – done high – & curled at the back. Then I powdered it snow white. Everyone said my hair was magnificent – in fact I got so much praise that night that I became callous.

I held a levée of Mitchells . . . here when I was dressed – I had a very tall stick with a crook. A bunch of flowers tied round near the top, with yellow & brown ribbons – this was like Peg Woffington. . .. I shared a bus [cab] with Alice Woods – Mr. and Mrs. Hogben – So the bus arriving at 10, I departed in the same – amidst cheers from the assembled family (figurative) all of whom unfeignedly admired me – even Mary was enthusiastic – while Sara said it was not so much my dress as my face she admired – nice Sara –

. . .The Hogbens having been taken on board we went to the Castle – I was now in fine humour, so arriving at the Ancestral Halls – I told the gentleman of the party, Mr. Hogben, I should need his arm up the steps – my high heeled shoes being difficult. So I descended from the bus with great dignity – & giving my stick to a lackey – my arm to Mr. Hogben, tripped up the carpeted steps – proceeding to the cloakroom up wide staircases – & down narrow corridors – I felt (it was all the dress) quite at home in the last century & quite used to lofty halls, and ancestral mansions.

I had my poetic feeling of the fitness of things gratified, as a gentleman of my era (Sir Hubert Miller in the uniform of the [Coldstream] guards of the 18th cent) stepped down the oaken stair dressed in powdered queue – richly gold laced scarlet coat & sword. . . On to the cloak room – where I awaited my chaperone. I found some friends there, Olivia [Crooke, who went as 'Night'], Primrose – & a Bunch of Keys – we had amiable Conversations & I gave my name & style to an attendant – both attendants of course being old friends – low acquaintance – and, on the arrival of Mrs. Frend & Mary – the latter in fine red plush cloak & silk gown – as Millais' Portia – proceeded to the Ball room – at the entrance of same I had the gratificiation of hearing a flunkey bawl my name & those of my companions – & made my entry & my salutations to Lady Rosse & also to the Earl – with much dignity. They are very pleasant Host & Hostess – I like the Host best.

All of the Crookes were there, even Douglas (referred to as G. Crooke): though Susan danced freely with whoever invited her, their engagement still being secret.

> As to the dancing – I got on very well – I expected a lot of sitting but hadn't so very much. My partners were neither numerous or costly, but I was ready for anything – G. Crooke – Mr. Hogben – Mr. Moore – Mr. Marshall – Captain Templar – Freddy McSheehy – Bill Frend & there were more I forget – in the Cotillion, I had a lot of dancing with Harry Bennett – also Tom Drought – also G. Crooke – also a man staying at the Castle – in one figure – I think Sir West Ridgeway – also a Mr. Trench – such a handsome youth. Considering that the dancing was a scrimmage, I enjoyed it a lot – I got some of my lace torn in the mob – but suffered no more. . . altogether I enjoyed myself as I had not done for ages.

The *Chronicle* of the day fills in her account of the ball with descriptions of the decorations: the flowers illuminated by the electric lights installed by the Earl, and the lighted wax candles. The ballroom with its rich moulded ceiling and brilliant gilt upholstery, the graceful draperies and massive mirrors, the trailing ivy and evergreens arranged by Sir Hubert Miller. The colossal sideboard of the dining-room laden with silverware, the walls festooned with flags, and every space filled with orchids, roses, palms and ferns, the portraits of past aristocrats peeping out through gaps in the floral abundance. At the top of the room, Sir Laurence Parsons, the first baronet, in his steely armour, gazed from his canvas, down the line of many coloured lamps, at the enormous supper, with every-thing conceivable that was in season ready for the theatrical throng.

Doors had been removed, so as to ease circulation, and maize-coloured lampshades cast a harmonious light on the brilliant costumes. It happened to be a densely dark night, yet the paper reported that inside the Castle was more like daylight than night time. Lady Rosse dressed as the Queen of Charles I, and the Earl as an 18th century Sir Laurence Parsons. Miss Evans came as a paper lamp shade, in yellow and green paper: but the most imposing costume of all was that of Mr. Henry Frend, who made a magnificent impersonation of his royal name-sake, Henry VIII.

The crowning event for Susan was the last dance of the programme; and Douglas took her out on the floor.

> The Cotillion began about 2 or 2.30 – & G. Crooke was my partner for it – you have a partner for the whole concern – & every time Cotillion is called you may take a wild whirl with him – but you can have heaps of partners in the figures – Sir Hubert & Lady Rosse led it – some awfully pretty figures – I am told I was very well in it – that is I was chosen for some figures – & as such a lot were dancing of course it was lucky for me – for instance that figure mentioned in the Chronicle – a lady placed at the end of the room – & two men told to jump through a hoop to her – I was rather proud of being in that – as there were only 2 or 3 girls in it before me – & they were very pretty.

Sir Hubert came over & called me out. – Jennie Crooke said when she saw me advance alone to the end of the room where I stood in solitary expectancy, she did not know me – I was radiant & tapped along on my highheeled shoon – I stood & waited while 2 men went for the hoop held by Sir Hubert they both jumped – & a tall handsome youth reached me first & we whirled off together – he was Trench – we waltzed round in the ring of spectators – & Jeannie said it was the prettiest sight of the evening.

At this point of her narrative, Susan checked herself, realising she had been totally carried away in her memory of the fantasy of the night.

You will say I am very vain – but I didn't feel like myself & I think now I am writing of someone else – so you will pardon – & I know you thirst for every item – & really if you heard all the things were said to me of my appearance – you would laugh.

'I am sure this letter is awfully flippant,' she excused herself, hesitating about the delight she took in the ridiculous headiness of the festivities. 'But the Celtic buoyancy of nature will out – & goodness knows the depression is bad enough when it comes.'

The fairy story of the Ball finished crisply with a sarcastic 'Here endeth. . .' Susan felt she had overdone her ecstatic description – even for her faithful 'Pair' for whom she had probably been shaping the detail while still dancing. But the truth was that her pen was growing fertile: and she confessed that she had been writing some essays recently, 'very caustic & spiteful – but rather amusing. Some day you will see them – they are about people here.'

The major event in Birr, in 1892, was the passing of Uncle Adam. He had been to church on the morning of April 24, particularly anxious to be present at the institution of the new Rector, and had become ill when he arrived home – 'a sort of stroke – paralysis of the brain', she told Johnny. George had been down for Easter Monday and Tuesday, which had given Uncle Adam much pleasure, though George thought he looked poorly.

It was all so sudden – seeing him at church as usual in the morning – & seeing him dying last night – poor Aunt Barbara is in a fearful state – it is harder for her – because he was unable to speak to her, & she feels this very much.

Two of Adam's sons, Tom, his heir, and George, the youngest – who was somewhat older than Susan's brother George – were with him when he died. Adam did not arrive in time.

For Susan it was not only the end of an era, whose authority she approved though she could not accept its narrow principles, but it was the final break with the past. Uncle Adam was the last of her father's brothers. She deeply regretted that neither Jinny nor Tory had met him, and that George and Johnny were unable to come to the funeral.

> I was sorry – as of course it was a wonderful affair – and I would have liked our Father to be represented at it. However George could not apply for leave so soon again – & it is very hard for Johnny to get here from Kilrush – if Sligo was not such a journey we might have had Gilly – after all Uncle Adam was the head of our house.

Adam Mitchell

She could not go to the service, as neither of her two cousins, Susan and Sara (who lived at Walcot – daughters of Adam's brother, the late James Daniel), would come, and she did not care to be the only woman of the family present. Mrs. George Mitchell, wife of Adam's youngest son, sent an anchor-shaped tribute made of primroses: and one of the chief mourners was Adam Mitchell's old friend, Milward Crooke, who preached a tribute in St. Brendan's the following Sunday.

Susan gave her own tribute to her sisters. Her Uncle Adam, she said, was a major loss.

> The universal feeling here is one of regret – he was considered a very able & great man here – one of the old stock – & he was a great benefactor to the town & specially to the Church – the pulpit put up to Fitzroy is really a noble gift . . . I hope the new head of the house will try & grow like his Father – & keep up the prestige of his name – but you know he is not much of a favorite here – though not really a bad sort, when you get beneath the disagreeable husk. The sons' grief for their father is very genuine – Adam – my favorite was specially fond of him – though he tries to let people think he doesn't care – he is a queer fellow, but has wider sympathies than the rest – & a good marriage – a wife with a high ideal – would have made a man of him.

She felt sorry for Cousin Adam. She would have liked to have been friends with him and his family, 'but I can't stand the lot in the Queen's Co. – consequently I think Adam feels a little huffed about my not going there.'

You will think I am giving a lecture on the Mitchells – but they naturally interest me much at present – there is a strong family clannish feeling amongst them – & they ought to be an immense power here – they wont go into society – at least this generation – but if the next get fair play – & Tom at least is giving his sons every advantage – they will be a great power in the countryside.

Uncle Adam's wife, Barbara, and Mary their only daughter, who was unmarried, were overcome with grief: and Aunt Jane and Aunt Margaret hurried over to Walcot to stay with them. There was much reminiscing about the family. Aunt Jane told how her grandfather, Thomas Mitchell of Fortal – Susan's great grandfather – who had died at Riverstown when Jane was only two, had had a funeral three miles long. It stretched the whole way from Fortal, almost into Birr.

Susan felt isolated while her aunts were at Walcot. 'I hate being by myself', she told her sisters, 'but never mind. The summer is coming – & then Tory you'll come with it.'

EIGHT

'Knowing the Ritual in my Blood'

PAROCHIAL RITUALS FOR A LEARNED AUNT

Susie, writing from Birr, shaped her letters particularly to suit the recipients. For Tory, she concentrated on curates, with a special accolade for the departing 'paragon of curates',

> Mr. Stanistreet, words can't convey the niceness of this curate. He is delicate – Baby! suffers from post nasal catarrh! – sympathise. But he is all right now – he plays beautifully – he was in here the other night – shared our car in from Riverstown & stayed to tea with us – he was sweet – lit the lamp, drew the curtains, played accompaniments – even tried the bass in a duet – talked & was everything the fondest curatolater could wish. – Alas he is gone & none can supply the loss . . .

She expected, even demanded that curates be entertaining. Mr. Fletcher was 'cultivating a most extraordinary style of walk – it resembles a dance – & may indeed be some medieval ecclesiastical measure!' Harry Armstrong, 'dear little man . . . Of course he is the princeps of curates, but I would like to know what kept him so long without being priested. . . ?'

Baby coincided with Susan in Cavan early in the summer of 1892, where Bidz was recovering from her bereavement. Susan herself was adjusting after Douglas Crooke's departure to his commission in the Suffolk Regiment, a handsome sight in his scarlet uniform with white facings. 'What with officers – & curates to tea etc. it is hard to find leisure', Susan found. Diana (Baby) wrote to Mamma about the tennis parties, and of happy visits to the Somervilles, to pick and eat raspberries and gooseberries. They both liked Mr. Fleming, who sat between the sisters at the Sullivans' tea party, and who insisted on pouring black currant jelly on to Diana's plate, after which he left to prepare his Sunday sermon.

Diana met old Mr. McCausland at the stationer's and introduced him to Susan. 'You would have laughed to have seen 'Auntie' walking down the street with her Cullen air beside the old Rector,' she wrote jokingly about Susan. The future poet seized the pen from her sister to interpolate – 'There is no knowing now where 'Auntie' will stop. I suppose in the Vatican – at the feet of the Holy Father, & in the bosom of Holy Mother church'.

She could now talk with authority on church matters, because she was on close terms with the new Rector of Birr and his wife. She tried to explain to her 'darling Pair' why she hadn't a minute of time in her 'incoherent sort of life'.

> Last night after practice I waited to speak to the Rector about a woman – & he said promptly, "come into the vestry". Of course the curate drew up, of whom I took not the slightest notice . . . then Mr. Taylor, seeing me about to go in the vestry, came up smiling & said, "What is the meaning of this, are you let through here – I think I will come too." "Very well", said his cousin, Henry Fletcher, "come with me."

> Then both Taylor & myself saw an imposing looking thing on the vestry table. Flagon shaped, with a cross on the lid – & the Rector said, "look at the Ritualism", Fletcher's ritualism – I think he said – so Henry came back, took up the vessel & said, "Have you seen this, Miss Mitchell."

> So we all admired it – I think Taylor said he gave a shilling towards it – Henry Fletcher collected money for it – it is a thing for filling the font. I don't know the proper name. The Rector kept saying – "this savours of Ritualism, a cracked jug would be the right thing." Then the curate & Taylor melted away. . .

> The other day we had a great chat, Mrs. Hemphill, Sam & myself – we thought "ritualism" would be a good bold thing to discuss. I said it was the name people dreaded, not the thing, as they did not know that here, or were ever likely to. We spoke of how ceremonial & ritual was a part of everyday life – entered into our common intercourse, our society manners. I mentioned the Salvation Army ritual of drums & tambourines, its vestments & its orders. Sam speaking of the lengths they go in England – said a great part of it was really the aesthetic movement, & that some was due to curates & ladies – at which we both (Mrs. H. & I) laughed & asked if they were the same species.

> "These young curates like to fancy themselves priests", he said. I spoke to him of what you said as to the Archdeacon's attacks on dissenters, whereat he cried out, "the man is a fool to cut his own throat. Half the Protestants in Ireland are descended from dissenters, for my part, I am descended from Presbyterians": & again he said the other night, "I am convinced these bodies have their raison d'être".

'Knowing your love for Sam', Susan said, 'I do not apologise for long quotations from him'. But she indicated what direction her own form of aesthetic ritualism was taking when she told the story of her 'comforting the sick & indignant' out of the monies Sam had given her in the vestry to help the poor woman she had spoken to him about.

> I made grand beef tea for Mrs. Fagan today, first I ever made – took it to her & saw her drink it, & sang "She wore a wreath of roses" the while.

Susan, with her secret betrothal diminished to become a wavering ghost hovering in the veil of the future, was finding herself absorbed more and more into the daily rituals of the parish. She sang in the church choir. She worked with the Girls' Friendly Society. 'I am at present stumping for papers on Vivisection & Feathered women to be read at G.F.S. Monday 29th. I find it hard to get writers, the subjects are horrid. We are to make it a sort of debate, & the Rector has entrusted the working of it to me, gay for me.'

She begged the intellectual Jinny to cooperate – 'Do get some papers about either of these subjects, ask McClean, anyone, & either write yourself – of course, Baby wouldn't being only an ass! or else send the paper to me . . .I know nothing of Vivisection & can not tell which side I should take. For goodness sake come to my aid.' On another occasion, she wrote 'a great Essay on "Church Music"' for the G.F.S. that had cost her 'some honest work in the shape of reading', but she did not begrudge it.

She and the Rector made plans for a literary society, on the lines of the famous one run by Davidson Houston in Sandymount Church in Dublin – 'for men & women both. It would be awfully nice, some object for which to read & write'. When the Dorcas Guild met to sew for the poor at Mrs. Shannon's house – 'I hear she has asked everybody in Birr' – Susan decided to sing and read Tennyson. She so comported herself that at the Fultons she was

> accounted worthy to take a part in Shakespear – a poet hitherto sacred to the Best Society in Birr. To tell you the truth their interpretation of the Immortal Bard is very meagre, his utterances at these sceances being read for the most part in such mysterious whispers as to be unintelligible to the Philistine minority who ply the needle of the seamstress.

When Susan went to stay with Bidz in Cavan in May 1893, she found Bidz was expecting another child. Bidz hadn't told her, as she feared Susie might change her mind about coming: though she had written to Mamma joyfully about 'this business of mine', and explained why she would not go to Sligo for her confinement.

Susan was holding the fort in Farnham Street when Mamma came, an ever energetic Kate conscious of her years. 'A homely woman' pulled her into the train at Inny, and the guard was very attentive. 'The country looked lovely', she wrote to Jinny, '& I had a splendid view of Edgesworthstown House & kept thinking all the time of the Authoress of "Belinda".

> Susan and Turk met me at the train. . . We walked from Train, met Jimmy half way, were greeted by Miss Badger from the Window in passing. We are to go to the Rectory to eat Fruit if it is fine, looks very dark just now.

Susan was picking red currants, supposed to be helped by Turk [her niece Kathleen], who was far more interested in the 'Cow catcher in front of the Train' – explained to her by her learned Aunt, 'who is full of information on all subjects.' Kate secretly admired this daughter whom she knew least of her children. Rarely had they been together for more than a few days.

Susan left for Sligo some days later; and Bidz Dora Brabazon, who would outlive the rest of her family, was born on July 26. Kate could write to the Trio in Sligo that 'Bidz and the Baby are so well that it has become monotonous.' She hoped the party up the lake had been a success – 'I am always relieved when I hear Lake parties are over'. She was interested in the beaus. Jim Vernon was 'a great bear'. 'It was mean & low of him not to bring his handsome Uncle to the party, but I suppose he is jealous of his splendid physique, for where would you see a finer man?' Kate's sense of humour, like Susan's, revelled in the irony of certain items of news from home. 'The Archdeacon turning Nationalist beats all. . . Sligo is going to the dogs!'

One family event of 1893 that Susan found hard to stomach was George's marriage. He was thirty-two, the second of the independent-minded Mitchells to venture into wedlock. Like Susan, he had spent most of his life away from home: but he visited the family every year, looked after them when they visited Dublin: and was the oracle on financial matters.

He took to wife a devoted Roman Catholic, a Miss O'Neill, from County Kilkenny. It is to the credit of the close-knit, upper class Protestant Mitchells that they did not allow any rift to develop. And the next generation, likewise, though reared as was the custom in the Catholic faith, refused to ignore George's Protestantism, and – defying their mother – insisted that he had a Church of Ireland burial. Susan, of course at the time, was well aware of the potential problems, and, when, years later, Johnny decided to get married, she wrote to Jinny, 'Thank God she is a Protestant.'

For Susan, with her liberal views, and conviction about the Catholicity of the Church, religion was not the major stumbling block. It was a matter of upbringing. Manners, tastes, habits, were seminal to her appreciation of personality, and Ellen, she felt, was wanting. 'Ellen is most goodnatured', she wrote to Johnny, after visiting George and his wife with their first child in November 1894, 'though hopeless as to her ever taking polish.' She found the house comfortable, the baby a nice little girl – 'or rather big girl – for she is powerfully strong looking – George . . . carries her about & fusses over her generally. . . seems so delighted to have one in his house.'

Her letters to her brother Johnny were not so full of uninhibited fun as those to 'the Pair', though, when describing characters in whom he might have a particular interest, she displayed the same fascination with human idiosyncrasy. She had lately made the acquaintance of the RM, Mr. Shannon – who was a cousin of Mr. Taylor, the DI, and also of Mr. Fletcher, the curate. 'This relationship is a little embarrassing if you want to abuse any of the 3 to the other 2.' But she liked Shannon, who 'tells very pleasant stories, uses the choicest language – it is a lesson in elegant English to hear him talk, indeed one is inclined to form oneself on his style, as you may fancy I am doing, from the longwinded phrases in this letter.'

Susan mentioned in her letters the standard English poets she was reading, but made no reference to the writer who was in vogue in the eighteen-nineties, and who influenced her own first mystical verse. John Greenleaf Whittier, the American Quaker poet and associate of Emerson and Longfellow, wrote passionately in support of freedom and humanity. His efforts in the cause against slavery, and the fact that his sister Elizabeth was also a poet and his closest friend, impressed her. In the summer of 1895, she acquired a small volume of his poems, bound in ivory cloth, and she read and re-read them, marking verses for their advanced spiritual ideas as well as for their gentle compulsive rhythms, some of which she adopted for her own poetry. She seems to have used poems such as 'Andrew Rykman's Prayer' for personal meditation, underlining phrases and marking couplets.

> I alone the beauty mar,
> I alone the music jar.
> Yet *with hands by evil stained*.
> And an ear by discord pained,
> I am groping for the keys
> Of the heavenly harmonies.

She felt totally at one with a mysticism inspired by nature: and content with Whittier's religion of love. A verse in 'The curse of the Charter-breakers' seems to echo in her own 'Ode to the British Empire' written years later. The lyrical thoughts of 'Tauler' affected her more than anything –

> one who, wandering in a starless night,
> Feels, *momently, the jar of unseen* waves,
>
> And hears the thunder of an unknown sea,
> Breaking upon an unimagined shore'.

Her delight and frustration with Mammon was stirred by all around her in Birr, and Sligo and Dublin; but in Whittier she found the silent muse which set her on the path to her own original poetry. She was already writing religious verse: but she now knew what form the blood-inherited ritual could take within herself.

182   *THE RANGER.*

Down the locust-shaded way ;
But away, swift away,
Fades the fond, delusive seeming,
And I kneel again and pray.

" When the growing dawn is showing,
And the barn-yard cock is crowing,
  And the horned moon pales away ;
From a dream of him awaking,
Every sound my heart is making
Seems a footstep of his taking ;
  Then I hush the thought, and say,
    ' Nay, nay, he's away !'
Ah ! my heart, my heart is breaking
  For the dear one far away."

Look up, Martha ! worn and swarthy,
Glows a face of manhood worthy ;
  " Robert !" "Martha !" all they say,
O'er went wheel and reel together,
Little cared the owner whither ;
Heart of lead is heart of feather,
  Noon of night is noon of day !
  Come away, come away !
When such lovers meet each other,
  Why should prying idlers stay ?

Quench the timber's fallen embers,
Quench the red leaves in December's
  Hoary rime and chilly spray,
But the hearth shall kindle clearer,
Household welcomes sound sincerer,
Heart to loving heart draw nearer,

140   *ANDREW RYKMAN'S PRAYER.*

Not for sport of mind and force
Hast Thou made Thy universe,
But as atmosphere and zone
Of Thy loving heart alone.
Man, who walketh in a show,
Sees before him, to and fro,
Shadow and illusion go ;
All things flow and fluctuate,
Now contract and now dilate.
In the welter of this sea,
Nothing stable is but Thee ;
In this whirl of swooning trance,
Thou alone art permanence ;
All without Thee only seems,
All beside is choice of dreams.
Never yet in darkest mood
Doubted I that Thou wast good,
Nor mistook my will for fate,
Pain of sin for heavenly hate—
Never dreamed the gates of pearl
Rise from out the burning marl,
Or that good can only live
Of the bad conservative,
And through counterpoise of hell
Heaven alone be possible.
For myself alone I doubt ;
All is well, I know, without ;
I alone the beauty mar,
I alone the music jar.
Yet, with hands by evil stained,
And an ear by discord pained,
I am groping for the keys
Of the heavenly harmonies ;
Still within my heart I bear

Two marked excerpts from Susan Mitchell's copy of Whittier's Poems

NINE

'A Fragile House . . . of Broken Memories'

ORPHANED FOR A SECOND TIME

On October 19, 1896, Aunt Margaret died at Cumberland Square. She was seventy-seven, the youngest of Michael Mitchell's surviving sisters. The funeral was held four days later, on a Friday, at Mount Jerome in Dublin, following the arrival of the 8.20 train from Parsonstown.

Aunt Jane died the following April, on Good Friday. She was ninety, in possession of all her faculties, and passed away peacefully, mourned with her sister by all of Protestant Birr for her unostentatious charity and evangelical piety. A drenching day did not deter mourners from coming to hear Dr. Hemphill pay his tribute, as her bones were lowered into the family vault at Eglish. The chief mourners were her nephews and great-nephews.

Now Susan's ordered home, the omphalos of her adult existence, which had reflected the more cultivated side of her father's origins, had been removed. Her aunts, she told Lily Yeats, 'were such lovely people, so amazed and secretly proud of the duckling that had appeared amongst the docile Mitchell hens, and ready to battle the whole family on my behalf all the time'.

Years later she ruminated on the cocooned life with her aunts, and how, until that period of separation, in spite of her early irritations, she had never fully questioned her orthodox upbringing. She had had 'that pathetic longing to be like the herd, that the uniformity of a girl's education indicates to her as the proper path for those who aspire to belong to what I had hitherto known as society'.

Educated as she had been, and living in Birr society in the midlands, through the Land League troubles, and the 'great times' of Parnell: even standing in the crowd at Parnell's funeral, she had been 'but lightly moved'. She had been virtually unaware of the turmoil of change and struggle in the political Ireland of those days. It was obstinacy of temperament that kept her from adopting the 'respectable' views accepted in her aunts' circle.

Now, of course, the question was what should she do with herself, orphaned for a second time. She had a small private income, but not enough to

Charles Stewart Parnell, by Sidney Hall, 1892

live on; and certainly not enough to satisfy the needs of an active mind with ambitions, however undecided.

Jinny, always businesslike, had taken over the Sligo infant school with Diana, when the Misses Blyth retired. So Susan went to Sligo to work with her sisters for a short while. Bidz's eldest daughter, Kathleen, was taught recitation by Aunt Susan. Afterwards she remembered being called a 'wooden stick' for her rendering of a poem, 'The enchanted shirt'.

In the more liberal atmosphere of Sligo, Susan's growing antipathy to 'the walled world of the Ascendancy' dilated once more. She was at a prize-giving in a convent about this time, at which the Catholic bishop of the diocese officiated.

> . . . it was to me as if the solid ground had fissured beneath my feet revealing an underworld entirely unsuspected. In the narrow pride of my

> Ascendancy I had never dreamed of a Catholic Ireland that had its own
> presiding lawn sleeves, its own yards of white muslin billowing in restless
> rows, representing money that could be paid and was paid for teaching
> in French and the piano and the violin, all the very same trappings of
> education that I believed only to exist among the Ascendancy under
> whose shadow I was nurtured. . . The whole solid ground of my experi-
> ence trembled. . . The walled garden of the Ascendancy was no more to
> me a world, but a walled garden, and I another Eve, curious as the first'.

Six months after the wrench of Aunt Jane's demise, Susan experienced a further, more private shock. This may have been the cause of the chronic illness
that was shortly to afflict her, and bring about a complete change in her life. She
was extrovert and outspoken in her letters about friends, acquaintances and
current public follies, even about her own shortcomings: but she was always
reticent about personal emotions. Apart from the first bubbling announcement
of her engagement to Douglas Crooke in 1890, she made no reference to him,
except in passing. In society of the time, since Douglas was a sergeant and not
an officer, it was not proper for the couple to be seen in public together, or for
the engagement to be official. But the family liked and approved of him. She
had accepted that the engagement would be a long one. Then, instead of pur-
suing the desk job she proposed, and eventually some colonial appointment, he
had finally got the commission that at heart he wanted, and went on active
service in an emergency area of the Empire.

Susan must have kept hope glimmering in the 'fragile house' within her.
With her deep and affectionate nature, and determined character, it is unlikely
that she could have fallen in and out of love easily, though, from the beginning,
she had been strongly aware of the intellectual gap that divided them. Among
her papers is preserved a newspaper cutting, with a photograph of Lieutenant
G. D. Crooke, giving a brief reference to his death in action in November 1897
on the Indian Frontier.

The Indian border campaign, organised as an offensive against Afghanistan
by the Indian Viceroy, the Earl of Elgin, had taken its toll of the British army.
The stubbornly independent tribal peoples of the northwest frontier continued
to make their protest by guerrilla tactics: and according to Indian commenta-
tors were forced into aggression. India in 1897 had been enduring a number of
natural calamities, famine, plague, earthquake and flood: and the high-handed
British army, with its repressive measures, burning villages, blowing up forts,
taking over civilian houses, only agitated the local population and inflamed the
bitterness of guerrilla resistance.

The British army saw it differently, as a series of heroic deeds in the course
of subduing a dissident population. Early in November of 1897, General Kempster
led an expedition up the Waran Valley, and, returning to camp on the 15th,
there was a fierce battle. The main company managed to make their way suc-

cessfully; but as they descended to the Valley, two companies of the Sikhs were suddenly attacked by the guerrillas. 'The Sikhs fought splendidly', 'behaved brilliantly', one newspaper report reads. It was dusk and the enemy were coming from all sides. The Sikhs stormed the enemy's blockhouses with bayonets, and forced their way into one. The weather was bitterly cold, but the wounded soldiers were cared for by putting them on the hot floor of a blockhouse that had been recently burned. The regiment then marched into camp the following morning without further incident.

But while all this was going on, the detachment of the Dorsetshires in which Douglas Crooke was serving had lost its way in the dark, and was surrounded by the enemy. Lieutenant Hales, Lieutenant Crooke and nine of their men were killed, 'virtually extirpated by a swarm of sharp-shooters who knew every inch of the ground, and had been dodging behind rocks on the heights,' reported the *King's County Chronicle*; 'the enemy are admittedly among the first of marksmen.' The group of lost men, cornered in the darkness, had no chance of survival. The night after his premature death, Douglas was buried with all the obsequies possible on active service.

George Douglas Crooke, thirty-two years of age, was praised at length in the *King's County Chronicle* – which gave a full account of the incident. 'From childhood', it stated, 'he had a military spirit, inherited from his parents.' He had been as popular as a private and sergeant in the Seaforth Highlanders, as he had been as a youth in Parsonstown, when he captained the football team. He was 'the heart and soul of chivalry'.

Susan was left with a newspaper cutting from the *Daily Graphic*, showing a shy intelligent young man, with deep-set twinkling eyes and fair moustache, a trim figure in his uniform. Not long afterwards she penned the following lines in the leather and brass-bound occasional book Rosa Holzer had given to Jinny as a New Years' present:

> I walk within my heart and take
> The roads he led me dear and dim
> To where a fragile house I make
> Of broken memories of him.
>
> Without, they build me stately halls
> They call my comrades, near and far,
> Ah, heart, more dear the wavering walls,
> Where all thy broken treasures are.

TEN

'A Wonderful Society'

DISCOVERY IN LONDON

L ate in 1897, Susan joined the Yeats family in London as companion to Lily Yeats, who had never fully recovered from the experience of work-ing for May Morris, and the typhoid she subesquently contracted when in France. Susan too was ill. She had to undergo treatment for the tuberculosis that was to afflict her for the rest of her life,[1] 'spoiling her beauty', as she would say, and leaving her very deaf. An office job, and training in how to index, were to be an asset when she returned to Dublin two years later. But, more than that, was the actual experience of living with the Yeats family.

Even before Jinny's first meeting and instant rapport with Lily Yeats in l890, as she set out on her journey to Germany, Susan had received a lasting impression of the father of this remarkable family, when she had sat on the step of her aunt's house in Wellington Road, and watched him walk up the 'sacred' path to the Pursers' house next door. A hostility had grown up in her juvenile mind, despite her 'natural feminine admiration for a handsome man.'

> Something had been said in my presence that suggested that Mr. Yeats admired & painted red hair of a shade different to what mine was at that early and glowing period, red hair as straight as mine was curly, hair I could not conscientiously approve of at all, I whose ruddy locks were for the first time in their history admired & thought worthy of recreation on canvas by the hand of Miss Sarah Purser.

Some part of that feeling of hostility remained, she recalled years afterwards, so that when she met Mr. Yeats in his own house in Bedford Park, there was at first between them 'a faint mist as of frost'. The frost wasn't long in dissipating. 'In contact with so stimulating a personality as that of Mr. Yeats, one may become furious, but one is never frozen,' she commented.

---

[1] The operation on her nose for 'lupus', a skin infection caused by reaction to the tuberculosis organism, was probably treated with a skin graft.

JBY,[2] for his part, noted initially that she was a pretty woman who sang rather well. He soon found her singing soothed him while he painted. As he grew to know her, he came to relish her appearance and personality, her intellect and her wit, comparing her with a kitten – 'so playful and tender, such big eyes, such soft paws, and such claws'. Next she was sitting to him, one of the sympathetic characters he craved, whose conversation and listening ear meant as much to him as the image he recreated in oil. He coveted Susan's presence, as that of Lily, in a house that he found 'a desert', since Lolly was making her career outside, and his wife was a total invalid in a world of her own, unable to respond to him either benignly or irritably. He was fond of his wife, who – according to Katherine Tynan – he 'always knew would be the mother of a poet'; he was intrigued by her remote nature, but frustrated by her passivity which lapsed into melancholy.

Susan, accustomed to elderly aunts in their failing years, would have been a welcome visitor in Mrs. Yeats's room: but she never made reference to her. Lily became a lifelong friend, JBY her confidant and creative mentor.

Apart from the Yeats family themselves, there was London. 'The greatness of London', she wrote later, 'was not in its literary persons, but in the city itself.

> It submerged me, and I instinctively raised myself on the shoulders nearest me. It was doubtless luck for me that these shoulders belonged to such as the Yeats, Martyn, Moore, Lady Gregory, Ashe King, but at first I did not know my luck. I thought that these people were merely ornaments for the drawing-room; afterwards I realised they were ornaments for the world.

'The talk in the Yeats household turned ever Irelandwards', she remembered. The Yeatses, after all, came from the same kind of Irish background of business and spiritual affairs as Susan had been discovering in her own descent. They had landowning forbears as she did, and had the same amused relish for the more extravagant aspects of such life, in the shadows of which they all dwelt.

JBY's grandfather had held a college living at Drumcliff, County Sligo, 'almost within hail' of Susan's great-grandfather, Rector of Manorhamilton in Leitrim.

> Lily Yeats, who has great talents as a chronicler, once told me that my clergyman great-grandfather kept fighting-cocks in the Vestry. This would account for the fact that in my family I never heard any ill spoken of her great-grandfather. The moral obliquity in my ancestor that permitted

---

2 JBY, the artist's initials, are used regularly to distinguish John Butler Yeats from his son Jack; and he will be referred to from now on in this manner.

Sketch of Susan Mitchell by JB Yeats, 1899

such practices would of course render him incapable of seeing any pec-
cadillo short of murder in hers! . . .

In the house of JBY, in Bedford Park, she found herself 'in what seemed . . .a
wonderful society.' Ideas were valued above all other possessions. 'Normal conversation ran on subjects some of which I had indeed thought of, but which
thinking I regretted in myself, as one might regret a harelip or other abnormal-
ity differentiating one from one's fellows.'

> But here was society, & a society in which my harelip far from being a
> deformity was regarded as an ornament. Here I might pour out voice
> and heart without obstruction, here pride of country, intellectual specu-
> lation, creative aspirations were fostered & not frowned on. I had had
> affection, companionship, tender guardianship all my life, but now I was
> as a fighter with one hand tied behind his back suddenly liberated, my
> powers were doubled.

She admitted that she did not realise at once that, in the Irish men & women she met under Mr. Yeats's roof, she was having her first contact with a movement that was bringing about a revolution in thinking and feeling in her own country'.

In Bedford Park, she met Willie and Jack Yeats, Dr. Todhunter, Edward Martyn, Lady Gregory, T. W. Rolleston, Katharine Tynan – 'most agreeable society'. She had only gradually become aware that she was meeting face to face with the protagonists of Ireland's awakening consciousness. She felt she hardly knew what they were doing, though Willie had already written *The Wanderings of Oisin*, *The Island of Statues*, *The Land of Heart's Desire*, and *The Countess Cathleen*, and Jack Yeats had 'indicated a new path in drawing with his titan tinkers, & his horses, centrifugal force personified, stampeding on little country racecourses, truly inadequate to the immense momentum that drives them'. George Moore, she mused later in her satirical book about the novelist, though then virtually unknown in Dublin, was already meditating a sensational incarnation 'in our unsuspecting city'. Perversely, because WB had forbidden his sisters to read it, she 'gulped guilty pages' of *The Mummer's Wife* when she went to bed at night, intimidated at 'its merciless probing into life'.

She realised for the first time, now, what conversation meant. John Butler Yeats, head thrown back, eyes smiling, said daring, witty things 'full of old wisdom & young folly, but said . . . always with a distinction & grace that made the mere saying significant. What a revelation it was to one who had never realised that talking meant something far beyond asking intelligibly for what one wanted & grunting unintelligibly when one got it; that the expression of ideas was an art as music & painting & literature were arts'.

Susan, with Lily and Lollie, sat with needlework in the company of Professor York Powell, 'his eyes overflowing with light behind his glasses', who listened also '& himself said admirable things'.

> Always the talk turned back to Ireland & it seemed to me that in this London suburb I saw Ireland truly for the first time; as one cannot see oneself in a mirror by pressing one's nose against the glass, I had to leave my country to find her.
>
> In the Yeats' house I picked up a key to my own nature, & it was an Irish key, that was its significance. It was to unlock many doors.

Susan spent eighteen months in the Yeats household. In February 1899, when she had a week off from the office because of ganglion – little tumours on the long tendon of her right hand caused by excessive writing – she received news from Sligo that Victoria Diana, still 'Baby' to her, was to marry. Victoria's diffidence, because her fiancé, Harry Franklin, was Jewish, was demolished by her elder sister, determined to avoid any of the strain George's marriage caused.

Sketch of Jack B. Yeats by his father, JB Yeats, May 1899

She had guessed that Baby was attracted by Harry, and it had been obvious that the liking was mutual. He was so nice, so clever, so tall, so goodlooking, and both of them so musical: and, if he was younger than her, what about Jack and Cottie Yeats ? – 'shining examples of the nonsense of all that sort of thing'. Susan was delighted that Victoria was not to be as one of the Blyths, and spend her life in teaching. She was far too pretty. Lily was to begin at once on her wedding present, embroidered bodices and a petticoat. Jack Yeats sent a sketch, an 'allegory' of himself, her old schoolfellow, mourning in the foreground, as she, Victoria, was being carried off in the distance. Susan sent 'oceans' of love, with characteristic warmth and excitement. 'My darling young sister', she wrote, 'I wish I was near you to see your happiness, & to tell you how happy I am that you should be happy'.

Susan of course would go home for the wedding. JBY wrote to Jinny in May lamenting the talk about Susan's return to Ireland. 'Your sister is greatly appreciated in this house. I do not [at] all enjoy the idea of her going away. I hope when she goes away it will only be for a time'.

Susan was prompted to look for other keys to her nature besides the Irish one. Before she left London, her curiosity about the occult was stirred – perhaps through Willie Yeats – by George Pollexfen. Pollexfen read her hand, and promised to send her his interpretation of her horoscope. He apologised for the delay in sending it, but

> as . . . you might possibly wish to get some of your friends (the Poet for instance) to scan over your natal figure I herewith send you the Map of the Heavens at your birth, with my reading of it so far as I have gone. . .

> You may possibly remember that when I looked at your hand I thought the Sun and Venus would be your strongest Planets. Then at the Point I thought the Moon and Venus. Well by the Horoscope these three Planets are powerful. . .

> The Sun's dominant Influence gives you a very sunny and bright disposition in general – while the brooding saturn being in your ascendant in conjunction there with the moon (Imagination) brings periods of depression and Introspective reflection, etc: . . .

He himself, he said, had Saturn in the same position in his ascendant, and the moon in opposition, 'and I know how Saturnian depression glooms at times.'

> I had not thought that you were a mars person, but it appears by your horoscope that that fiery planet was ruling the ascendant at your birth. The Sun, however, as you will see by what I have said in your horoscope, was a very dominant Planet at your birth and very Largely influences

your personality: the 10th House the Midheaven is generally taken as the mothers House and you will see Leo of the suns sign upon that house so that I should opine that you take your Sun disposition and characteristics from your mother.

He made another interesting comment in the postscript. A student of astrology looking over her horoscope, not knowing whose it was, had said she should be very careful of her health for some time, and not travel more than necessary: 'so I give you this for what it may be worth: It seems a safe advice in any case.'

At the beginning of June, as a prelude to her departure from Blenheim Road, Susan's heart was lifted by a bouquet of lilies, roses and narcissi which arrived 'beautifully' from the family garden in Sligo – 'a joy to the senses'. The heat was delicious. She was enjoying the blazing hot sun. There was a visit to Chatham, when they would have been happier to sit out in the garden – 'smuts & all'. But Harry, Matthew Yeats's son, who invited them and paid their train fares, treated them 'en prince'.

He was a naval engineer, and had just built a torpedo boat destroyer, *The Cygnet*, at Thornycrofts, and was waiting at Chatham for it to be commissioned. He met them at the station with a carriage, took them to the dockyard,

Jinny, Susan and Victoria Mitchell in Sligo, 1899

and showed them battleships, cruisers, torpedo boat destroyers, and then took them on board the Old Pembroke for luncheon – 'soles frites, lamb cutlets, chickens 'à la something', cherry tart & three wines'. They then went to see where the French captives were buried, and after a carriage drive had tea at the Swiss café before going back to town. Susan was impressed with Harry in his engineer uniform, not unlike Douglas Crooke, with his shining deep set eyes. She kept his photograph. He gave her a box of Fuller's sweets.

Susan planned to leave Bedford Park with Lily on June 14, and had bought one hundred 'at home' cards, so as to be quite ready for the fray. Her idea about the wedding was that it should be exceedingly simple and exceedingly pretty. Cottie hoped to lend her veil. Susan would look at hats when she was in Dublin to see how she might carry out designs for tulle toques, and she would look for a hat or a bonnet for Bidz that wouldn't be rashly extravagant. She herself would be bringing some of the smaller items of Baby's and Jenny's toilet from London – shoes and etceteras.

Other matters occupying Susan's mind in this June of 1899 were Cardinal Logue's regret about his pronouncement against WB's *Countess Cathleen*, and the new Dreyfus courtmartial – she delighted that the villainy of Messrs de Claur and Esterhazy had been found out. Captain Alfred Dreyfus had originally been found guilty of espionage, as he was thought to be the author of a bordereau (memorandum) announcing the dispatch of certain confidential information found in the German Embassy in France, but Commandant Esterhazy had now been revealed as the author of the bordereau.[2]

She noticed, too, the real heroism of the raw boys, undersized and under-fed, filling the departing trains with anguish and fear, on their way to the war against the Boers. In later life she would remember this image as she mused on the tin-pot heroics of the 'tawdry and tipsy processions headed by a whiskey bottle in Hammersmith Broadway, with the trays and baths and tin trumpets wherewith respectable suburban London signalised a British victory.' South Africa to her seemed very far away, and England a 'tipsy bully lashing himself into what he believed was a similitude of Elizabethan greatness'.

Closer to home was the deafness caused by her illness, very bad this week, though a self-inflater ordered by Dundas Grant had given her two delicious days of good hearing. The cloud had come back on her good ear, and she was disgusted. She wondered would they all hate her when she became a fixture at the Mall: though she refused to be downhearted, and looked forward to the Sligo house, with its crumbling appendix and her room. 'They must remember that her artistic sense had been 'educated up to its top notes at the Yeats!'.

---

[2] At the new court martial in 1899, however, Dreyfus was found guilty with extenuating circumstances and it was not until 1906 that he was finally pardoned.

PART TWO

Susan – 'A Kind of Renaissance' (1899-1926)

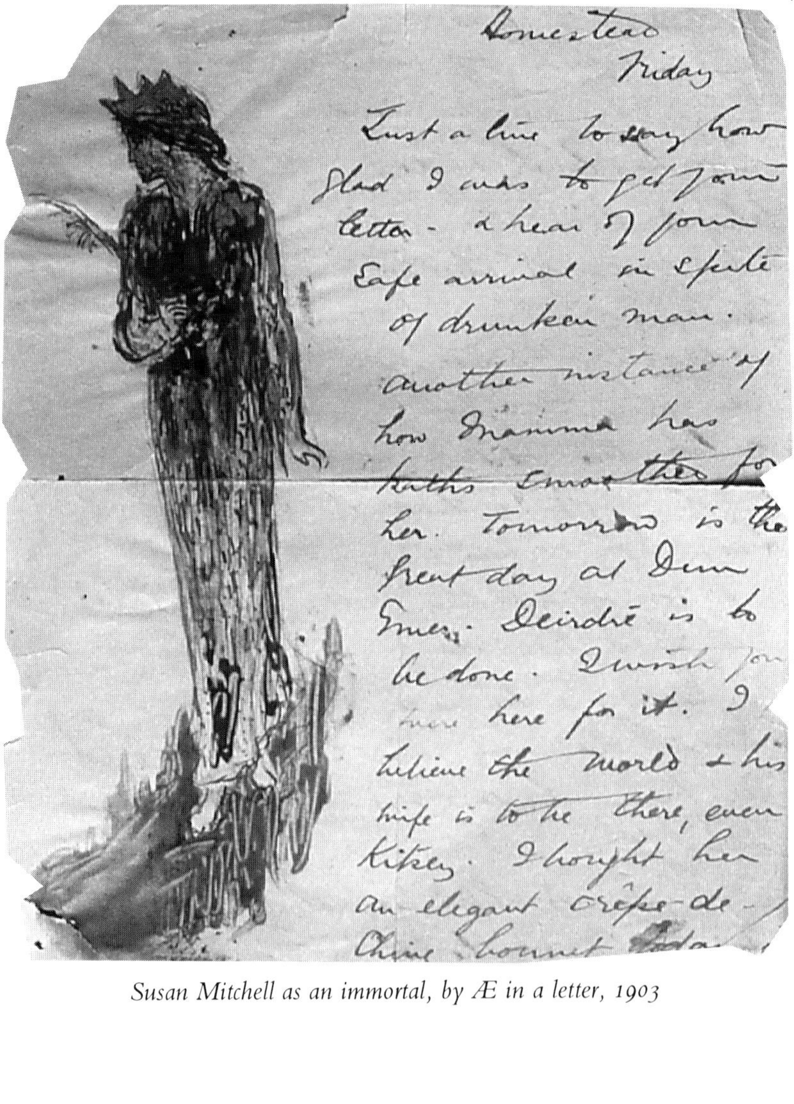

Homestead
Friday
Just a line to say how
glad I was to get your
letter - & hear of your
safe arrival in spite
of drunken man.
another instance of
how Mamma has
paths smoothed for
her. Tomorrow is the
great day at Dun
Emer. Deirdre is to
be done. I wish you
were here for it. I
believe the world & his
wife is to be there, even
Kitty. I bought her
an elegant crêpe-de-
Chine bonnet toda

Susan Mitchell as an immortal, by Æ in a letter, 1903

ELEVEN

'The Lordly Dream of Ireland'

THE IRISH HOMESTEAD

Returning to Sligo after the revelations of Bedford Park, Susan was intoxicated by things Irish. Nationalism still paced the streets of Sligo relentlessly: and the battle for the franchise had started in the western town two years before with the foundation of the second society in Ireland fighting for the vote for women. But from these she was detached, knowing at last her ambition, which was to write.

For the moment – herself composing a few poems – she persuaded her mother to put down her reminiscences on paper. Hearing the Yeatses talking made her question her mother once again about her own ancestors. She had been raised by the Mitchells, and had fed her imagination on the antecedents of the Mitchell stronghold of Protestant Birr. Now there was the opportunity to hear about the Cullens.

Kate at first hesitated to write. It seems she was encouraged to talk, and then to dictate to whichever of her children was near at hand. 'Of my early life, I have the most pleasing recollections', she began, on November 12, 1899, telling of the pampered childhood revolving about Manorhamilton, Carrick, Clare and Donegal. She was cajoled by Jinny into a detailed description of the Cullen's ancestral home, the great house, Skreeney. Susan then took up the pen, writing in her firm flowing hand as her mother reminisced about the bedrooms, and her elegant elder sisters sitting up late at night, 'burning too many candles, which action of theirs had to be looked into & stopped.' The attractive formal phrases were written down, a few pages at a time. Kate, whose one desire for her children had been that they should have a sense of humour, must have valued her own sense of humour as she looked back over the mixed fortunes of her own life.

For the time being, Susan settled into no. 12 the Mall, behind the fanlight with its plaster moulding, the only adornment on the plain facade that looked on to the broad street of the rural town. Jinny and Gilly were still at home. A few doors away was the house Uncle St. Leger had built. Both gardens dropped down to the river and the weirs, to the romantic tree-shaded water. The bridges and streets of Sligo were full of associations for Kate's family – and so for Susan.

The beginnings of a possible career were owed to her mother. Colonel

Wood-Martin, who had coached Gilly while Kate worked as manageress of the County Club, and who entertained and instructed Sligo with lectures on archeology and ancient Irish buildings, was preparing a handbook on Irish primitive traditions.[1] Susan was asked to make the index. Wood-Martin included 'the Anglo-Irishman', as he called Willy Yeats, in his scathing criticisms of 'the absurd theories started by visionary antiquarians of the last century.' 'M. Jubainville', he wrote,

> a recent French writer, affirms his belief, in which he is followed by Mr. Yates [sic], that the narratives of the battles between the Dedanann and the Firbolgs are simply twisted and distorted allegories, representing the contests between the powers of Light and Darkness, or of Good and Evil.

Susan, still heady after her sojourn with the poet's family, noted the reference in the index, correcting the spelling to 'Yeats, W. B., archeology of'. She found the index a chore. She was still at it after she moved to Dublin. Before that, she, Jinny and Mamma were in Youghal, staying with Bidz who had moved there, exploring the lanes which led up the hill to the city walls. Through a long narrow street, past the church and chapel, they found 'such funny houses', 'the natives . . . sitting at their doors making lace'. They paid visits, came across Mr. Crosthwaite – 'he is not pleasant. He might be described as a pale young curate but he is really a rector.'

The curate – of whom they approved – at once set about looking up Great Uncle Carn Cross Cullen's funeral in the church books for Mamma. They looked on at tennis; played croquet with Miss Ronayne, while Mrs. Ronayne looked on. 'They are very nice (Catholics) and are coming to call on us'. Generally they liked Youghal: 'the people are not poisonous like in Sligo.'

Shortly afterwards, Susan moved permanently to Dublin, staying with Sarah Purser until she found herself suitable lodgings. At Christmas, George informed his mother that Susan would spend St. Stephen's day with himself and his family. In his usual dry way he added some political comment in his letter, that the South African situation was not encouraging for the British. 'I see the military authorities have abandoned the contemplated thanksgiving service. This looks like passing a vote of censure on the Deity!'.

Susan was absorbing her first impressions of a new kind of Dublin, quite different from the ascendancy capital of her youth. Through Horace Plunkett's intervention she had found herself in the midst of 'an agreeable literary society', 'an ideal home for clever talkers', whose acoustics, George Moore – arrived there shortly after her – remarked were 'perfect', so that whatever jest was whispered in the closet never failed to be heard on the remotest house-top. All

---

[1] W.G. Wood-Martin, *Traces of the Elder Faiths of Ireland*. 2 vols., 1902.

Portrait study of Sarah Purser (Werner & Sons, Dublin)

this she would report later in her book on George Moore. Yeats, Æ, John Eglinton and the sculptor, John Hughes, talked 'the most excellent copy'.

Susan had entered the 'agreeable' literary world as sub-editor of *The Irish Homestead*, whose office was in a red brick building beside the back gate of Trinity College. Horace Plunkett had founded *The Irish Homestead* five years before as the official publication of his flourishing Irish Agricultural Organisation Society (IAOS). In the co-operative movement, he seemed to gather together truly imaginative talent, to pursue – despite his own fundamental unionism – a nationalist aim. Plunkett's overriding ambition was to improve his country and his fellow countrymen's self-respect by encouraging cultural as well as material progress: and he saw that this could only be done by laying aside any personal prejudices.[2]

His most inspired appointment was that of George Russell, the young poet

---

[2] See T. West, *Horace Plunkett: Co-operation and politics*, 1986, *passim*.

Horace Plunkett by JB Yeats

and painter – to become better known under his pseudonym Æ – as banks
organiser of the society in 1897. Æ was promoted to become Assistant Secretary of the IAOS shortly afterwards.

Harry Norman was another inspiration. Norman had been working in the
Dublin office of the London and North Western Railway Company: but his
heart was in the music criticism he wrote in his spare time. He became a friend
of Æ when he joined the Dublin Lodge of the Theosophical Society: and followed him into its successor, the Dublin Hermetic Society. He was an ideal
editor for the IAOS journal, appointed in August 1900, shortly before Susan
arrived. Deeply opposed to emigration, his leaders advocated more education
for farmers in order to develop higher standards and more prosperous farming
at home. He also supported the Gaelic League through the pages of the paper,
and, the year after his appointment, introduced stories and poems by contemporary Irish writers among the agricultural articles. His policies were maintained
by Æ when he took over the editorship in 1905.

With Jinny, Susan enjoyed the contradictory reports of the proclamation

of Edward as King that circulated in Sligo. Susan already deplored Queen Victoria's indifference to Ireland. According to the *Sligo Star*, of February 21, 1901,
Sligo was indifferent to her successor, and the celebration passed off 'in a very
tame fashion'.

The *Sligo Independent*, with an extra two days to think the matter over,
offered the headline, 'A brilliant and enthusiastic reception.' 'Never before was
a public function carried out in this town with such a patriotic and enthusiastic
spirit . . . the sun broke out in all its glorious splendour, lending radiance to the
brilliant scene. Flags innumerable fluttered gaily from the houses of all loyal
subjects in the town, making a very pretty display. It would be impossible to
adequately describe the immense concourse of people . . .' – who assembled in
front of the County Courthouse to hear the High Sheriff, George Pollexfen,
read the Royal Proclamation.

The *Sligo Champion* was more caustic, describing the celebrations as a 'great
day' for the Loyalists, and being sarcastic about the 'extremely miserable' outside show at the Wine Street Police Barrack, who had to recruit some of the
county police to ornament the procession. 'High command of the police bri-
gade was allotted to Generalissimo Newell, KCB, who kept the monocle on
his right eye the whole time, giving him a very valiant appearance.'

Susan's author, Lieutenant-Colonel Wood-Martin, was noticed, resplend-
ent in a cocked hat and a "yellow" belt. 'He was really too utterly utter!' exclaimed
The Champion. 'The High Sheriff and Sub-Sheriff only wore Piccadilly walking
suits and violet bauquets' (or 'bouquets' – an extravagant way of describing the
ornamentation of their buttonholes). About noon, small detachments from three
regiments marched into position, 'and there was a splendid gathering of ex-
policemen who took up a rear position.' *The Champion* summed up: 'As a
display of Toryism, officialism, military and police, the function was all right,
but the popular element was wanting – sadly wanting', and 'it should be added
that more than one voice in the outside crowd cheered for the Boers and De
Wet.'

Such fuel fed the fire of one who was shortly recognised as bard and
Gilbertian-style chronicler of the national literary movement. Susan had shown
her fascination for human perversity in her early letters. Ballads and their artless
wisdom had always intrigued her. The sarcasm and ridicule of the eagerly scanned
provincial papers were yet another source of leaven for her political lampoon-
ing.

For the moment, on the *Irish Homestead*, signing herself 'Bríghid' (probably
in honour of her grandmother, Bidz), Susan launched into some of the *Household Hints*, which became famous, she told Lily and Lolly Yeats: though a 'cheap
plum cake', designed for Christmas, caused her some misgivings, and she did
not continue her contributions to the series for long.

A captious critic in Cork discovered that I invented a cake which was to

Sketch of Harry Norman by JB Yeats, 22 March 1902

be made of a stone of flour, wet by a pint of milk. This I need hardly say was a printer's error – (it was also the subeditor's error, who thought there seemed to be a good deal of flour, but didn't suppose a few lbs either way made much odds).

She got on well with the editor, Harry Norman. A quiet wise man, with his mind on music and mysticism, Norman was bound to strike a common chord in Susan. They lunched together, and she encouraged him to visit her family on his holidays in Sligo. She wrote to Jinny saying that she had received a letter from him from the Mall, 'delighted with his reception, & greatly pleased with you all. Were his clothes awful – & had he a dickey? He is an awfully good soul.' Jinny experienced an instant rapport with Norman, found they shared the same birthdate.

Susan herself was making a new friend while Mr. Norman was away. The Assistant Secretary – usually on his travels about the country – took over his post temporarily, his tall awkward form, the twinkling blue-grey eyes above the tangled red-brown beard and the sagging, shabby suit, somehow transforming the office. 'Mr. Russell & I are having a lovely time,' Susan told Jinny.

> I never met so pleasant a man, & he is awfully kind to me, makes jokes on me & at me all day long. I send you a series of notes he wrote on me. Show them to Mr. Norman if you see him. I think they are very funny, & awfully good. Mr. Norman will be delighted, but be sure & return them. He repeats poems & talks weird talk. He is an extraordinarily sociable man.

Æ told Sarah Purser that he found Miss Mitchell 'placid and charming'.

Susan Mitchell was to become closer to Æ than to any other member of the literary movement, partly because of their similar sense of humour, partly because of their mystic bent. Her ardent and unrelenting dedication to the nationalist cause sometimes astounded him: but she was in total sympathy with his 'lordly dream' of Ireland, which looked for a Celtic avatar to lead the country to inspired independence. In his book, *Co-operation and Nationality* (1912), Æ expressed his conception in an idealistic language that Susan might understand, but not everyone could grasp –

> True, it cannot be done all at once, but if we get the idea clearly in our minds of the building up of a rural civilisation in Ireland, we can labour at it with the grand persistence of mediaeval burghers in their little towns, where one generation laid down the foundations of a great cathedral, and saw only in hope and faith the gorgeous glooms over altar and sanctuary, and the blaze and flame of stained glass, where apostles, prophets and angelic presences were pictured in fire: and the next generation raised high the walls, and only the third generation saw the realization of what their grandsires had dreamed.

This was dreaming from the roots, which was what he encouraged in fellow writers. Even Moore, with the exhilarating experience of late impressionist Paris, felt at their first meeting as if somebody had put a hand on to him and led him away into a young world he recognised as Arcady. Æ restored Moore's confidence in life, he said, and when Æ parted from him it was as if a certain mental sweetness had left the air.

At a metaphysical level, Æ's spiritual struggle, as a disciple of Madame Blavatsky, paralleled Susan's own journey by different ways. Under the influence of Whittier, and other poets, she strove towards a renunciation of her rebellious self, longing for union with the invisible everlasting spirit of the uni-

Sketch of George Russell (Æ) by JB Yeats

verse. Her writings of this period, started before she met Æ, reflect her struggle, recording a deep pain when emotion and spirituality fail to fuse.

Meeting Æ helped her to put her long-felt thoughts into words. 'The army of the voice' was the first of her hermetic poems to be published, appearing anonymously in *A Celtic Christmas* of 1902 with an illustration by Pamela Colman Smith. It is a clear renunciation of institutional religion, of 'the tireless voice of God's armies', 'jubilant and strong'.

> To the great silences in dreams I go,
> Where my own mountains brood eternally,
> World-old the heart I lean my heart unto'.

While within her the poet was budding, Susan at the same time was finding great enjoyment in the external world. Quickly committed to the Gaelic revival, she told Jinny that she had been trying to get a buckle of ancient Irish design from Hopkins for a wedding present, but he was so slow she had given up in disgust. She told Lily Yeats on October 11, 1901, of the nice black dress she was doing up for the exhibition Sarah Purser was organising for John Butler Yeats and Nathaniel Hone. (Sarah Purser was scandalised at the Royal Hibernian Academy's neglect of these two major painters: and by showing their paintings was instrumental in inaugurating JBY's most successful phase as a portrait painter.) She had invited Susan to breakfast on Tuesday morning, or to look in on Monday night, and Susan thought she would do the latter – 'Miss Purser is full of business and was awfully nice though she checked me in a half-formed desire to upholster myself in yellow poplin'.

In black, Susan decided, she would wear 'a look of that subdued yet reflected glory that is to dazzle in my cousins the Yeats.'

She was disappointed that Miss Purser would not hang the portrait JBY had painted of her in London, despite York Powell recommending it. 'She knows best, and I feel like the worm that hasn't begun to turn to think of it.' However, she did think Miss Purser unsatisfactory in the matter of encouraging JBY to come over for the event.

> I'd love to see him walking about and looking handsome. He'd be a distinct ornament and distract attention from that bundle of pretty manners, George Moore. The deference paid to that man makes one very impatient, and yet one can't help being amused at him, the obvious and dull things that he says with an air as if each were an epigram.

Lily and Lolly were to come to the exhibition. Lily would stay with Miss Purser. Lolly would lodge with Susan, as she had done before, at Murphy's in Upper Pembroke Street. On that previous occasion, 'after the first friction', they had dined with all the Yeats relatives, and Lolly had been delighted with Susan's brother, George, when they met in the Bank, and wished she could have married him herself.'

JBY did come over from London after all for the exhibition, which was a great success, well reviewed and well attended. It was the restoration of a warm intimacy for Susan, made easy because JBY stayed in Lower Leeson Street, within walking distance of her lodgings and office. When they met, they compared notes about their financial straits. 'All her money is in Grand Trunks',[3] JBY wrote to Lily and Lolly, 'in Debenture stock. She had noticed that last time they paid her a smaller dividend.' Susan wondered why the nice people were poor. She was often behind with her rent, but thought her landlord Murphy approved, 'and grovels much more than when I paid to the day, is more the well trained servant, & less the independent houseowner'.

Reunion with JBY was stimulating. She wrote to Lily and Lolly on January 28, 1902, to say that she and JBY lived for each other 'at intervals of months. He is looking well, & we had a great afternoon when Jinny was here – lunch, Edisons pictures (*animated* Lily!) & tea at the D.B.C. where he did a sketch of me which aroused such interest in the waitress that she asked me did I think he would do one of her'.

Susan and Harry Norman were favoured with a first reading of JBY's story, 'An Irish Penelope'. They were enthusiastic (George Moore who heard the first part was not so sympathetic). In April 1902, Susan came to JBY's lodgings at 43 Harrington Road, to sit for one of four panels of the Seasons – Autumn, which he was doing for the D.B.C. Restaurant.

Meanwhile, Susan was writing mystical verse, with the encouragement of Æ and her friends in the Dublin Hermetic Society. She copied the completed versions of her poems into a notebook with a linen cover, now in Armagh Museum: and from time to time added in more, while Æ illustrated her text during the first years with drawings in watercolour and gouache. The opening verse in the notebook is romantic:

> A darkness heavier than night hung over Sligo Bay
> What a dawn awoke in me –
> When I saw a ship of flame come sailing under Knocknarea
> Up the river from the sea!

Æ's boat, surrounded by salmon-coloured flames, moves up the channel, bearing a shining avatar to the yearning dreamer standing among dark trees.

The passage which follows is unusual among Susan Mitchell's prose writings, which are generally satirical. It is a mystical vision in the form of a dream, evidently fermented in her imagination after some hermetist meeting.

---

[3] Stocks of the Grand Trunk Railway of Canada.

> Once upon a time I fell asleep, and it was a sleep of which I had been in
> great dread, for oh brother and sister hearts the sorrow is upon me that is
> on you all, & though my way had been a way of pain, & though I had
> stumbled and fallen ever & ever in my going, it had seemed to me as to
> you that the path of all mankind was the only path, & that outside it there
> was no place or only a wilderness horrible with blackness and evil forms,
> and so I dreaded & doubted all that was not within sound of the ticking
> of the clock, and when my time came that I should be asleep, there was
> a restlessness & fear upon me.

Fear, she goes on, melted away in the darkness as she encountered a vision from
her childhood days, which had since lain 'a hidden living spark on the altar of
the heart'. She found herself seated beside the River of the World, the sacred
river Ganges. The accompanying sketch by Æ shows an angelic being, leaning
over a girl floating in the river.

> I sat beside the river, yet the river was myself, and as it reached each
> bourne I knew that I had lived a life, one of the 60 or 70 years of the
> human life of this earth, & when I had reached each bourne I came to
> myself and as it were home to my immortal comrades, those whose be-
> ing was a self welling fountain of eternal gladness & whose dream had
> never swung itself inward to that central core of fiery will whence it
> must fling itself outward again & into a painful labour of being which is
> the life of man.

Æ drew a girl stretching up to a dark blue being, who leans out from a row of
seated hieratic figures wearing crowns of flame. He was to repeat this image, of
a woman united with a supernatural being, in an oil he later presented to her.
'The immortal glad ones', according to her narrative,

> at each return of mine amongst them asked me always the same question
> of my earth life & if I had suffered much therein – they whose rhythmic
> life of joy knew nothing of the anguished sweetness wrung out of those
> broken chords that make the melody of pain. And I whom the high tide
> of death had flung spent & weary on those immortal shores answered
> them always with an insistent reiteration that longed to trouble their
> uncomprehending joy, how that in my journeying that portion of my
> being of which the years took count had felt the pain & weight & labour
> of the years, but that the soul, the source & stream of being, was always
> conscious of whence it came & whither it was going.

The four pages, written in pen, contain the core of the theosophical philosophy
that underlies Susan Mitchell's mystic verse. There is a spiritual optimism whose

height she rarely reaches elsewhere. The final paragraph, where she describes
waking 'from the light of darkness into the darkness of light', recognises a
change within herself, from fear – 'of all that lies beyond the ticking of the
clock' to an understanding of 'the adventure of the soul'.

> I who felt that to drop out of the hours and days was an annihilation & a
> confusion knew that the hours and days are but as little booths upon the
> banks of that river through which the untiring spirit flows. Time was –
> where I rested my eyes. To the eyes indrawn it was no longer, and as I
> willed it was or was not.

There is a further shorter passage in the Armagh notebook, which names the
'uncomprehended chain of the light that moves in darkness' as only one of
many ties that bind the worlds together. She perhaps thought specifically of her
deceased fiancé Douglas Crooke when she wrote:

> Nearly a million years away that restless fire-garment flutters by whose
> light I see the dear eyes of my friend.

Among the poems of dream and vision, there is one that describes such a love
– severed irreparably by the division of the divine and material worlds. It is
entered without title in the notebook, and later published as 'Incompleteness' –

> I wander on without the eyes to see,
> If I go up or down, still wanting thee,
> You go alone another path than mine,
> But always upwards . . .

In her uplifted mood, however, she was experiencing a universal mystical love,
expressed most clearly through the words of an immortal to an earth lover in 'A
dream', which she did not publish until 1906, when it appeared in *A Celtic
Christmas*.

With the exception of 'Homeless', which is dated July 1902 in a manuscript among the writer's papers, it is unclear when the poems in the Armagh
notebook were composed. Some were undoubtedly drafted before Susan
Mitchell met Æ and joined the Hermetic Society. The initial prose passage was
probably written under the influence of Æ, in the latter part of 1901. After it
comes 'The army of the voice', describing her struggle between Christianity
and Theosophy, 'A dream'– which brings heavenly and earthly lover together
for a space – 'Loneliness' and 'Incompleteness'. These are all illustrated by coloured visionary drawings by Æ, as are 'The Faed Fia', 'The wind bloweth
where it listeth', 'Homeless', 'The roads of heaven' and 'Love's mendicant',
whose title was added at a later stage. It appears that this earlier part of the

> it reached each hourne I knew that I had
> lived a life, one of the 60 or 70 years of the
> human life of this earth, & when I had reached
> each hourne I came to myself and as it were
> home to my immortal Comrades, those whose
> being was a self welling fountain of eternal
> gladness & whose dream had never swung itself
> inward to that central core of fiery will
> whence it must fling itself outward again &
> into a painful labour of being which is the
> life of man. The immortal glad ones at
> each return of mine amongst them asked
> me always the same question of my earth
> life & if I had suffered much therein – they
> whose rythmic life of joy knew nothing of
> the anguished sweetness wrung out of those
> broken chords that make the melody of
> pain. And I whom the high tide of death
> had flung spent & weary on those immortal
> shores answered them always with an insistent
> reiteration that longed to trouble their
> incomprehending joy; how that in my
> journeying that portion of my being of

Extract from the Armagh Notebook

manuscript was assembled under the influence of the Hermetic Society, which
was dissolved for a time in 1904.[4]

A more specific dating can be reached through individual poems. After the
second – 'fire-garment' – prose passage, come 'The way of grief' (illustrated in
the notebook with a reproduction of a Pamela Colman Smith painting), the

---

[4] In the autumn of 1904, the Dublin Hemetic Society amalgamated for a short period with the
Dublin Theosophical Society.

final version of 'Love's mendicant', and 'The hidden home' – which is the original version of 'The roads of the heart'. 'The San Grail', which follows these, was to become her most famous poem, published in the Christmas number of *The Irish Homestead* in December 1903, under the title 'The living chalice'.

So it would appear that the first section of the manuscript dates from 1901-2 and the early part of 1903. Two untitled poems following this first part were published as 'Ireland' and 'The dark way' (later called 'The tryst') in *A Celtic Christmas* of 1905; after which there are 'The heart's low door' and an unfin-

Æ illustration in the Armagh Notebook

ished poem, 'I asked but for the opened eye.' A few late poems, and some verses from her collection of 1908, *Aids to the Immortality*, are copied in at the end.

Working with Æ obviously affected Susan's mystical verse. It is much more personal than his own poetry, but grounded in a similar figurative vision. His drawings depict the soul, or human yearning, in the shape of a girl, who relates to or is unable to relate to some shining being. In the three verse poem beginning

> My wild will spreads its wings & flies
> To reach your heart my dove
> The winds of love on which I rise
> Gather in clouds above
> And drift me from my dove

– which was revised to become 'Exile' – one of his typical winged spirits hurtles downward through poem itself.

Æ liked to discuss his own poems with Susan. In August 1902, he wrote to her with nine lines of a poem about a peasant, begging her to come to his rescue: his demand was partly a way of providing a distraction for her because she had become ill again – worryingly ill. He told her to get him 'out of the bog' into which he had fallen. 'I wouldn't wonder if you did not sweep the poor three last lines away with the mantle of your psyche when you swept through me', he joked. 'Restore me my three lines, oh peculator of other people's affections & ideas'.

Over the years, they collaborated on humorous verse, Æ being the first to hear, and offer suggestions, about Susan's satirical songs. They published the scrap of opera they worked on together (*Leaguers and Peelers* in *The Irish Review*), and 'a grand song to the Shan Van Vocht' ('The Irish Council Bill 1907'), but both appeared under Susan's name – they were written largely by her.

The Dublin Hermetic group, which met regularly on Thursday evenings in the Dawson Chambers, brought Susan together with the other poets discovered and encouraged by Æ. Pádraic Colum, Thomas Keohler, Seumas O'Sullivan, Ella Young and George Roberts, are all represented with Susan Mitchell in *New Songs*, the collection Russell edited in 1904. Henry Summerfield has described how the group, numbering about ten, would meet in the dimly lit shabby room each week to hear Æ – sitting at a table, with a copy of Blavatsky's *Secret Doctrine* nearby – discourse on some aspect of the divine, after which he would ask his disciples to lend their spiritual or literary ideas to the discussion.

Some of them pinned their verses to the wall. Not all were serious, and everyone relished any chance for wit. The impish quatrains preserved in Æ's handwriting in the Houghton Library, Harvard, were said to have been declaimed at a meeting by Susan's actress friend, Helen Laird. Helen herself –

My wild will spreads its wings & flies
To reach your heart my dove
The winds of love on which I rise
Gather in clouds above
And drift me from my dove.

Loves self I sought & in thy heart
I thought his home must be
Though all his storms sweep us apart
My homing wings to thee
Flutter continually.

Where shall I find thee? To & fro
Thy homeless bird is driven,
For ever lonely must I go
From every shelter driven.
Wing-weary under heaven.

Æ

Susan Mitchell's poem, 'My wild will spreads its wings', illustrated by Æ according to the parody – had no need for any exotic deity – 'Plain God is good enough for me'.

Each of the regular members of the Hermetic were lampooned in this rhyming skit: Keohler for his homely frankness, Seumas O'Sullivan for his scholarly diffidence, Roberts for his domesticity, and Ella Young for her 'territorial view of God': while Susan was said to regard the divine being as an obstructer of love affairs. Æ was noticed crooning to the deity as 'his mighty mother'. The personal nature of the witty Harvard verses suggests that Susan herself had a hand in their composition.

TWELVE

'Down by Sligo'

A WESTERN INSPIRATION

Susan's entry into literary Dublin had been a rapid matter as a natural consequence of her being part of the Yeats circle in London. Dublin, at the time, was a domestic-sized city. The cultural élite were 'At Home' on particular evenings, when tea was taken, and every subject discussed: and those invited were encouraged to bring relatives or friends. Unexpected relationships were discovered.

Susan was pleased to recognise a link with the Gore-Booths, through the Wynnes of Sligo. Constance Markievicz's aunt was married to Owen Wynne of Hazelwood, a connection of her mother's family, the Cullens. This made Susan a 'cousin' of Constance Markievicz, who with Æ, her husband Casimir and others, would soon form a group exhibiting landscapes and paintings of a visionary kind. More important for Susan, she saw a place for her own family, so active in the cultural life of their province, as part of this new nationalist creative ethos. Her own emotional self-identification with the West of Ireland was charged.

It rejoiced her heart that Jinny had found an 'appreciator' in George Russell. She told Lily and Lolly Yeats,

> He thinks there is a delightful atmosphere about her & he went to see them in Sligo. Ordered Mamma to make me an orange cake, giving full directions, & that cake arrived I can tell you in double quick time, was eaten at the IAOS tea & finished to the last crumb by Shane Magan.

Lily and Lolly she urged to come over from London to live in Dublin – 'quit the City of Destruction and set out for the Land of Promise'. Dublin, she said, was exciting. She had been seeing and hearing much Wagner and had many invitations from friends. She had always had a deep admiration for Douglas Hyde. With Jinny, the linguist of the family, she set about learning the Gaelic tongue, earning for herself the name 'Siobhán'.

She wrote to Jinny purring about the Mitchell presence at the Sligo Féis, at which Baby (Victoria) and her husband were always prominent musically. Jinny had acted as master of ceremonies, reading out the names of competitors, and her dignity 'must have struck terror into the native.' Johnny and George were down in Sligo for the Féis too – and noticed a great improvement in Gilly's health.

Susan, now a thoroughly liberated woman, told Jinny,

> I was much amused about your remarks on stays. I have cut the Gordian knot figuratively & literally & discarded them altogether. 'Ah I couldn't be bothered with them'. I have been reducing them by degrees till they came to be simply a Swiss belt, made of ribbon & a couple of bones.

Still instinctively vain, and attentive to fashion, she had 'stolen' and altered Helen Laird's green blouse – 'needless to say I didn't stay with her without levying some contribution on her clothes.' Lodging with Helen, while Murphy's rooms were being repapered, she had contrived a sort of sailor collar, and wore it with a simple band of black velvet round her neck fastened with an antique brooch.

She had just had a visit in the office from Father Meehan of Greenlea – 'so cordial': when she told him she was a native of Leitrim, and that Mamma was a Cullen, he had become very animated and told her that the Cullens were as well known in Leitrim as the O'Conors in Sligo.

Louis Purser, one of the dancing partners from Cavan days, she told Lily and Lollie, she had met in the street one day when she was with Jinny – 'he came up behind & hit me on the back with an umbrella'. 'He was clean & bright – & wore a tall hat'. He was telling her of the people he had been seeing in Birr when he broke off short to help the Provost of Trinity over a crossing 'with his own energetic gentleness.'

Though she had spent her childhood in Dublin, the western origins she shared with the Yeats sisters and with Constance Markievicz began to mean more and more to Susan. The most potent images of her poetry are the bul-rushes of the Shannon, the 'awful spaces' of the dominant western sky, the haughty mountains, the petulant rain and wind, the scent of spicy grass, and the salt sea. This landscape was more aloof than Æ's terrain in Donegal with its russet floor of woodland, 'the dim blue mantle of the mountains' and 'the fawn-coloured shore'.

Her Sligo roots had been planted first in the public buildings superintended by her Uncle Noblett St. Leger during his years as County Surveyor: in the two handsome bridges, and the Point Road and the Mardyke, which he built: in Uncle Noble Shepperd's Congregational Church, and the Ulster Bank opened by Uncle James Mitchell. But beyond that, there was some indefinable quality in the air of Sligo with which she, the Yeatses and Constance Markievicz felt akin. Constance carried a picture in her memory of

> a beautiful, enchanted Western coast, where we grew up intimate with

the soft mists and coloured mountains, and where each morning you woke to the sound of the wild birds. . . In Connaught, the traditions and soul of Ireland were trampled into the mud by alien feet, and left for dead. But they only waited the day of resurrection, for they lay deep buried, too, in the hearts of a noble people, as unconquerable and great as their own Atlantic.[1]

As child and adult, Susan knew the sandy beach with rolling breakers at Strandhill (An Leath-Ros) on the southern point of the sickle of Sligo Bay, under the shoulder of Knocknarea, blotted out, more often than not, to a beige-grey stain when a feathery cloud of rain settled over it. Coney Island was reached by foot at low tide. It stands out in the bay, between the two rosses, with seabirds strolling or darting on the wing across the weedy sand, oblivious of the fine white mist.

Lough Gill, where her father, as a young man, and her brother Gilly walked at different periods, had secure white stone cottages on its treed slopes, which opened here and there into fields edged with reeds or meadowsweet, or little bohereens lined with brambles, bracken and loosestrife, and every kind of wild flower, gorse and heather. She walked these roads herself after her return from London, and saw the inland of Lough Gill in green light, and in dark sunlight. Further up the coast, the fossils of Streedagh Strand were scattered beneath the black bricks of its cliffs, which opened on to a bubble of salt water.

Susan located the root of her poetic inspiration in the Greenlands, the broad grassy plain at Rosses Point where she had holidayed as a small child with Kate. She recalled the occasion in her charming pasticcio poem,

> I went up the Greenlands at the Rosses long ago,
> Running, stumbling, just a child, small and very wise.
> It was well I came from heaven to see the blue bells grow,
> And the bright sun's happy thoughts unfold before my eyes . . .
>
> I held within my little hands the keys of life and death.
> From every leaf and blade of grass an old sweet wisdom came,
> And in my heart strange flowers sprang up with every hurrying breath,
> I saw Ben Bulben as a god, amethyst and flame.[2]

Sligo was near to heaven. But for the moment she was in Dublin, now in her mid-thirties, loving her 'cage', despite the recurrence of the dreaded illness she

---

[1] 'Memories', *Éire*, 18 August 1923, p. 5.
[2] 'The Greenlands' was first published in *A Celtic Christmas,* 1904, p. 17.

George Russell (Æ) by JB Yeats, 1903

had sought to cure in London. Dr. Woods had been scraping both sides of her nose with cold steel in January 1902, which made her quite sick, and she temporarily abandoned her lodgings with the Murphys at 9 Upper Pembroke Street to be 'petted' by her aunts' friends, the Legges, in Wellington Road. She had all her meals in bed, and she left the 'little Editor', Harry Norman, 'staggering under a load of unread newspapers'.

Æ thought she was getting better in August, when she took her holiday at Rosses Point, and he told Sarah Purser that she was in good spirits. While she and Harry Norman were away, he had become 'Editor and Miss Mitchell rolled into one.' He wrote to Susan affectionately, addressing her as 'Alannah', or 'child':

> if the tide of cheerfulness rises above the horror, why you have got the upper hand, and if it raises its head above the surface pop it down again & drown the little devil. Don't say you have got dull to beauty. That's not true, my dear, when you are so anxious about your own nice face.

Everyone, he told her, including her Hermetic brothers and sisters, were enquiring after her. 'Do not think we are not sorry for you', he wrote to her from the office, telling her that if Jinny refused to be to her all that he had advised he would supply the deficiency by putting himself en rapport through the astral light.

> I will upon the Wild Jews Harp
> With her be sad or gay
> Though I be here in Lincoln Place
> And she on Sligo Bay.
>
> And Harry here, the Editor,
> Who has no harp to play
> Will chatter on his teeth meanwhile
> And go as near he may.
>
> And never such a harmony
> Could be since time began,
> As Susan's song, the Wild Jews harp.
> And the teeth of the editor man!

'It is excess of grief which has gone into a kind of hysterical reaction,' he explained, adding,

> We have heard reports from two doctors that you are a very healthy person and are all right. We know that the idea of your being healthy

will cast a gloom over you, but still if you consider it the truth is not unpleasing, and you can easily find something else to grumble at, as for example your uncertainty whether you will have good health in your next life or not, and your uncertainty whether your place in the Homestead will be kept open for you in that life, and many other things.

The weather, as can be imagined, was not prepared to assist in raising the spirits: and Æ had to make every effort to cheer Susan. 'My poor forlorn Hermetic sister', he teased her,

> I picture you looking out on a drizzling atmosphere with a big lump in your throat and the tears trickling slowly down your cheeks. I feel ashamed to write to you because I know you will feel quite rightly indignant that I a mere stranger should have stolen your share of fine weather at the Point and crammed it all into one selfish fortnight. I had intended to write to your sister instructions how you were to be amused, how she was to make you merry, gambol before you in your walks, but seeing how it is with the climate I think the only thing she can do is to transpose herself into a footstool for you. When you are sorrowful let her cry to keep you company, and when you are in better spirits let her turn delighted somersaults, and wag the tail of her dress.

He was able to give her news about 'less serious matters' – Evelyn Gleeson's hunt for a suitable house in Dublin where she and Lily and Lolly could establish an arts and crafts industry. Lily would train girls in embroidery. Lolly, after a course at the Women's Printing Society in London, would establish a private press, in keeping with the times, but with an eye to contemporary Irish writing, and with the interested support of her brother, Willy. Evelyn Gleeson, who was a fine painter, but also a skilled weaver and tapestry maker, had plans to develop a weaving and tapestry industry.[3]

'Lolly Yeats was in here a couple of times', he wrote,

> and I expect her up some night with Miss Gleeson to talk over these enterprises. The house at Dundrum is still on the dim and distant horizon and retreats before their ardent advances as the pot of gold buried at the root of the rainbow did before the seeker.
>
> I believe if the landlord finally does come to a decision they will find it was only a fairy house after all and it will mysteriously disappear like Aladdin's wonderful palace. I never yet heard of anybody getting exactly

---

[3] The enterprise would be developed as the Dun Emer Industries and the Dun Emer Press, taking its name from Emer (wife of the legendary hero Cúchulain), a skilled needlewoman.

the house or thing they wanted, and I don't believe it can happen now and break all precedents. The only way to get things is to pretend seriously to Providence that you don't want them, in fact to get them would be a burden, harder than you can bear, a cross which you pray you may not have to carry, and then, if you have not revealed by the faintest indication or twinkle in your aura that you are a hypocrite, Providence will cram the object of your desire down your throat and will facilitate its transfer to your possession, and will even precipitate matters in its desire to chasten whom it loves.

This is the basis of the oriental calm, the indifference they inculcate in the sacred books as to the happy or the unhappy life. Everyone of course would prefer the happy life, but when it has been well grounded into people that they must not have preferences, it perplexes Providence and you have a chance, a good chance, of being happy. So spider like weave the tissue of your web, and then retreat into yourself as if you only spun it for fun or out of sheer boredom, and perhaps you may catch the celestial fly. I write to you as to one advanced in human wisdom, one old enough in experience to understand. It is not the common or garden teaching which the uninitiated receive which I communicate, so be proud and flattered.

Negotiations for Dun Emer were, in the event, successful. 'Dear Mitchell', he wrote slightly later,

We have been tormented here by the constant stream of sub-human people who are all faddists. Varian, who ought to have been a fowl, and whose appearance in human form I consider is a shameful neglect of His duty by the Deity is the type of this class, and Almighty God never knew I am sure the harm He was doing when He created him, or He would have made the sticky part of him into glue and turned the rest into a turkey. I apologise for even mentioning him. It is to recall unutterable sorrow: but I feel easier after the above.

The House in Dundrum is taken at last. The way it came about was a complete vindication of my view expressed before. Miss Gleeson gave up the idea and thought after all it would not be a good house, and Providence straightway threw it at her. The Gleeson, Henry[4] and Lolly Yeats have gone out there today to get a house for the latter.

---

[4] Augustine Henry (1857-1930), the distinguished botanist, lodged with the Gleeson family when they lived in Athlone, and became a lifelong friend of Evelyn Gleeson, assisting her financially with the foundation of Dun Emer. *See* Sheila Pim, 'Dun Emer – an unrecorded chapter in the life of Augustine Henry', *Moorea* vol. 3, 1984.

But they don't really know how to get a house. The best plan is to fix on the nicest inhabited house and ask the people in it to clear out. This method has never been tried, and at first it might be successful. If they did not agree you could make it disagreeable for them by sending ghosts to them. This would be easy and there is no law against it at present. Anyone who thinks intently could create a ghost to haunt other people with. I have done it in my early days and only I made him a soft kind ghost with no terror about him, I would now be a millionaire.

Whether Æ's house-finding method was successful, or whether the Yeats sisters needed to enlist the help of a ghost, they did find a suitable place for themselves and their father in Churchtown. They named it Gurteen Dhas, 'nice little field', and could walk every day to Dundrum to work at Dun Emer.

Augustine Henry heard about Susan's illness while in France (he had no doubt met her through Lily Yeats, and his continual concern for her health suggests more than a passing attraction). He wrote in November to Evelyn Gleeson. 'I am very sorry about Miss Mitchell and hope the doctor's diagnosis is incorrect; for consumption of the throat is awful'. He urged her to get Susan to the very best doctor even if she had to go to London: and was prepared to pay if she hadn't any money. 'Let there be no dallying – it is too terrific a fate.'

He wrote again, shortly afterwards, 'I want another kind of world where friends would be friends without so many difficulties. Apparently my idea of friendship is chimerical. One can't even be kind without it costing all sorts of pangs. I should like . . . to send Miss Mitchell a cheque for £50, so that she should have a trip to the Riviera: but that is impossible – and so on – and so on – of course I don't know Miss Mitchell, except as a chance acquaintance'. And a week later he was again enquiring and hoping for better news.

Susan, though somewhat better, was 'so desperately done up' after the *Samhain* plays that she hadn't recovered sufficiently when writing to Jinny in Sligo to 'think [her opinion of the plays] out clearly', and had asked her editor Harry Norman to send her sister an account of the evening. (She was going to Dr. Woods for further consultation that day – Dr. Woods, who all Dublin said had proposed to her as soon as she came to Dublin.) 'I thought Deirdre lovely', she told Jinny. 'The Pot of Broth is good – W.B. is boiling over with conceit & arrogance. I'd like to beat him'.

Harry Norman undertook the task of drama critic cheerfully, telling 'Miss Jeannie',

> I am asked by my chief, the Sub-Editor, whom it is, as you must know of old, a living death to disobey! to write you an account of "the plays". Now this reminds one of the orders given by some of the tyrant-kings of old time to the Court Jesters. It requires considerable imagination to execute, partly because of the difficulty of the task in itself, & partly

because, of the plays I ought to describe, there were two that I did not see. These are, I am sure, the two your Eastern Potentate of a sister would demand that I should describe in full.

He thought Jinny must have seen *Kathleen Ni Houlihan*, and the other was *Connla*, 'the work of Mr. Cousins whom you saw I think as one of the "lights of valour" in Deirdre.' He described the play as 'a sort of cousin-german to Deirdre'.

I did laugh, though, at W. B. Yeats's "A Pot of Broth" which was put on on Thursday night. It is an old story of a man who gets the better of a parsimonious housewife who refuses him a meal. . . W. G. Fay who played Beggarman in the caste was inimitable. I really never sincerely enjoyed a farce before!

The Building of the Foundations was even more amusing because it appealed to the mind as well as the emotions. It was a satire on Corporations and pseudo-nationalists who traded on the industrial revival, and pretended to be working for the country.

One of the parts . . . was taken by our friend Miss Laird whom I think

Sketch of WG Fay by JB Yeats, August 1907

Edward Martyn by JB Yeats, 1899

you met. A good story (true) is told of her acting at Mr. Edward Martyn's expense. Miss Laird adopted a Limerick accent for the occasion – a real good strong Munster brogue. Asked how he liked her acting Mr. E. M.'s answer was: "Capital. She should make a great actress but you know you never could make anything of a woman who has an accent like that"!

Deirdre was too beautiful for words, the acting beyond praise. He thought Mr. Russell's feeling that influences not directly human were at work in its production was justifiable. 'Four persons saw the figures of the Sidhe mingling with the actors. I felt that the air was alive with vibrating things. I know one person who was much moved and would have sobbed aloud . . . and one lady says she nearly "went away" in trance.'

Susan was looking better, Harry thought. However, in April 1903, Augustine Henry was writing to Evelyn Gleeson from Nancy saying that the illness was serious: and that as she would only take half measures the outlook was grave. 'Her own hopefulness is really a bad sign. The consumptives are always hopeful: the blindness of the mind with them is dreadful.' He went on

> I happen to be writing to Norman today. . . & I have spoken to him very
> frankly regarding Miss Mitchell. If she has tuberculosis, it is madness of
> her to continue to work in an office – & so on – But what to do. The trip
> to the Alps will do good for a time, temporarily check the malady. That
> is all.

Susan, however, took a less deadly view, and, while she planned a trip to Swit-
zerland in June in search of restored health, sat to John Butler Yeats for his
'Autumn' painting, and had her brother George to sing during one session.
JBY, who didn't have fires going on 'ordinary' days would have a fire lit when
she came. York Powell, who had had a clash with Susan in January on a 'point
of patriotism', in which he believed she had indulged in over-sensitivity, told
JBY he would 'give a lot to hear her sing again. . . She must sing and be happy.
She makes other people happy'. He hoped she was really better.

But JBY, writing to Rosa Butt about a successful party with Madame
Markievicz, who had retired to Dublin and was 'gay & original & sociable &
pleasantly bohemian – having a real aristocrat among us raised us all in our own
esteem', told how Susan had been to the doctor. He had discovered a new spot
on her throat and put caustic on it, so she could not come to the party. 'Her
brother left us for a few minutes & crossed the road to see her in her lodgings.
Afterwards when he sang 'The Snowy Breasted Pearl' in Irish he for the first
time in his life forgot the words. No doubt the disappointment about Susan &
this fresh symptom was the cause. Why are people so tormented?'.

Susan always remained optimistic – on the surface at least. In late spring she
told Jinny that her bicycle was 'in great order', and Kilmashogue was only
about half an hour's ride away from Upper Rathmines, where she was staying
with Helen Laird. She enjoyed living at Miss Laird's. They went shares in food,
and shared a sitting room.

> I've got a funny little room there covered with advts of cigarettes. A
> large card hung up in one corner announces the "Holly Quadrille Club"
> and *Extra* in another conspicuous position. I took 6 waistcoats off the
> door & put them in a drawer – & there is a trousers in a distant corner that
> I haven't dared to remove! I think it is the room of the young masa of the
> house, whose name is Reggie, & who is very grand!

Her throat, she told Jinny, was feeling awfully well, and her nose seemed all
right. Æ had finished her picture, and she thought she would give it to the
Hermetists, who had new rooms – 'owned by Starkey, Kohler [sic] & Roberts,
and they are much cleaner & full of books & bookshelves & have a carpet
which I believe deadens the spirituality.' Mr. Ireland was to be brought to the

next meeting, and would be 'the only parson except Carmichael who ever ventured among the mysteries.'

'Wasn't Maud Gonne splendid, and Edward Martyn', she exclaimed to Jinny, referring to Maud Gonne MacBride's outspoken words during the Parliamentary Fund meeting at the Rotunda. 'That most picturesque but impracticable of lady politicians, Madame MacBride,' the *Irish Times* commented, 'whom we had hoped had permanently retired to Paris', had organised a protest about King Edward's visit to Ireland. ' I'm sure it'll do a lot of good in spite of the lying local papers,' said Susan. Æ referred to the event as 'the most gorgeous row Dublin has had since Jubilee time. The Rotunda meeting was a free fight and two M.Ps are incapacitated. The *Freeman* tries to depreciate the effect of the row, but the *Irish Times* and *Express* and *Independent* give good reports and do justice to the scrimmage. Martyn has heroism thrust on him . . .'

Susan herself continued to think of Sligo. Harry Norman hadn't been able to get to Sligo during his travels each weekend to adjucate the Stop Emigration Prizes. He was coming back looking quite fat – 'he dined with 6 priests in Tagoat, & you may be sure that was a dinner!' But she followed the fortunes of the Sligo choir at the Dublin Féis. 'They sang with such taste and if one may use the word, spirituality. One felt they had not lived between Benbulbin & Knocknarea for nothing.'

She had been dining with Mrs. Roe, the Hermetist her niece Kathleen lodged with, 'who replenishes the Hermetic fire out of a biscuit bag'; and she took tea with Miss Wilson in the garden, where the only other guest, besides Miss Laird and Miss Joynt, was a tortoise called Shule Agrá ['Walk, Love'].

> Sure enough, as soon as I began to sing, it began to walk, walk, slowly, slowly, down the garden, having been hitherto quite motionless. It is evidently primitive Irish.

'I am sure Sligo is looking lovely', Susan sighed to Jinny. 'It is perfectly beautiful here with the fresh, early green of the trees. I suppose we are going to Switzerland end of June. I'd rather be going to the Point'.

THIRTEEN

'Persons are my Medium'

A SHY VERBAL CARTOONIST

Susan's mother, Kate, whom Seumas O'Sullivan later remembered in his *Essays and Recollections* as the handsome old lady who gave 'regal hospitality' at her home in Sligo, suffered from rheumatism about this period, which took her on regular trips to Lisdoonvarna in County Clare to drink the waters. Harry, her son-in-law, wrote to her delighted that she was improving, the family pleased that she had decided to extend her visit in Clare. 'Take all the open air, & rubbings you can get,' urged the courtly musician, 'for I hope to have the pleasure of lending you my arm, & "walking" you home from the station next week!'.

He told her, for Jinny's benefit, that Roberts and some of the lady members of the Irish Literary Theatre were stopping at the Point (Rosses Point) – they had met them at Father Brennan's concert there the previous night: and Æ and Starkey were to arrive as soon as they had gone.

Kate Mitchell with one of her granddaughters, c.1900

Augustine Henry, at the same time, was worrying about Susan and never done writing with pessimism to Evelyn Gleeson, warning about the seriousness of her illness. In a surge of sympathy, while on the Continent in July, he went to visit her in the clinic at Yverdon, on the Lac de Neuchatel, near the French border of Switzerland. He sensed her tension and frustration. 'I found Miss Mitchell like an Andromede, chained to a barren rock', he wrote to Evelyn from Nancy, telling her that Belalp was an ugly hotel, perched on a bare mountain beside the biggest and dirtiest glacier in Europe.

> Everyone rushes off all day, fooling about on the glacier, & Miss Mitchell I think was desperately tired of the weird ugliness of all of it . . . the snow mountains are lovely in the distance: but parts of the country are really hideous, barren rocks without beauty & even lakes that are dismal pools surrounded by dirty snow. The English tourist accepts it all as beautiful & . . . for him & les eile there are wearisome hotels, where the people discuss inane subjects. I really pitied Miss Mitchell. She is not well: but you will see her. I think she liked my going to see her, what was rather a wild and hasty expedition: but I had an idea she was bored to death. . .

The fact that Susan never refers in her writings to her experiences at Belalp confirms Augustine Henry's gloomy description of the cold airy landscape where she sought new health. Even after her return, she continued to be depressed: and, judging from mentions of her in Henry's letters, she continued in poor health until November, when Evelyn Gleeson told him that Susan was 'looking bright & pretty'. 'You can tell her to continue so', he replied.

Susan owed her power to survive through chronic illness to a pertinaciously detached and humorous view of life. 'Persons are my medium', she was to write later in the introduction to her book of satiric verse, *Aids to the Immortality*; and, whether in sickness or in health, she enjoyed the idiosyncrasies of those who came her way. While at Belalp, or shortly afterwards, she was able to scribble some verses about her doctor, on apropriately black-edged note paper.

> He stands amid the Jura
> A figure spare & small
> He calls aloud to Europe –
> And Europe hears the call.
> "Come, ears and throats & noses,
> That fear the fell catarrh,
> Come lave yourselves at Yverdon
> Where baths of sulphur are!"

She arrived back, deafer than ever, to a Dublin divided about the visit of the King. The Corporation had declined to recognize Edward VII as Sovereign of

Ireland. Susan, likewise, coming in on the tram from Kingstown felt 'richly indignant against the foes of Ireland' because loyalty was rampant. However her feelings reduced during the day, because her editor, Harry Norman, was so black with disgust that her sympathies began revolving towards 'Ned'.

She wrote to Jinny from the office in Lincoln Place:

> The King makes his entry today. So Norman and I are secluded here from the gay world, and eating sweets. I arrived this morning at Kingstown 5.50 am. Ned arrived 9 am. I'm sorry I missed him, they weren't at all pleased with him at Chester yesterday, because he didn't stop there. However *we* stopped there a couple of hours, so no doubt he is forgiven by now. . .

> Norman & I are now going out to lunch, as we think it would be best to be engaged eating as the procession passes. The act will be symbolical in some way I'm sure. Norman is in an awful temper on account of the procession. I can't hear it of course, & I have made him delirious by suggesting that as my indignation against Ned was waning, I ought to go out & stimulate it by seeing the procession. Tell Æ he'll appreciate this suggestion. . . . I wish to goodness Æ was back or that Norman had not too good principles to make some Royal jokes, its as dull as Belalp, all because Ned is here.

Susan had passed through Paris on her way back from Belalp and spent two pouring days shopping with the remains of the money she had borrowed for the 'tour', rapidly choosing a few cheap gifts. A mauve wrap would do for Mamma, and Victoria might find the white shawl useful for herself, or for her new son, Michael Hermann – Susan was 'greatly pleased' with the names, she told Jinny, reviving a family memory as she quoted the graceful phrase used by the Cullens' old butler, Burke.

She coaxed Jinny to come up to Helen Laird's house when Helen was away, and when Susan herself would be more free. Susan could have Helen's sitting room and bedroom, and come into town indefinitely, if Jinny could get away, and if she did not mind leaving Sligo while Æ and Starkey were at the Point.

Jinny had another concern, the safe conduct of Kate from Lisdoonvarna to Sligo, in August. They arrived intact, 'despite the drunken man' wrote Susan, on the 21st, congratulating her sister: 'another instance of how Mamma has paths smoothed for her'. She was writing on the eve of 'the great day at Dun Emer. Deirdre is to be done. . . the world & his wife is to be there'. She wrote on paper painted (see back cover) by Æ in oil, with a maiden crowned with gold walking barefoot on grass, and told Jinny that Æ had decorated the office with 'the loveliest fairies'.

Harry Norman wrote to Jinny on February 25, 1904, about the new performance of *Deirdre*. He thought it, if possible, more beautiful than the previous one: and said that an English drama critic who was there thought that the players' speaking voices were superb. Miss Walker took Deirdre now, instead of Lavarcham. 'George Russell looked fine in a new Druid's robe of purple with a "golden sword of Mananaan on the breast" and silvery fishes round the skirt', embroidered by an admirer, Mrs. Law,[1] who sat up till two embroidering, and continued the following day till just before the performance. 'The fact is it's not finished yet'!

> We also had a new play "Riders to the Sea" – very lugubrious but powerful. If the "corpse" and the "chief mourner" had not had frequent sallies in the rehearsals and one's sense of humour had not clung desperately to one's expectations of what they would say and do when the curtain fell it would have been too harrowing for words. I am sure that life is not very unlike this and that we go back to reality when the curtain falls upon our life.

Jinny, who had a gift for languages, was learning Irish, but was distracted by too many other interests. Susan approached the matter with less dedication. She was enthusiastic, exchanged 'Guidheanna Croidheamhla' ('heartfelt wishes') and 'Slaintí' at Christmas time with May Kelly and Eilis Ní MacLeagáin.[2] Her bent, however, was still towards mystic matters. In October 1904, she told Jinny about the 'orgie' at the Theosophical Society – 'the Hermetic has now joined the Dublin T.S. and is going in for a course of serious study on subjects with most mysterious names. I suppose its the "best thing".'

She was now one of the group of young Dublin poets who used to meet in a College Street restaurant at lunch hour 'by common consent' at Æ's table. James Starkey, as Susan then knew him – the name he was born with had not yet been ousted by the nom de plume 'Seumas O'Sullivan', taken from his grandfather – Starkey remembered that she was lovely to look at, lovely to listen to with her deep musical voice, 'her glorious and irresistable laugh which lit up the stream of the witty talk, like sunlight on a river. She was one of the few wits I have known,' he wrote forty years later, 'whose wit and satire held nothing malicious. She was, too, one of the most unopinionated of people, and for all her appearance of assurance, one of the shyest.'[3]

---

[1] Mrs Law, who built AE's studio at Marble Hill, was the wife of the Nationalist MP for Donegal, Hugh Law.

[2] About this time Susan and Jinny were members of the Gaelic League, though it has not been possible to ascertain at what date they joined. Susan had a deep admiration for Douglas Hyde throughout her career.

[3] *Essays and Recollections* (1944), p. 123.

Seumas O'Sullivan was shy too, and Susan teased him about this when he was hesitant to take up an invitation to visit her in the Lincoln Place Office. But they readily found a common meeting-ground in their hermetic experience, as well as in their love of local hills, and in poetry – where they could help each other. She had probably met Starkey first in 1902. Writing to congratulate him on his poem, 'The sunset path' – under the pseudonym 'Oghma' – which appeared in the *Southern Star* of 31 May, 1902, she was ready with the mild criticism the group of poets must have administered regularly to one another. 'I think this is subjective enough', she said. 'You must use the terms of external things & images to suggest the inner self – which as yet has hardly a vocabulary of its own'. However she liked his image of the 'fiery foam of the sunset' which 'brimmed and lay level and rippled / To our feet like a sea of gold', and commented 'There is a sunset behind your sunset'. On another occasion she told him how his 'Calvary' – a poem he was to include in *Verses Sacred and Profane*, and which contemplated the sin and sacrifice of love – had been greatly in her mind.

Her own poems she sent to him for approval, or recited aloud as all the Irish poets were inclined to do, in the office. '– Did I tell you my last poem – 'Vanity', I'm sure I did but I'll retell it!' she announced in one letter. One of her experiments of this period was the libretto for *Etáin – an Opera*, composed in 1903 for children, who speak the prologue on behalf of their distressed counterparts on the streets of Dublin. It is the Celtic story of the wooing of Etáin, treated in an esoteric way, and written in the same passionate outflow that characterised her account of the mystic dream she described in the Armagh notebook. The idea of the lovers, Eochaid and Etáin, one in this world and one in the next, recurs repeatedly in her poetry. 'I send you a few songs out of my Etáin opera', she wrote to Seumas in November 1906, when she was working on the opera again. 'They are not very noble verses, but they sing.. I did the duet last night & it has the first fragrance of delight about it still. . .I have done a prologue & nearly all the first act. It isn't much good – but it pleases me to write songs & sing them for myself'. And she quoted Etáin's song,

> I hear music rising falling
> Old-remembered voices calling.

Æ was excited by this group of young poets who gathered about him, because he felt they 'revealed a new mood in Irish verse'. He dedicated his new book, *The Divine Vision* to them – Tom Keohler,[4] one of the earliest members of the

---

[4] Tom Keohler, who changed his name to Keller, also published *Songs of a Devotee* (Tower Press Booklets, Maunsel, 1906). Harry Norman published an appreciation of him, 'Unheard music: in memory of Thomas Goodwin Keller', *Dublin Magazine* 17 no. 3, pp. 26–30.

Dublin Theosophical Lodge; George Roberts the Northern-born printer, who had left Belfast to join the new movement; Ella Young and James Starkey – calling them 'Comrades in the craft'. Susan came first in the opening dedication of *The Divine Vision*: and was probably the inspiration of the valedictory poems, 'A farewell' and 'The parting of the ways', which speak of a deep love and common mystical experience shared by two beings, who must seek their destinies separately,

> . . . unfolding lonely glories, not our own,
> Nor from each other gathered, but an inward glow
> Breathed by the Lone One on the seeker lone.

There were compensations for such loneliness.

> Brought by the sunrise-coloured flame
> To earth, uncertain yet, the while
> I looked at you, there slowly came
> Noble and sisterly, your smile.

New Songs: a Lyric Selection was the title of the collection he planned from March 1903, in order to encourage the young poets, and in inspired recognition of the totally new mood, and strengthening spirit, of the literary renaissance. He included all the 'comrades' to whom he had dedicated *The Divine Vision*, together with Pádraic Colum, Eva Gore-Booth, and 'the sheeogue', as he dubbed Alice Milligan. Some of the poems had already appeared in *The United Irishman* and *A Celtic Christmas*, but the greater part were manuscripts entrusted to Æ 'by writers too shy to venture on even the momentary publicity of a weekly paper', as he put it in the introduction. He felt that there was no indication of the tradition of *The Nation* (Thomas Davis's paper) infecting any of the writers represented in the volume – 'there is not a patriotic poem in the book', he wrote to W.B. Yeats. His sole aim was to show some of the new trends in contemporary Irish poetry. He admitted that he had hardly ever performed a task with greater pleasure than the editing of these verses.

Alice Milligan's 'A song of freedom' – alone among them – admits a tincture of the Davis spirit. Instead the verses lean either towards mysticism – as all Susan's do, and those of Ella Young, George Roberts, Seumas O'Sullivan and Thomas Keohler – or to a love of native land, rather than to overt patriotism. Colum contributed 'A drover', 'A portrait' – a description of a poor scholar in the 'forties' – and 'The plougher': all of them now famous. The explosive jerks of the opening phrases of the latter opened up a totally untrodden direction for Irish poetry. Jack B. Yeats's frontispiece, with its robust figuration and illuminated sky illustrating 'The plougher', fitly indicated the earthy quality of the lines to come – a style Æ had recommended himself when he wrote rather wistfully to William Dara[5] in August 1901, 'I started from the stars and never succeeded in getting my feet firmly on the earth, but if you start from the earth you can go as far as you like'.

New Songs was published in March 1904. York Powell, now in his last illness, received a copy as an Easter present from Lily and Lolly Yeats, and was delighted with it, and with Jack's frontispiece. 'Susan Mitchell's poems are beautiful, far the best in the book. Pádraic Colum best of the men's, but far below hers'. Oliver Elton, writing in the *Tribune*, picked out Seumas O'Sullivan and Susan Mitchell, remarking that there were lines in each that few poets would not have wished to have written.

Susan was probably one of the 'too shy' writers Æ referred to in his introduction. She had published only one poem, when Harry Norman set about typing her contributions for *New Songs* in October 1903, and that anonymously: 'The army of the voice' appeared in the Christmas number of the *Irish Homestead*, of 1902, with an illustration by Pamela Colman Smith. With more daring she owned authorship of 'Homeless' and 'The living chalice' (illustrated by Æ) in *A Celtic Christmas* the following year.

She was still diffident about publishing her sung satires, and 'The voice of one', a dramatic skit in blank verse on Yeats, Martyn and Moore, was unsigned in the same publication. She continued to publish her various satires anonymously, could it be because she held them to be in the tradition of street ballads?

The three mystic poems named above were included in *New Songs*, together with 'Love's mendicant' – a poem written, it would seem, in answer to Æ's 'A farewell' and 'The parting of the ways'. She also contributed 'The lonely' – later renamed 'Loneliness' – and 'Amergin' – where she applies Celtic mythology successfully to her mystic mood.

While *New Songs* was received enthusiastically, and established Susan as a contemporary writer, it was her wit in company, and her unashamed delight in parodying politicians or men of letters that pleased literary Dublin. She had always enjoyed the Irish lampoon in traditional ballad form. She knew Percy French through Jimmy Duncan (later of the Arts Club) and his wife, whose daughter Molly, a gifted soubrette entertainer, accompanied French on his Irish tours, joining him in stage sketches, and doing some monologues. Susan possibly introduced her brother-in-law, Harry Franklin to French, when Molly Duncan gave up the touring. Harry became Percy French's business manager, and occasional accompanist on violin, and the Franklins knew all of his unpublished songs.

Susan's own first attempt at parody probably dates from her period with the Yeatses in London. It is a humorous and slight piece, which she hoped her brother George would revise:

---

[5] 'William Dara' (William Byrne) published a book of poetry, *A Light on the Broom*, in 1904.

WB Yeats by JB Yeats, 1900

Have you ever thought of England
In comparison with France,
For while over here they grumble
In the other place they dance.
Let me state, tho' it seem funny,
And in fact is rather rum,
While a Frenchman's temper's sunny,
An Englishman's is glum!'

Susan was always intrigued by traits of character. Her first published comment on Irish idiosyncrasies was the scrap of verse drama, 'The voice of one', in which she takes an amused view of the attempt of Yeats ('Bates'), Edward Martyn ('Barton') and George Moore ('M'Clure') to create a modern drama for Ireland. In Shakespearean metre, she parodies their foibles and dissensions, tracing the historical happenings in Dublin theatre after Moore's return from London. After their efforts at collaboration dissolve with the departure of M'Clure in a huff, followed by the stalking off of Barton in a rage, Bates has the stage to himself where he can hatch his 'little plans', as Susan put it.

I for my plays will find a simple hall;
My stage – Shall I have any stage at all?
"The world's a stage," a well-known writer states.
It is well said – though Shakespeare isn't Bates!
I'll have no stage, then I'll no scenery need
(Article two of my dramatic creed),
My players' clothes I will have wan and plain –
Ah, I forgot, from clothes they must refrain.
A pious thought, and near to Nature's plan,
My theatre of the primeval man! –
A thought I hold by one long gleaming tress,
A thought of delicate, dim loveliness.
The Drama of to-morrow draweth nigh,
I its inventor, its creator I.
No theatre, no scenery, no stage,
No clothes the roving fancy to engage,
No actors either, for their gestures rude
Break in upon the spirit's solitude.
And neither shall my plays have any line –
The straitened word the winged thought confines.
No, I will cause that a new thing shall be,
Plays shall be played in wordless wizardry. . .

This impish burlesque suited the humour of Dublin, relieving the heightened pitch of aestheticism. Susan was a cartoonist using words instead of pictures in spontaneous pleasurable ridicule that teased rather than judged. Yeats received another quasi-trouncing from her two years later in the *Dublin Evening Mail* during the *Playboy* row – when the audience made plain to the Abbey management their reaction to the word 'shifts'.

'You're quite too dense to understand
The chill – the thrill – of modest loathing
With which one hears on Irish land
Of underclothing'.

The Playboy yielded two further songs. Another controversy, that of a doubtful Corot, she parodied earlier in 1905, in 'The Ballad of Shawe Taylor and Hugh Lane', when her sympathies were all on the side of 'Apollo / And his servant, Hugh P. Lane'.

Hugh Lane, enthusiastic to found a modern art gallery in Dublin, had persuaded the executors of the famous Staats-Forbes collection of nineteenth century art to exhibit a large number of the paintings for sale in Dublin, along with some pictures of the same period owned by himself, and a selection provided by the dealer, Durand-Ruel, the proceeds to be donated towards the proposed gallery.

When the exhibition moved to the National Museum, the Director, Colonel Plunkett, showed his disapproval of the 'modern' paintings by supporting those who queried the authenticity of a Corot. He pinned up photographs of the Corot painting and a landscape by the Hungarian artist, Meszoly, side by side, suggesting that the Corot was merely a preparatory sketch by Meszoly for his own painting. In her rollicking ballad Susan described the 'heroic' action of Lane's cousin, Captain John Shawe Taylor, who, as an army man, dealt with the situation in a pragmatic manner. He marched to the Museum with a screw-driver, and removed the offending photographs from the wall. She extolled him as the champion of 'Art and Liberty'.

In her ballad, she condensed cultural Dublin of the day in two of her dis-arming verses, digging gently at the characteristic mannerisms and little vanities of each personality.

> A.E. was there with his long hair,
> And Orpen, R.H.A.,
> Sir Thomas Drew[6] was in a stew,
> And looked the other way,
> But Martyn, who had left the stage
> To play the patriot's part,
> Called for Hungarian policy
> In everything but art!

> And John B. Yeats stood near the gates
> With mischief in his gaze,
> While W.B., the poet, he
> Pondered a telling phrase,
> You'll find it in the *Freeman*
> After a day or so.
> And Moore was there – the same who is
> High Sheriff for Mayo.

Thomas Bodkin, in his book on Hugh Lane, recalls the way in which she sang the naughty ballad in Dublin drawing-rooms and studios, 'in a pleasant throaty voice'.

George Moore, the brilliant but self-opinionated art critic and novelist, who had made it known that he had decided to return to Dublin to 'reform everything' – and was to be quite vicious, when he left, in his criticism of his Dublin friends – became the permanent butt of Susan Mitchell's gentle wicked

---

[6] President of the Royal Hibernian Academy.

Sketch of Sir Hugh Lane by JB Yeats, 1905

parody. The year after 'The voice of one', in December 1904, she contributed another unsigned stanza to *A Celtic Christmas*, as part of 'The Celtic Renaissance Birthday Book'. There were twelve entries in the 'Birthday Book'. Susan herself was parodied as 'The Muse in the Wardrobe'.

> 'What do I want of thee
> No casual grunt of praise
> Nor silent love. You see
> Famous I long to be
> And wear becoming bays';

a quintuplet Sarah Purser remembered when painting her satirical portrait of Susan, wearing a crown – not of bay or laurel, but of vine leaves. Susan's contribution on Moore was 'Moods and Memories' for 'January 5' of the 'Birthday Book', which became the final verse of 'George Moore crosses to Ireland' in her collection, *Aids to the Immortality of Certain Persons in Ireland*. She dug gently at his pose as a reformed libertine and promotor of the Gaelic cause – 'Some day you'll all discover how respectable I am'.

She provided four more unsigned satires for *A Celtic Christmas* in 1905, as 'Ballads of the Year 1905' – 'selections from an unpublished Irish comic opera'. At the same time, she sent a jaunty pen-and-ink portrait of herself in a smart hat and suit, with brimming lace collar, to her brother Johnny at the Provincial Bank in Kilrush. Posing, as if on stage in a musical comedy, she offers best Christmas wishes 'from The Original'.

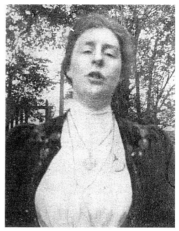

There is no doubt that she had the performances of Gilbert and Sullivan[7] from youthful days in mind when she put her verses to popular folk tunes at Dublin gatherings, and that she thought of her satires fundamentally as sung entertainment, to be enhanced by the singing, and to be received in the mood of carefree mockery in which they were delivered. She felt sufficiently confident in her role as balladeer of the literary movement to send a postcard to friends and relatives in Sligo at Christmas 1906, with a photograph of herself in full voice among trees. The caption read:

Susan Mitchell in full voice, 1906

> Come gather round me, neighbours, and listen while I tell
> Of how I sang of bards and peelers, not wisely but too well:
> 'Till some said I was a Fenian, and some a Unionist,
> And still I went on singing. I couldn't hould my whisht.
> You know my little foolish songs – but, please, don't take it ill
> If I wish you a merry Xmas – and go on singing still.

She may have been the author of 'Now and then', a Home Rule ballad signed by 'Sinn Féin', published in the *United Irishman* on October 21, 1905; though its robust sincerity lacks the apparently artless needle wit that became her hallmark. Her individual tone, however, is sounded in her vigorous attack on the new Irish Council Bill in 1907, her verses set to the melody of the popular Irish ballad, 'The Shan Van Vocht', and embellished with its persistent refrain –

> Is it this you call Home Rule,
> Says the Shan Van Vocht;
> Do you take me for a fool. . .'

---

[7] Gilbert and Sullivan seem to have invited parody throughout the English speaking world. Augustine Henry in his letters referred to *The Gondoliers* being burlesqued in Shanghai in March 1896.

In her indignation at the Liberals' new Parliamentary Bill, she condemned the Lord Lieutenant, the Metroplitan Police, 'monumentally obese', and most of all the Irish M.P.s, who had betrayed Parnell and Plunkett, and, in order to earn their 'screw', spent their time serving the Sassenach. 'All your promises are vain,' she concluded, 'I'm turning to Sinn Féin.'

Arthur Griffith's republican paper, *Sinn Féin*, received so many letters in protest againt the Liberal Home Rule Bill in 1907 that he decided not to publish any, but, on May 18, he printed only the Shan Van Vocht verses by Susan, under the pseudonym 'M.R.'. According to Seumas O'Sullivan these had a 'devastating effect' on those around Griffith in the Sinn Féin movement.

Susan went further in her satire of the political situation and composed her 'Ode to the British Empire' in May 1908, which she dedicated to the Archbishops and Bishops of the Church of Ireland. She was in fiery mood, rankling after hearing the praises of the British Empire 'sung in our churches on May 24th'. She deplored the ambivalent position of Irish Unionism, then rife in the southern provinces. The British Empire was the God of the Irish Protestant, she opined. The Empire was the 'Lord of our proud Ascendancy': and in her 'Ode' the Protestants complain to the Lord –

> 'We did your dirty work for you,
> And incidentally likewise
> To us some profit did accrue
> (You'll understand and sympathise).
> Now one by one of each asset
> You've robbed us, this we can't forget. . .

Susan Mitchell's ballads became famous at Dublin parties. Augustine Henry was one admirer. Planning a novel, he told Evelyn Gleeson that he ought to get Susan to write a verse for each of the thirty-three chapters. Æ, however, had for a long time been encouraging her to publish a book of comic verse, with illustrations by Jack Yeats, which, he thought, would sell like wild fire. After initially being terrified at the idea, and the notion of such publicity, she was persuaded because Harry Norman and Thomas Keohler added their influence. Seumas O'Sullivan was to publish the first volume, and she became quite excited.

He informed her about some criticism of her 'Ode to the British Empire'; and she wrote back, 'No, I am not offended. I am highly delighted at the prospect of my book of Satires . . . And I am not going to change it in spite of those two nice men, Messrs. S— and G—. As I am a Protestant & they are not, I may be expected to know more about Protestant feeling than they do. The Mitchells have been Protestants since Luther & probably long before, & not only Protestants but Orangemen – rise sons of William rise! We are the Ascendancy & we are not afraid of hard knocks. The timid people in this island are not Protestants. I would sing my Ode at the General Synod without a qualm. I hate timidity. . .'

She was sufficiently aware of the seriousness of the criticism to add in her preface to *Aids to the Immortality of Certain Persons in Ireland*,

> If anyone should object to the "Ode to the British Empire" on the grounds of religion, my reply that the British Empire is not the Deity, ought to be perfectly satisfactory. If the Irish Protestant has been making this mistake all along, no one will be better pleased than he when he discovers his error. A better fellow than the Irish Protestant never stepped in shoe-leather. I am not obliged to be careful what I say to him, he is not the man to turn his back upon a blow.

She promised Seumas however that she would write a Catholic Song to match her Ode: she would take a turn at her 'step-brothers', reminding him that she was born under Mars. The new Song would be called 'The Ode to the new Ascendancy'. She told him she was planning a drawing to run along the top of the new volume, silhouetting the principal characters who appear in it. She hoped Jack Yeats might do the drawing, though she feared he might not, 'as WB gets such a slating'.

The 'Catholic Ode', however, would not come. Susan confessed that she had written verses upon verses, and the Lord was not in them. 'I know my own church, & better the devil I know than the devil I don't know'. The two 'Catholic' verses that survive in the Armagh Notebook lack the punch of the 'Protestant Ode'. But her diffidence was gone. She had no compunctions about appending her name henceforward to the 'Ode to the British Empire', even though it had been attacked as 'low, scurrilous, blasphemous and ribald dog-gerel' – 'I am bound in honour now to put my name to it'.

She did admit to being afraid that her little jokes looked 'dreadfully small in print or writing. I am sure I will one day blush for them. You know I am really a serious person driven to extremities by the gloom of living'.

FOURTEEN

'Art, the Most Strait-Laced Lover'

I907 was a sad year for Kate, and one of upheaval for the family. On St. Patrick's Day, while walking within sight of his home, Gilly, who was epileptic, had a seizure, fell over the wall at the end of the long garden into the river, and drowned. The Sligo branch of the Bank of Ireland, where he had been a 'most faithful and conscientious official', and the Dublin office of the Bank, wrote to Kate offering sympathy: as did the members of the local Congregational Church where Gilly was a Deacon, and had adorned the walls with illuminated texts.

Augustine Henry called in to Lincoln Place on his way to the Holyhead Steamer in early April to give a word of comfort to Susan. Finding no one there, he wrote to her instead. 'Poor little world of a moment', he reflected. 'How it hurts us always, the inevitable'.

In December, Susan published her own words of mourning, in the deeply moving poem, 'Immortality', where she muses on the moments of the present – 'a bulrush's brown head / In the gray rain' – 'a child drowned and a heart / Quickened with pain'.

> Awhile we walk the world on its wide roads
> And narrow ways,
> And they pass by, the countless shadowy groups
> Of nights and days;
> We know them not, O happy heart,
> For you and I
> Watch where within a slow dawn lightens up
> Another sky.

By May Mamma and Jinny had made up their minds to move. Gilly because of his indisposition had been permitted to pursue his career in the home branch of the Bank in Sligo: and, though it was a wrench for Mamma to leave the long associations and dear friends of the Sligo Church, Susan's idea that they take a house in Dublin, now that Kate was infirm, was practical.

The Mall in Sligo had been a magnet for all the relatives in need of holidays: though lately George, while his daughter Elinor went to her grandmother in the West, found a stay at Rush, north of Dublin, less expensive for a family holiday, and immensely enjoyable.

> It is a very quiet place and more rustic than Rosses Point. All the inhabitants are fishermen & farmers and the finest potatoes in Ireland are grown there. The people are most industrious, all the girls earning about 6/– a week embroidering stockings at home for the Balbriggan factory. The air is very strong and I could have gone to sleep at any hour during my stay.

George had brought 'several learned books' down to Rush but never opened them, and found it difficult to read even a sensation novel. 'Spent most of the time smoking, sitting down with my back against a rock.'

There were still family in the West, Johnny at the Bank in Co. Clare, and the Brabazons in Westport, where they had moved from Youghal, Bidz playing the piano and designing the childrens' costumes for the parish's Christmas plays. The rector, James O. Hannay (better known as the writer George Birmingham) wrote thanking her, and apologising about the piano. 'I know that it would try the temper of an angel (angels are musical)'. 'I always think that in theatricals as in most other things in life the most important work is done behind the scenes & gets no applause from the audience'.

Susan was glad to establish a permanent home in Dublin, where for six years the only relief from lodgings had been the few days spent with the Legges and the Crichtons, or with her friend, Helen Laird, now married to C.P. Curran. She would see more of Jinny now: and more of the family when they came to Dublin.[1] 16 Frankfort Avenue in Rathgar, was a small classical-style house of red brick with stone cornice, in a terrace, not unlike the kind of dwelling Kate had been used to in Sligo. The centre of Dublin was reached by a short tram ride. Æ and his family were not far away in Rathgar Avenue, while Constance Markievicz also lived in the vicinity.

Constance Markievicz had rented half of the O'Connell-Fitzsimon's cottage at Balally in the near hills, where she entertained her bohemian circle, and trained her boy recruits. Her husband, Casimir, would have nothing to do with the boys' club, but could be found, according to Seán O'Faoláin in his biography of the Countess, '. . . up at Lamb Doyle's at Stepaside on a summer Sunday for a drink as a 'bonny fide', and a glorious view back at Three Rock, or out

---

[1] Bidz's daughter, Kathleen, at boarding school in Dublin, remembered visits to Frankfort Avenue. 'My grandmother [Kate] was not at all a typical Victorian grandmother: she smoked the odd cigarette. I remember her sitting at the piano, and whistling most beautifully to her own accompaniment.' (K. Brabazon, *Family Memoir*.)

over the whole of Dublin, its chimneys coldly smoking or plumeless, and the dark sea fading beyond the clouds behind Skerries'.

Following the move, Kate's faithful servant, Mary, died of a tumour: and it was as much because of this as because it needed explanation that Susan set Kate working on the supplement to her memoir in which she straightened out the individual histories of the immediate members of her own family, the Cullens, describing their traits and their ultimate fates, after the fall of Skreeney.

Another break with the past was the departure of JBY for New York. He and Susan were still close friends: and would become regular correspondents, as he prolonged and prolonged his precipitate vacation so that in the end he died in the States fourteen years later without returning to Ireland. He kept Susan in mind constantly, making her the heroine of his unpublished American story, 'The Last of her Sex'.[2] The singer, Mollie Fitzgerald, is ultra feminine, with dark red hair and a deep voice. As she sings, every note reminds her of the west of Ireland and her people there. She is 'a woman artist whose chef d'oeuvre is herself'. Her art – her radiant appearance and her voice – is 'the art of being a woman' and of making herself pleasing to others: and JBY praises her self-discipline and self-denial.

"'Dear clever affectionate old friend'", says Mollie to the narrator, who questions her about her single state, "'I love you better than any one in all the world except my mother" – "my dear mother who used to pervade the whole house – along the passages along the corridors into every room and closet her spirit entered to give love and help"'. "'But" – and then came one of those bursts of humour which she could never resist – "marriage is like a game of chess – when it is mate in three moves".'

To JBY, Mollie was the epitome of womanhood, whose secret every American woman should learn. In America, according to the latest femininist doctrine, every woman should please herself: but for Mollie, though there was much in her that longed to have its fling, never for a single day or night would she indulge herself – her joy was in pleasing others. She had 'an ingrained pro-priety of mind'. "'Is it because I am Irish that I am the last of my sex?'", muses Mollie in the story: stating that though there are many present who are lovelier, younger and more elegant than herself, she is the only true woman in the room.

It was when Lily was going to New York, as a representative of Dun Emer at the Irish Exhibition, that JBY suddenly decided to accompany her. Æ and Susan saw JBY and Lily to the boat in December 1907: and JBY wrote to his friend Rosa Butt referring to how close the two *Irish Homestead* colleagues had become.

---

[2] Professor William Murphy very kindly drew my attention to this short story, as well as to other SLM references in the unpublished letters of John Butler Yeats.

> I am sure they are a great happiness to each other. I think everyone is glad that it is so. Mrs. Russell never knows anything about anybody and finds her children and life generally a bore (but all this is for your faithful bosom. You must not betray them. You and I make each other happy).

JBY knew that, with her 'ingrained propriety of mind', great happiness was sufficient for Susan, and that her heart was given to 'Art, the most strait-laced lover'. The innocence of her intimacy with Russell can be measured by a letter from Æ to Sarah Purser in early June 1908, thanking the artist for a tie. He adopted the same joking manner he used with Susan: though Sarah Purser he addressed as 'Sarah Purser'.

> A thousand fundamental ideas bless you, through me, for the green and blue colour which has thrilled them multitudinously up to their sources in the divine hierarchies. I have just returned from a trip west & have gloated over the tie. It reminds me of Mananán Mac Lir as a mystic of the depth, of the green woods, & of green fields as an agriculturist, of the seas as a sailor, of the Abbey Theatre poetic scenery as a dramatist, in fact all my nature is brimmed up to overflowing & blesses you. The sub-editor has volunteered to put the necessary shape on the thing so that it can take its place under my beard with the long line of memorable ties which have made history in Ireland. I am off to Donegal I hope at the end of this week to paint & I feel that I can do much better work having a tie that suits my beard.

Shortly after this the two poets said farewell to their office in Lincoln Place. Susan had been Assistant to Æ since he had succeeded Harry Norman as editor of the Homestead in August 1905: and in November 1908 they moved to Plunkett's new grander office in Merrion Square. 'Few people know Sir Horace Plunkett', wrote Susan some years later; 'though he is the most approachable of men, he is reserved as only your frank Irishman can be. . . he is a statesman, a large-minded, clear-thinking, most witty and most courteous gentleman'.

She saw Plunkett as a man who did his own thinking at the same time as – with a dispassionate mind – taking into consideration the opinions of others. 'One can always trust him absolutely in every circumstance to take the noble point of view'. And something she personally appreciated – 'he is gifted also in a way that is not perhaps generally realised with a wit that bites like mustard.'

These were things that she was yet to find out, for at the time she and Plunkett had hardly spoken with each other. Plunkett was probably as fearful of her wit, as she was shy of him. However, others who already knew and ad-mired him had presented him with Number 84 Merrion Square, partly in recognition of his political and social achievements, but also to assist the con-tinuation of his work with the Irish Agricultural Organisation Society.

One of Æ's murals from his office in Plunkett House, 84 Merrion Square

Standing in the elegant doorway, the cupola of St Stephen's Church may be seen to the right. Turning to the left, the rusticated classicism of the National Gallery is apparent on the west side of the Square, beyond the railed-in shrubbery and lawns. Within, the whole house with its white rococo ceilings radiates spaciousness. Plunkett's office was reached through a pillared vestibule on the first floor, up the small staircase approach to the original ballroom. The back rooms face on to the distant hills: and, one of these, with bow windows, on the third floor, Æ chose as the *Homestead* office.

He wrote to Susan, who was visiting Bidz in Westport as the IAOS were moving quarters, offering to have food at the office on her return if she needed it, wondering had he paid her salary up to date. 'Dear S. . . . I am beginning to get cheerful already as the time comes for your return.' He had begun two illustrations for *A Celtic Christmas*, one for Dunsany's story: and had verses from Ella Young and James Stephens. 'Have you written your customary Celtic Xmasy poem? Don't forget. One serious & as many humorous as you can. It will need a lot of humour to outweigh Dunsany. . . & don't forget to tell me whether food would be nauseating to you on your arrival in Office or not'.

It was not long before Æ was covering the wallpaper of the room, over doors and fireplaces, with symbolic murals. Faery-like beings move among water-plants and fauna, part of the unseen life of vision he claimed to see beneath the material landscape.[3] For Susan he painted a girl with flowing dark red hair (her otherworld self) in sunshine, outside a cave on a Donegal strand, gazing into the eyes of a figure bathed in an aura of flamelike light. She hung the canvas above her roll top desk.

1908 was Susan's year of glory in Dublin's literary world. *Aids to the Immortality of Certain Persons in Ireland . . . Charitably Administered* was published by Seumas O'Sullivan at the New Nation Press. Susan enjoyed the preparations. She dedicated the 'little stale crumb of humour' to her mother, 'whose most fervent prayer for her children was that they might have a sense of humour'.

The book is small. The prologue (with apologies to Yeats and Ronsard), the four satirical ballads she dared to print, and the George Moore history, are supplemented by an 'author's review' and a comic list of autumn publications. The author claimed in her review that having 'launched herself out upon Great Personalities' she was 'upborne thereby': and she consoled the victims of her jesting with the thought that

> One Woman loved the foolish souls in you
> That made you perfect subjects for her Art.

'I feel dreadfully sorry about those whom I have not mentioned,' Susan added, ' they may feel that they have lived and loved in vain. But I implore them not to be discouraged, everything cannot be said in thirty-seven pages. I may write another book'.

Her hope that Jack Yeats might do a drawing for the cover came to nothing. Instead Beatrice Elvery supplied the outline frieze which decorates the upper half of the cinnamon brown cover. George Moore looks out meekly from under his halo; Yeats gestures inspiredly at Hyde who confronts him; Lane, Orpen and Shawe Taylor, of 'The Ballad of Shawe Taylor and Hugh Lane', are gathered at the other side of the frieze; while near the centre are Æ, 'with his long hair', and Plunkett who 'got the sack' from Westminister – the two men she most admired.

The tasteful humour of the modest cartoon is perfectly in keeping with the openness of the provocative lines, whose author, up until the end, was unsure about their publication. 'If you think these dedications bad – don't use them', she wrote to Seumas, asking restlessly for the proofs. 'Comic verse makes me unutterably sad. . .', she said. Yet it made Dublin merry. The five hundred copies sold 'in record time', the entire edition almost having been bought up a few days after publication 'by the persons referred to therein, their modesty

---

[3] These murals are now in the collection of the National Gallery of Ireland. *See* 'Æ's Merrion Square murals and other paintings' by J. White in *The Arts in Ireland*, 1, no. 3, 1973, pp.4-10.

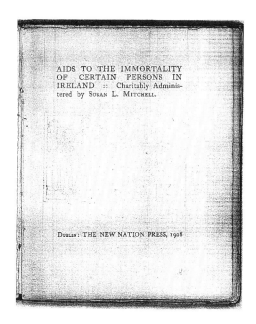

First edition of Aids to the Immortality of Certain Persons in Ireland, *(a) title page, and (b) frontispiece by Beatrice Elvery, representing (l. to r.), Edward Martyn, WB Yeats, George Moore, Sir Anthony MacDonnell, Æ, Sir Horace Plunkett, Hugh Lane, Sir William Orpen, Captain Shawe Taylor*

impelling them to take steps to shorten such immortality as was offered by the authoress' – or so Æ thought.

The Living Chalice, her most memorable book of verse, was published in December. Another pocket-sized volume, barely six inches high, the collection of mystic poems has a blue cover, marked with the tower adopted as the symbol for the Tower Press Booklets, edited by Seumas O'Sullivan and published by Maunsel. There are just twenty-four poems, with the dedicatory verse. John Butler Yeats felt the book showed her to be 'poet through & through & with intensity – a beautiful intensity that only half unveils itself – she has naiveté and is full of 'particulars' and she has the impersonality of true personality – she gives herself to what she touches'.

Love, intensity, dedication are what the poems convey, right from the initial lines in memory of her late brother, where she compares their two lives:

> Fire fell from heaven on me, who, negligent,
> Had brought to Love no sacrifice. . .

This constant struggle between enjoyment of the ephemeral mortal pageant, and craving for initiation into the inner – permanent – reality, are her perpetual theme. She seeks, she rejects. She has momentary visions, yet is drawn back to the warmth of the world she knows. It is a pattern of her own life, where the domesticity and frivolity of her family experience were as important to her as the detached role and esoteric fulfilment she achieved as a writer.

In the title poem, 'The living chalice', she realises the essence of the problem. The Church has prepared her spiritually, and in conventional manner, for communion with the divine. She is eager to concur.

> The Bridegroom's Feast was set and I drew nigh –
> Master of Life, Thy Cup has passed me by.

Next, finding the established way has failed her, she remembers her dreams, where her heart drank deep from 'the wondrous Cup of Flame'.

> The Feast of Life was set and I drew nigh –
> Master of Life, Thy Cup has passed me by.

Finally through pain and suffering she understands why conventional faith, and why dream, or an absolute idealism, have not led her to revelation. What is necessary is an unconditional sacrifice of her being. She must offer up her whole self, with its agony and love and inspiration, and without any preconceptions.

> Master of Life take me, thy Cup am I.

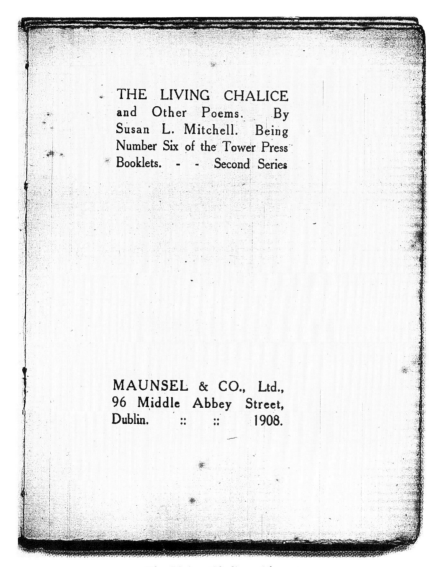

THE LIVING CHALICE
and Other Poems. By
Susan L. Mitchell. Being
Number Six of the Tower Press
Booklets. - - Second Series

MAUNSEL & CO., Ltd.,
96 Middle Abbey Street,
Dublin. :: :: 1908.

The Living Chalice, *title page*

The fact that she changed the original title 'The San Grail' for the more con-
crete notion of 'The living chalice' confirms that the experience described in
the poem was earthly and real rather than some vague esoteric fancy. It is the
poem most closely associated with her: and, referring to it, Sarah Purser, could
create a most imaginative portrait of her some years later with the underlying
notion of the Fall as a central image.

In the head and shoulders portrait, a Susan
not unlike the Susan who sings on the 'Come
gather round me neighbours' postcard rests her
beautifully painted hands on the bough of an
apple tree, her head crowned with the clusters
of her Vine. Around the branch of the tree
twines a serpent, which reaches up its glittering
head to confront her steadfast acrimonious gaze.
The witty motif, together with its essential truth,
must have been enjoyed by both artist and
model, who had known each other's wry humour since Susan was a child. It was exhibited
years later as a portrait of 'Eve'.[4]

Susan Mitchell by Sarah Purser

Returning to Susan's book, *The Living* Chalice, another poem, 'The extravagant heart', reiterates the contrary pull she feels between 'the awful spaces
of the skies' and the friendly 'sounds of waves and woods', or between 'the
high built towers of heaven' and the warmth and glow of her cabin in the dusk.
'I could have taken world after world out of my pocket & spent them all down
to the last blade of grass', she told Seumas O'Sullivan: 'but the mood changed
to niggardliness & I don't care for that poem'.

The pull of earth had inspired 'The beleaguered heart'. She had told Seumas
a couple of years earlier, 'when I was with you on Saturday, while you were
engaged I was looking out at some enclosed space with trees & had for a moment one of those sudden full heart throbs which are after all the only beats that
count in that perpetual systole & diastole (do you call it?) by which we live'.

Later, while she sat 'elaborately prepared to make verses for Xmas cards,
some one suggested the idea to my money grubbing soul', she had made a
poem she liked – 'carefully avoiding Xmas'. After a few small alterations, it
became the question and answer octuplet in which she concludes that what
prevents her heart remaining impervious to the demands of time, with its ebb
and flow of seasons, is 'wilful memory', which refuses to be locked out.

Seumas had admired 'A dream', when Susan had written it out (Æ illustrating it) for *A Celtic Christmas* in 1906; though Susan had replied that she couldn't

---

[4] In *Pictures Old and New*, Dublin 1923. The portrait is discussed in my article in *The Irish Arts
Review Yearbook* 1991-2, 'External things and images: the portraits of Susan Mitchell, poet, pp.165-
170.

think good. In the poem the heavenly lover is pulled to the beloved on an earth which appears 'dim and grey / Beside the light I lived in that long day'. 'Who could in any words describe that star garden against whose flowers I leaned my head that morning when I wakened', she lamented to Seumas.

The book, whose title immediately poses a dichotomy, dwells on the darkness of the spiritual journey as well as its light, on the glory of love with its loneliness, on the pleasure and pain of beauty, the freedom of eternity and the cage of reality. The originality and strength of the poems rests in their personal quality – the writer's struggles with deafness, spirituality, and deprivation of love, and her overwhelming emotion for her own land, which she must inevitably abandon when Death calls.

The style is undoubtedly old-fashioned, the metres carefully measured and crafted to strengthen the emotion of each poem, and loath to experiment. Less painterly than Æ, though obviously given confidence and influenced by him, her manner is more robust and specific. It shares the perversity of Emily Dickinson, but owes more to her first love, Whittier. She is conscious of Yeats and Hyde, and of the ballads and the Bible she grew up with, and quotes from them all. Perhaps she influenced James Stephens to a slight extent. They both grew in the same Protestant ethos, if at opposite ends of society, and like Seumas O'Sullivan reacted in varying degrees to the constraints of convention and establishment practice. Each related warmly, if differently, to multi-denominational nationalism.

Seumas O'Sullivan, with whom she worked closely, had the same problems of conscience as Susan, and she could exchange positive advice about writing – and encouraging banter – with him. They met regularly at the various Dublin 'At Homes', which could make 'a harmony out of the discord of the week'; they met particularly at Alice Stopford Greene's house. 'I missed you . . . the other night', she said once, when they were still formal, and he was 'Mr. Starkey'. 'I put on a dress that I felt had some of the finish of a sonnet about it, but you did not come to hear my sonnet.' His poem, however she admired. 'I like the "Royal Quiet of your silver ways", the whole measure has caught the rhythm of swinging branches'. 'You are wonderful to write so many poems. I wish I could. Poems never come my way'.

She was aware of his essential need to be independent. 'Like myself I daresay you feel when asked to go one place, you are absolutely compelled to go another!'

FIFTEEN

'By High Ideals Fired'

A DUBLIN FULL OF TENSIONS

Founded in 1907 through the efforts of Ellen Duncan, and meeting in the Lincoln Chambers (next door to the Irish Homestead office), the United Arts Club was a great stimulus for Susan's entertaining wit. There were other cultural groups, which she dismissed in her book, *George Moore*.

> I once was present at a social gathering in Dublin which tried to imitate what we have grown to believe – it is probably fiction – was the life of the Latin quarter in Paris. There was just one person present who was native to that life and at home in it and he was not Irish. The others! My goodness, how funny they were! Dear things, they had never learned to be anything but good, and they couldn't learn. They were as awkward as dancing bears. Conscience sat on them like Sunday clothes, the atmosphere was as gloomy as a church heavy with mea culpas. They drank pitifully, it was the only road they knew to Verlaine.

In the Arts Club, however, she had the company of professional artists, writers and musicians, at the height and in the centre of Ireland's resurgent creativity. It was what JBY missed most profoundly when he went to New York, hoping to be back for the publication of *The Living Chalice*. 'Never before did I know solitude – I have been alone for months together in London & in Dublin – but here it is being alone with a vengeance . . . it is against the nature of artists – *we must have people about us. It is the very meaning of the artist mind*'.

Susan wrote to him regularly, and he told her he wrote to her in the same way as he wrote to Lily and Lolly, because it cheered him immensely. They sent news of her singing, and how well she looked. He wrote to her 'describing an actress with all the enthusiasm of a boy at University'. She felt he was 'young, eager, spirited, mocking time . . . the product of a heartier time than ours'; and when lecturing about him some years later remembered him as 'one so in love with discovery'.

Soon after Lily's return from New York, the sisters had separated from Evelyn Gleeson and the Dun Emer Industries, to set up on their own in Churchtown, taking the ancient name of one of the roads converging on the royal residence of Tara as the title for their concern – the Cuala Industries. The Dun Emer Press became the Cuala Press: and for this Susan provided some of her poems for illustration by Jack Yeats – her favourite illustrator. Her poems, also illustrated by his wife and by Elizabeth Yeats, by Dorothy Blackham and Beatrice Elvery, became popular as greeting cards. With Cuala, in 1912, she published her Christmas poems in a charming pocket size volume called *Frank-incense and Myrrh*. Jack Yeats provided the hand-coloured frontispiece for the small book.

Her relations with the Yeats sisters, particularly Lily, were warm. She was the heart and soul of the parties at Gurteen Dhas; and she always remembered the period in their house in Bedford Park, adding to the inscription she penned in their copy of *Aids to the Immortality* – 'from The adder they warmed on their hearthstone'. In the 1913 edition she reminded them that they had 'fostered this grain of mustard seed until it grew into a deadly upas-tree' – the Javenese plant which dribbles a poisonous juice.[1]

The years in Bedford Park had of course meant a great deal to her, and the friendship perpetuated. But just in May 1909, the Yeats family experienced what it was like to be attacked by the adder, and poisoned by the upas juice. For a time relations became delicate.

Susan had turned on W.B. Yeats in the press before; but this time it wasn't satire. She was in deadly earnest. On May 8, 1909, in a fiery article entitled 'Dramatic rivalry', featured on the front page of *Sinn Féin*, Susan berated W.B. for causing the rift between the Abbey and the Theatre of Ireland. Alongside her article appeared a review of Seumas O'Kelly's *The Shuiler's Child*, in which the reviewer (Mise) praised Cluithcheoirí na hÉireann (the Theatre of Ireland) and Máire Nic Shiubhlaigh for achieving 'a turning point. . . in the Irish Theatre. We have got real living drama at last.'

Susan took much the same standpoint. By withdrawing permission from the Theatre of Ireland to act in the Abbey, she declared, Yeats had created formidable rivals, who had full houses while the Abbey was empty. She was urging W.B. publicly to treat the Theatre of Ireland with courtesy, and to unite with them against the commercial theatre. Máire Nic Shiubhlaigh 'looked beautifully' and 'spoke beautifully' at the Abbey, but she had never been allowed to act there: and, Susan believed, it was later, in a performance of Ibsen's *Brand*, with the newly formed Theatre of Ireland, that she had found herself as an actress.

> I remember her then, no Yeats's painted angel, no statuesque instrument
> for reciting beautiful words, but a tragic temperament for the first time

---

[1] These volumes are in the Trinity College Library Early Printed Books Yeats Collection.

struggling with the bonds of its convention.

'Oh, Yeats! Yeats! with your broken kneed heroes and barging heroines,' Susan continued:

> even your drawingroom Deirdre, tender, appealing, complex as she was, did not save you, who, with all your talk of tradition, have only suc- ceeded in producing on Kiltartan French and pigeon English some few passably competent comic actors and actresses. I feel very sad for you and for your loss in the possibilities that your futile dictatorship flung away.

'Pull yourself together, Man of Genius,' she advised: 'save your theatre. There is yet a little time.'

Susan had a strong case – the later establishment of the Dublin Gate Thea- tre, dedicated to the performance of European drama, would prove the soundness of her criticism. But the words could only appear harsh to the family who had nurtured her talent and whose careers were interwoven with her own.

There was a degree of literary politics involved as well, because Constance Marckievicz, and her husband Casimir, close friends of Susan, were supporters of the Theatre of Ireland. Lily saw a different twist to the story and attributed their involvement with the dramatic group to their fall from elegant society.

> Poor Cassie has we hear been requested not to go to the Castle again. He was too rowdy. So he and Madame now pooh-pooh the Castle and are all for Sinn Féin, Theatre of Ireland etc. . . . Madame will have trouble with her savage before the end,

she told JBY in a letter. She witnessed the savage in Madame herself at Jack's private view, in May 1909. Con had brought her dog –

> (she takes it to evening parties). It sat in the centre of the hall and was sick. When he felt much better, thank you, Jack saw what had happened and went off quietly to tell the porter. At the same moment Mrs. Coffey saw also and said, "tell Con it's her dog," and so she did. Con began to shout and drag the dog out – such an uproar.

The private view at the Leinster Hall took place the day after Susan's article was published in Sinn Féin, and Susan didn't go because Lily was so furious. Æ was there, in strapping mood, telling Lily that he was always perfectly friendly to- wards the Abbey: but even though Susan wrote an abject letter, 'really and genuinely sorry to have offended us', Lily said to JBY, 'I think she is at bottom quite proud of her beastly article'.

A year later they had made their peace, and one evening, when Lolly was out, Susan came to supper with Lily: and they had a good time sitting by the November fire, both being 'quite clever and witty over the difficulties of making a living when you are a woman'. Mamma was not well, which added to the expenses of the Mitchell household.

Susan had for a long time had strong views about the role of women in Irish society. In her days as the columnist 'Bríghid', she had advised young women not to put all of their energies into sport and ambition, but to concentrate on the making of a pleasant, well-tempered home. She had noted in the *Irish Homestead* the first outcome of higher education for women.

> The world is no longer made for the charming woman alone, for the beautiful woman alone, or for the lovable woman alone . . . they are of no value unless allied to that gift most coveted by the modern woman – cleverness. Do not for a moment think that I mean to undervalue intellect; and put beauty and charm in the highest place, by no means; in the highest place of all I would put heart, and cleverness has little enough to say to either intellect or heart.

Lily Yeats by her father, JB Yeats, May 1908

She saw cleverness as a 'horrible thing', bred of a short view of life, and the belief that success is the test of merit.

> Cleverness sees that "push" is needed to win that race for success – the heaven of the clever woman – so it pushes itself and values the pushing qualities in others.

Her attitude to contemporary feminism continued to be critical and questioning. 'The sex question shrieks at us from the covers of every modern novel', she commented in the introduction to the second edition of *Aids to the Immortality*. She was tentative about purely feminine issues, wholehearted about the influential potential of women in a rapidly changing society. She believed that women were only partially conscious of themselves, and relied on men to reveal what they really were – 'Man is our logos', she would write in *George Moore*, 'articulate on our behalf'.

Like Lily, who felt that Irish women were generally happy, and happier than English women, 'who are mostly a little unhappy because they will fuss about the little things that don't matter', Susan could only see women in a complementary situation with men, probably because, for her, equality of intellect was a natural thing, a matter of mutual respect, generally enjoyed among the well educated in resurgent Dublin. Social deprivation was another issue of concern, which, like the suffrage movement, had been slow to gain political momentum in Ireland, and neither the Mitchells nor the Yeatses were involved as yet. Susan was far more anxious about ambivalent attitudes to Home Rule and to the creation of an independent Ireland.

A contemporary commentator identified the apex of nationalist inspiration for the Dublin Protestant as St. Patrick's Day in 1908. Hitherto love of country or native language had generally been regarded as unfashionable, or sentimental or vulgar, despite the fact that each generation of Irish landlords had given birth to some Gaelic sympathisers, who either died for Ireland – or promoted the Irish economy – in neither case being exiled by their class. But Helena Moloney described this occasion as a watershed:

> A bright cold east windy day; afternoon service in St. Patrick's Cathedral with the friend who was going through similar experiences of conversion beside me; the sea of rapt faces; the familiar evensong service; the solemn music of St. Patrick's Breastplace; the preacher, Canon Hannay, with his fine grave face, and clear voice so easy to hear, telling, first the old tale of St. Patrick, then speaking of modern Ireland – "poor, divided, derided, the witmark and sport of the dull". All outwardly was quiet as the ancient banners above us, but surely my heart was not alone in its passionate response. It seemed to me that the whole congregation was listening to the call of the Irish, and consecrating itself to their service in

the old cathedral of St. Patrick, where, perhaps, many a Crusader in olden time kept vigil on the eve of his knighthood.[2]

In the evening she went to see the Abbey players, to hear the 'organ-sweet' voice of Sara Allgood: to delightfully enjoy the indulgence of her political disloyalty in Lady Gregory's Fenian play, *The Rising of the Moon*: and finally to gather together 'in one joyous calm' the torrent of the day's emotions in Yeats's *Cathleen Ni Houlihan*. 'The day's passions became first pure, then peaceable – St. Paul's vision of love.'

High ideals were rampant. About this time Constance Markievicz joined the newly formed women's political movement, Inghine na hÉireann: and in 1910 Lady Fingall, fired by slightly different motives, launched, under the auspices of the Irish Agricultural Organisation Society, the United Irishwomen, whose objective was to bring Irishwomen together to work for the social and economic advantage of Ireland.

Lady Fingall ascribed the inspiration for the United Irishwomen to George Russell. Susan also was behind the scheme, and it was Susan who thought up the provocative, or, as she described it in her article in *The State*, 'inspiriting', title, 'The United Irishwomen'. According to Lady Fingall

> Not long after Horace had been given Plunkett House, there was a gathering of his workers there. The IAOS had promulgated their famous slogan, "Better farming, better business, better living", and, at this meeting, it was Æ who pointed across the room to some of us women: "This is where you come in. We can do the better farming and the better business, but you must do the better living." Then started the United Irishwomen. And the United Irishwomen were always United and we never had a quarrel.

The United Irishwomen was seen as a society with a rural bias: and Horace Plunkett stressed, on its setting up, that its role was a social one in contrast with the political direction of Englishwomen campaigning for the suffrage. In a paternalist way, he envisaged hundreds and thousands of refined educated women, up and down the country, 'living . . . lives that are innocent, elegant . . . but a little aimless', rising to the call to help those sunk into poverty around them.

> I see the United Irishwomen drawing them out of their isolation, teaching them to teach others, and forming them into an ordered league of workers that shall penetrate every corner of our country and leave it a better and a happier place than they found it.

---

[2] 'The most exciting day of my life'. *Irish Statesman* 21 March 1925, p.42.

Susan rang Sir Horace at once to tell him how splendid his article was. She saw it immediately on publication. When he wasn't there to receive the call, she wrote to him enthusiastically, reiterating her cautious fundamental view:

> It is real clear thinking & clear writing, just what we want. No matter how present day life is pushing woman out into intellectual things she will always be a timid adventurer in the mind and will continue her old confidence in man as the *Logos* & expect him to say ideas for her, she will work at his ideas gallantly when he bids her, but he must speak'.

She suggested sending the pamphlet around the girls schools, as girls of twelve to sixteen were grand material, with wide awake minds. 'They should get a chance of hearing the new thought'.

The organisation started in Wexford, and spread to Donegal, Wicklow, Waterford, Tipperary, Cork and Clare, with second branches rapidly forming in the various counties. The central union and branches were governed by an executive committee which included the Countess of Fingall and Susan Mitchell, with her friend the writer, Katherine Purdon. The United Irishwomen were affiliated to the IAOS; and adopted many of the Society's objectives as to agriculture and domestic economy and health; but with a special emphasis on improving the quality of Irish life. This meant assisting the growth of traditional music, and supporting féiseanna, and encouraging cottage craft industries, in the hope of stemming the flow of emigration.

Susan composed a song for the United Irishwomen, 'To the daughters of Erin' (published in the second edition of *The Living Chalice*), in which she reminded them of the hopeless struggle for freedom in the past, and of the pessimism and self-mistrust this had induced – but without quenching the essential fire within.

'Rise from your knees, O daughters, rise!', she cajoled:

> Our mother still is young and fair,
> Let the world look into your eyes
> And see her beauty shining there.
> Grant of that beauty but one ray,
> Heroes shall leap from every hill,
> To-day shall be as yesterday,
> The red blood burns in Ireland still.

If 1910 was challenging, 1911 for Susan was a year of instability. In January George Moore left Dublin for London, and, as one of a few specially invited guests, she sang with deep throated lyricism at his farewell party. She liked the 'big baby and little devil', as she called him. But she was thinking of the absence of JBY when she wrote to John Quinn the following month, 'Conversation has become a lost art in Dublin since he left it: people only gabble now'. (She did extol elsewhere the excellent conversation of Sarah Purser.)

Health was a cause for depression, her own health, and that of her mother. Augustine Henry, still concerned about Susan, wrote to Evelyn Gleeson from Cambridge plaintively, 'Can't you get her by your Doctor to go on [the] lines of Sir A. Wright. There might be a chance of cure there'. Susan was more anxious about Mamma, and always finding it hard to manage, so that the contributions to the household of her brother Johnny, still a bachelor, were very welcome.

Setting worries apart, she could joke with Johnny about the approaching State visit to Ireland of the newly crowned king, George V, and his queen, Mary.

> The King's visit is exciting great mixture of feelings. I think it was splendid of Sheehy Skeffington & Madame Markievicz to stand up to the loyalists. They seem to find it very difficult to get a fitting adjective for George V like the "perfect tact" which characterised his dada! Postage stamps seem to be the only characteristic of His Present Majesty.

Indeed she seemed to find it hard ever to form an inspiring picture of this monarch: because years later in the *Freeman's Journal*, when she looked back to when she was in London at the time of the coronation, it was not the British royalty she remembered:

> I came suddenly in Victoria Street on a sight I shall never forget. A small company of Indian princes, in London for the Coronation of George V, had reined up suddenly to ask the way. They wore jewelled turbans, and their eyes outflashed the gems. Regal beings, they sat their horses with an ease and grace and power that I do not believe any European horseman could compete with. Their features were classically regular and beautiful, their complexions golden. Health, vitality, energy radiated from them. Their courtesy was as flawless as their pride.

She added 'these superb beings looked as much out of place in Victoria Street as would Michael the Archangel'.

Susan was contributing book reviews to the *Irish Times*: though, as her sister Victoria protested in a letter, it was impossible to recognise her style (the reviewers' names were never given). She was also being consulted by aspiring poets and writers. Lily told her father, rather cynically, of one instance, 'Mrs. Salkeld has taken to writing poetry, all about her soul's innermost feelings. Susan calls it naked poetry'. Advising a new friend, Dr. Bethel Solomons, and helping him correct proofs of a medical article, however, was enjoyable. They probably met at the Arts Club, and Bethel kept the words of the 'George Moore becomes the Priest of Aphrodite' song, which she performed and wrote out for him on the first of September 1910.

The fact that Bethel Solomons's sister, Sophie, was a singer, and his other sister, Estella, an artist and engaged to Seumas O'Sullivan, cemented the friendship. Attending Estella Solomons's parties, Susan was drawn into the company of Jack Morrow, and other Dublin artists; and in return Stella met 'poets and things' at Susan's evenings.

Susan wrote to Bethel from the Bank of Ireland, Dundalk, where the Brabazons had been for about eighteen months, in April 1911, returning his Christmas greetings. She was having further medical treatment. The clouds looming over her were heavy: she had been having the beauty of her nose 'marred by mutilating hands'. 'This is an aimless letter,' she concluded, '& I merely wrote to express a sentiment of goodwill towards the race of Solomon which has been gathering these many days'.

When next she wrote to Bethel it was in July, from hospital in Chelsea, where she had been for some weeks.

> The pain is nothing, at least it is short & I have a week between to recover. I am no heroine & I hate being hurt but dear Bethel it is good for me for inspite of all you say I don't feel very proud of myself . . . I like you very much and am awfully touched by your letter, so much so that I cannot write how much I feel it, and only clasp your hand in this letter.

Sophie Solomons, and Harry Norman visited her in hospital. Augustine Henry meant to, while he was passing through London to and from Sussex, but the plants of Kew had occupied him every day from six in the morning. He wondered would he be excused his neglect in the next world when he explained that he was writing a book and had to work. However, Susan had told Jinny earlier, one of the comforts of being in London was that no one she knew could see her and her poor nose.

There was another tragedy in early June, while she was receiving treatment in London, and this may have delayed her recovery. Bidz, second in her immediate family and her elder sister – a lovable active personality, whose gifts had been aired so sparingly – died prematurely of heart disease leaving a young family. Jinny went at once to Dundalk to be with Jimmy and the children, though, as Susan declared, Kathleen – the eldest, and perhaps her favourite niece – was a tower of strength.

Lily wrote to JBY to tell how she had called on the Mitchells. 'Jenny and Mrs Mitchell were alone and as brave as I expected – thinking only of the poor motherless children and their father.' The old servant had showed her in to where Mrs. Mitchell was half asleep in her chair. 'I stood by her till she woke up when she said, "There isn't anyone I wanted to see more than you". And JBY, writing to Susan said how Lily had told him of the afternoon 'when you were so filled with forbodings & you said that a time would come when you could look back on that day of forboding as a happy time − It almost seems to me as if life knowing your capacity for feeling had determined to test it to the full. For you have had far more than your share of sorrow. . . I cannot express how much I feel for you all'.

Susan didn't reply until September, when she was staying with Katherine Purdon at Enfield in Co. Meath. She also was struck by the bravery of Mamma and Jinny, who 'extract every bit of sweet that life has for them, no matter how cleverly it has been hidden away. . . You always taught me to be brave and to admire courage and I often feel all is not over yet for those 7 Mitchells born so long ago in Carrick.'

She had been thinking a great deal of her childhood.

> It is a curious thing all this year how I am living in Carrick-on-Shannon, the town I was born in. Everything recalls it, sound & sight & sense of smell. I think I must have drawn in a great deal of myself from the fields at the back of Shannon Lodge where we walked as children every day. I continually smell the summer scents there.

Writing to JBY, she praised Lily and Lolly − 'different to most people. Miss Purdon down here has an immense admiration for them both, says they look so handsome & well bred & when they come into the Abbey Theatre they give it great distinction'. She also criticised her own poetry. A Mr King had said the Americans thought it wanted 'concreteness': but she did not agree − 'I don't think my verse is vague − but I think it wants to be more pictorial & fanciful if the magazines are to take it.'

Back in Dublin, Susan was well, perhaps protected by the amulet, of which she sent a replica to Sophie Solomons. 'It is the Swastika or Thor's hammer. I do not know if you have it. Mine has brought me good fortune'. Domestic circumstances she found decidedly 'peppery: in fact we all think we have nearly come to the end of our tether'. One cause of strain was the loss and mysterious reappearance − on some one else − of Mamma's Castle brooch.

In October, *Leaguers and Peelers: or the Apple Cart (a Dramatic Saga of the Dark Ages in Two Acts*, was published in the new Dublin journal, *The Irish Review*. It was a lighthearted satire about the law and the Royal Irish Constabulary that Susan and Æ had tinkered with for years, and which now appeared as 'edited by Susan L. Mitchell'. Æ had always supplied moral support during the composing of Susan's humorous doggerel − as well as the odd contribution in the shape of words. Susan's predominance in the confection, however, is evident in the dramatic shape, which is based on *Trial by Jury*, performed first in 1875, and which she must have seen as a girl.

The plot and theme are simple, involving an apple vendor who breaks the law by advertising his name in Irish on his cart. Susan − choosing a setting

Sketch of Susan L. Mitchell by Æ

described vaguely as 'the dark ages' – is exhorting the anglicised establishment of her own day to take more pride in the Gaelic heritage of Ireland. She refers to a particular incident in May 1905 when Pádraic Pearse defended some street merchants known as the 'cart martyrs' for claiming a right in the form of no-menclature used. In her satire the choice of music – 'The British Grenadiers', 'Rule Britannia', 'Who fears to speak of Ninety Eight?' – adds a comic, also wickedly emotive, element to the artless words.

While the piece is slight, it reflects the continuing tension between the establishment – some of whom pursued the restoration of Home Rule with sincerity – and the idealists, like Susan Mitchell and Æ, who believed that a native culture was one of the essential components of social and political free-dom. There is an obvious pun in the idea of the apple cart, and its being upset during any major change in society. The opposition between the 'Leaguers' – or Gaelic Leaguers – and the 'Peelers' – or the representatives of the law – was very pertinent to the day.

Horace Plunkett, of whom Susan was still shy, wrote to her from Battle Creek Sanitorium in Michigan, where he was recouperating, and remembering that she was a fellow victim of disease last summer. 'By all means keep up the political satire. – no country needs it more & you surely can do the deed'. He wanted to bring out a modern edition of Berkeley's *Querist*, and encouraged her to start a collection of queries from her colleagues in the IAOS, Æ, Father Tom and R.A. Anderson. 'In the spring we can sort & arrange them & we might really bring out an effective new edition of that admirable little skit.' He thought she would be an admirable editor – 'Every *Homestead* suggests good queries'. The plan came to nothing, but strengthened a growing friendship.

Susan and Æ did feel that the nationalist writers were almost too aesthetic. As Æ wrote to St. John Ervine, in appreciation of his play *Mixed Marriage*,

> I thought your old Ulster mother the most human creature I ever saw on the Abbey stage. Yeats and Lady Gregory treat people in drama as Whist-ler treated his sitters turning them into arrangements and harmonies, & I was very tired of their world. I know Ulster being an Ulsterman myself.

He considered the country to be 'in a frenzy of politics': and Susan told him a comment by an English observer that Katherine Purdon had passed on to her: 'Ulster . . . is fast creating a new disease Ulsteria, and if it ever comes to a fight, which God forbid, it will end in their getting the biggest thumping of their lives – serve 'em right! – they are only a garrison of foreigners at the best, and they ought to work with the nation with whom their lot is cast'.

Susan firmly believed that the IAOS was a means of bringing diametrically opposed ideologies together, to work for the good of the country. In May 1912, in the South African paper *The State*, she said as much.

> We have in a country that has been torn for generations by religious and race animosities, a movement that can unite on its platform Catholic and Protestant, Home Ruler and Orangeman, the dark-browed lean-faced aboriginal Irishman and the red, white and blue Anglo-Irishman who seemed for so long to be his conqueror. All these have joined together in co-operative societies; and while their distinct characteristics have suffered no whittling down, their common work for Ireland has had very much added to it by the union of such strong individualities.

She pointed out that the members of the committee of the Irish Agricultural Organisation Society included Father Tom Finlay, S.J., and the Reverend Mr. Campbell of the Church of Ireland; and other co-operators included the painter, Dermod O'Brien – President of the RHA as well as being a grandson of the exiled patriot, William Smith O'Brien; Paul Gregan, the principal organiser, and a poet; George Russell, editor of the *Irish Homestead*, the voice of co-operation in Ireland, who was a painter and writer; Harold Barbour, a director of the linen industry; Sir Nugent Everard, the first grower of Irish tobacco; and numerous hard-headed Ulster farmers and fiery Munster and Connaught Nationalists besides. All were working heartily together, she declared, for the good of their common country, under the wise leadership of the secretary, R.A. Anderson, whom she described as 'the Ulysses of co-operation in Ireland'.

She put a word in for the United Irishwomen as well, who, she said, were now going to demonstrate the sisterliness of the movement, by improving the arts of life in rural Ireland, and by halting emigration.

> Ireland is now in a fair way of setting up her new housekeeping with a good share of her bright boys and girls at home with herself, new ideas have taken root, new activities are blossoming over the grey countryside. . .. Many of us will live to see a rural civilisation which will be more fascinating than ever was that of the cities, where the farmers' homesteads will be the guildhalls of the countryside and the co-operative societies its chambers of commerce, creating round them a rural Ireland such as that of which the Gaelic poets sang – yellow with grain, rosy with apples. . .

Susan could well be in high, idealistic mood. She was back from London, where her doctors pronounced her nose cured. She was for the moment free from disease.

SIXTEEN

'My Distinguished Sinfulness'

FRANCHISE AND FRANKINCENSE

Sensitivities were tender in Dublin when George Moore summed up the Dublin literary scene in his tripartite memoir, *Hail and Farewell*. Susan came out of it well, hardly mentioned; though Moore, at one time, had threatened Æ with the possibility of some kind of scandal. The first volume, *Ave*, was published in 1911. In the following January, Æ and Susan called on the Markieviczes after dinner while Augustine Henry was staying there, and talked about pictures till half past eleven. Augustine Henry wrote the next day, 'He is . . . in dread (fancied or assured or not) of the sort of religion that will be given to him by George Moore in the next volume'.

Susan's conscience was touching her on a more personal matter. Her brother George's marriage had been a source of awkward relations: somehow she had never been able to put that right. Now she seemed to be starting off on the wrong foot with her new sister-in-law to be. Johnny, close to her since Birr, was fifty, and decided to marry – a Miss Brew. Susan wrote to him 'strongly', concerned that he was marrying not out of genuine affection but because of his loneliness at the bank in Clare. Then she shrivelled up with compunction. 'As to your being a fool', she wrote again:

> I think you are wise to marry & if the girl is all you say, I am sure it will be better than being an old bachelor! It was because of George that I wrote strongly, but because of the difference of religion in his case it was worse, but in yours there is not this drawback.

She asked for Miss Brew's address, and promised to go and make friends with her when she came up to Dublin, with typical warm-hearted emotion determined to make every effort to be welcoming. 'I am not such a brute as to bully a girl for wanting to marry my brother, it only shows her good taste!'

She told Johnny that they had had quite a serious fire in Frankfort Avenue.

> The beam under the hearthstone in Mamma's room took fire. Lucky Jenny found it out. She and Turk flew down to the police station & the Fire Brigade were up in a minute, hatchets and helmets & hose. The

beam was hacked away & a fireman fell into the drawingroom narrowly missing Jenny & Turk who were moving the furniture. The carpets are ruined but luckily all else is saved. Mamma bore up bravely as long as the firemen & Police were pouring in. . .

Johnny's girl, Bessie Brew, came to town, as Susan packed off Jinny and Kate to stay with Frances Hogg in Blackrock, and stayed to cope with the tradesmen and decorators herself. Reporting on the state of the painting and papering, she told Jinny she had seen Bessie in Phibsborough, and 'it was a relief:

> She is the nearest thing to a lady I ever saw, in fact I would call her a lady! She is awfully fine looking, taller than Johnny & has a beautiful slight figure & the smallest hands & feet I ever saw on one of her size. Very pretty brown eyes & kind of bronze hair. . .She is very shy, which is nice & spoke to me so nicely, said she did not know if she would suit him, & she wanted him to wait & be very sure before he married her. Anything could be made of her. She has no brogue, but a gentle soft voice. . . I fancy Johnny will be able to rule there. . .

And she added, 'Thank God she is a Protestant. . . She is not a second Ellen, thank goodness'. Johnny, too, had been very relieved after the interview – 'the poor fellow is so happy. Kissed me again & again'.
Because it was the Mitchell household, the fire produced a ballad.

> . . . Susan and her mother heard
> The conflagration's roar,
> And Susan poured the water on
> And mother said 'Pour more'.
>
> Then suddenly six stalwart men
> With brassy helmets dight
> Filed past the bed where Granny sat
> A smiling with delight. . .

JBY thought that Susan had had '*psychic* anticipations' of the fire, telling her that her letter before the event had suggested this, being a little downhearted and anxious. He was gloomy because the artist, Clare Marsh, who had been staying with him, had left New York abruptly.

> On the day she left I meditated in mournful solitude on coaxing women & said to myself, I will write an article & describe in detail *you* and Clare Marsh – you & she are alike in this – that you always get your own way. Eve was like that – & so was the Venus de Milo, otherwise her statue

would never have been moulded – and as to Eve, why did Adam still a perfect man yield to her now become an imperfect woman? – we give way to such women because they are part of the primal poetry!

It wasn't the first time that Susan had been called Eve. But she nevertheless attempted to make expiation for her wilful personality as far as Johnny's fiancée was concerned. Johnny had been promoted to be manager of the Kanturk branch of the Provincial Bank, which was opportune. Susan invited Bessie to Dublin to do any shopping she might have to do. She chose the ring for the happy couple – 'what I would have liked myself which is always a good plan' – and suggested that Bessie and Johnny might like to be married from Frankfort Avenue.

> As Mamma is not able for very much excitement, a quiet wedding would I am sure suit you & Johnny & suit us all best. Rathmines Parish Church is near us, and would be convenient. You could have an early wedding and come back to breakfast. I will not forbid you to get your own wedding cake if you would like that best!. . .Have you settled on who is give you away?. . . If there is any difficulty in your relations getting away . . . I might do it myself! However when you come up we can settle everything.

After the wedding, Susan selected the china, while the couple were staying at the Waverly in London: the dinner service blue, with birds of a strange kind round the border, the tea service a long one, with rather high cups of a delicate thin kind of pale blue or lavender, and a touch of gold. Later she bought them the best house and table linen and blankets at McBirney, 'as they have a good old reputation'. She kept up a warm, encouraging correspondence with the new bride, apologising for her lectures on etiquette, appreciating the roses from the Kanturk garden, packed so carefully by Bessie, and sent up to Mamma.

When Susan became probably their first guest in the Provincial Bank in Kanturk, she had nothing but praise for the way Bessie managed affairs: and she told Mamma and Jinny how nice it was to be writing from a Provincial Bank once again. 'The house is at a corner & has shops opposite of course – but one side looks to the river – a tributary of Blackwater – & there is a fine bridge, poplars. . . copper beeches, & it takes away the town look. The back is all river, but it is a broad & beautiful one – & there is a lot of open space about it'.

Outside family matters, Susan was associating herself with the women's franchise movement, through the *Irish Citizen*, founded in May 1912 by her friend, James Cousins of the Hermetic Society, with Francis Sheehy Skeffington as co-editor. Not unnaturally the first object of the *Irish Citizen* was to obtain the vote for women, because for nationalists, men or women, freedom of person and the freedom of Ireland were synonomous. The *Citizen*'s declared motto was a laudable one: 'For men and women equally the rights of citizenship: From men and women equally the duties of citizenship'. Originating from the educated, privileged class, like the United Irishwomen, its supporters believed that the first stage in acquiring the vote should be obtaining the franchise for qualified women.

Susan joined the Franchise League, which together with nine new societies founded during the year formed the non-party, non-militant Irishwomen's Suffrage Federation, having its headquarters in South Anne Street in Dublin. (Edith Somerville, with whom Susan would cross swords briefly in years to come, was President of the Munster Women's Franchise League.) On July 18, a petition was forwarded to Mr. Asquith from the Irishwomen's Suffrage Federation asking for votes for Irishwomen. Many of Susan Mitchell's friends and associates were signatories with her, including Percy French, Evelyn Gleeson, Canon Hannay (George Birmingham), and Constance Markievicz: and when, in November, the voluble Mrs. Hanna Sheehy Skeffington, who was active on behalf of the less fortunate, was dismissed from Rathmines School of Commerce, Susan was one of the first to sign the protest against her dismissal.

Susan's association with the Franchise League never seems to have developed beyond a certain amount of active co-operation at the beginning. In subsequent years her name is absent from its published schemes. Ill health would have been a reason; but the militant direction of the League, and the bypassing of republicanism for what became a single objective, the vote,[1] did not appeal to her: though she no doubt appreciated the satirical tableau mounted by the Irish Women's Franchise League at the Daffodil Fete of 1914 (Constance Markievicz as Joan of Arc), which was reported in the *Citizen*.

She was still writing poetry: and in July 1912 published 'Light of lights' in *The Irish Review*, a religious poem showing a move away from the esotericism of her early hermetic days, towards the provocative lèse-majesty of James Stephens. The underlying message is still one of love: but JBY felt she needed to include her explicit experience to give her poetry strength. 'Every now & then I turn to your few poems', he told her, '& like them better & better.

> It is because you have such a poignant way of dropping suddenly into some personal "particular". It is what I call your naïvité – & because of it you have something which I find neither in Æ or in WBY. I think it might be called a quality of intensity. If you could write more & *use your own life more*, we should have not only more poetry, but it would be stronger & more intimate. . .

He saw her as a reflection of the Ireland in which she was living.

---

[1] R.C. Owens, *Smashing Times: a history of the Irishwomen's Suffrage Movement 1889-1922* (1984), pp.39-47.

> The world must learn to work less & reason less & feel more – & every
> man must get back into his environment & *saturate* himself with it . . .
> environment is the nursery of personality.

Susan's powerful yet self-accusing personality had fascinated him since the beginning of their acquaintance: and he now compared her with a lady he knew
in America, a Mrs Fleming, who had her 'wit & humour, also sudden irrascibility
– only she doesn't repent quite so quickly . . . She is very modest, thinks very
little of herself – *like you* – but whether a cunning pretence or a genuine thing I
know not in her case or in yours.' 'She is a perfect listener. . . *as with you*, I am
certain that underneath her velvet paws there are claws – but if she scratched
you, she would be so sorry'.

When he wrote to Susan again in December, he was comparing her with
the red-haired heroine of *The Bostonians*, by Henry James. 'It is easy to meet the
strong will & the strong intellect is not very scarce – *the combination is . . . entirely
out of the way & extraordinary* – not meeting with which Susan Mitchell has
remained unmarried, to her own loss & to everybody's loss'.

Horace Plunkett, with whom he had been talking at a dinner, and whom
he was delighted was to take 'a decided part in politics', had told him that Susan
was to publish another volume of poetry shortly: and he urged her again to '"*get
out of the idea & down to the particulars*", these words are Goethe's addressed to a
young poet – *you never* touch on "a particular" without touching the fount of
tears.' He also referred her to Keats more than once. Keats's 'delight in half
knowledge & his refusal to be imposed on by those glittering generalities which
were the daily food of Coleridge & Wordsworth etc. were part of his intensity
& his sincerity'.

The new volume was a tiny gem, *Frankincense and Myrrh*, a collection of a
dozen Christmas poems – a few of which had been in *The Living Chalice*. Susan
was also preparing new editions of *Aids to the Immortality* and *The Living Chalice*,
adding extra poems. She was interrupted in January by a letter from a Judge
Cullen in New York, who claimed to be a relative, descended from the family
in Manorhamilton – certainly a cousin of some kind. Susan had her mother's
writings about Great Grandfather Carncross Cullen's progeny: but it was difficult to make out to which of the sons Judge Cullen owed his existence. So she
went to the National Library to look up Burke's genealogies, returning only
with the lineage of Carncross Cullen of Glenade, which was of little help.

Her correspondence with Judge Cullen was friendly; but it roused in her
once more the need to identify some native Gaelic ancestry, to find some physical
key to explain her perpetual hunger for political freedom for Ireland. 'Things
rot without roots', as Yevtushenko has pointed out in *Wild Berries*. Susan particularly, orphaned by the death of her father at an early age, and brought up by
aunts away from home, had always had an extravagant interest in the family and
its antecedents, relishing each unexpected revelation with excitement.

THE DESCENT OF THE CHILD

Who can bring back the magic of the story,
The singing seraphim, the kneeling kings,
The starry way by which the Child of Glory
Mid breathless watchers and through myriad wings
Rode with the heaven behind Him slowly waning
Dark from His loss, unto the brightening earth,
The Young ennobled Star that He so deigning
Chose for the heavenly city of His birth?
Only the young child heart can dream the story,
The heart of youth so gentle and so wild,
It can renew the magic of that Glory
That dreamed Itself into a little child.

'The Descent of the Child' from Frankincense and Myrrh *with frontispiece
by Jack B. Yeats*

The Mitchells' presence in Ireland was traceable back to the seventeenth century, like the original Cullen, whose fidelity to Cromwell's henchman was something more happily forgotten than remembered. To have found a native Irish strain behind the Scots Gaelic descent recorded by Kate in the first pages of her family memoirs would have satisfied Susan. One faint hope lay in an undated newscutting of about this period, preserved among her papers, where the name 'Cullen' is said to derive from the Irish word 'coille', or 'wood': and an article in the *Roscommon Herald*, on September 7, 1912, noted that the Mitchells, or O'Maoilmichialls, a ruling clan in Roscommon, were descended from an ancient Irish monk, who because of his shaved head was known as Maolmichil, or 'Bald Michael'. This was going in the direction of Michael the Archangel (the Mitchell symbol and the nickname her father enjoyed) – but it was as far as she got.

However, there were more immediate realities to be faced at home. In early April, Mamma – Kate – Katherine Theresa Mitchell, née Cullen – died, aged eighty. She had been rheumaticky for a long time, something of an invalid for a year or two, her heart weakening: though, as Susan told Johnny, she had been out a few days before, and had kept her mind to the last, even if her memory was going. Susan had intended to write to Johnny, because, though the doctor was not worried, Kate hadn't seemed to rally from what they thought was just a cold. 'This morning after a very quiet night in which she seemed very tired, she tried to move on her side & died immediately. Jenny and I were with her. She did not suffer & it was a painless end to her long life.'

Kate, now, was lost to a Sligo that had been enquiring for her continually through Victoria. Victoria told Susan that Kippeen Scanlan, 'the one whose profession was "follying the Hunt"', was asking for '"the ould Lady", and that James Rooney greatly wondered why she did not come down to Sligo. '"Sure there'd be no delay to her to come down by the Mail!" He does not evidently realize that the Mail leaves at 7 in the morning!' And their old servant, Thomas

Ah heart, the seasons come and go
What is their passing unto thee,
Why shouldst thou heed their ebb and flow
Who hast thine own chronology!
Indeed, indeed, I bar my door
The Revellers make such a din,
But wilful Memory evermore
Breaks down my doors and enters in.

Susan Langstaff Mitchell.

Susan Mitchell's poem, 'Ah Heart, the Seasons Come and Go', illustrated on a Cuala Card by Jack Yeats's wife, Mary Cottenham Yeats

Farrell, who now had his own private hotel, wrote from Carrick-on-Shannon commiserating on the passing of 'the last of a good old Co. family & fancy what we are meeting nowadays.'

The Yeats sisters were an immediate comfort, and Lolly spent an evening with Susan and Jinny, which touched them warmly. Susan wrote to Lily,

> You appreciated Mamma & it is curious what it means to us to have those whom we love praised. You remember that night I saw you – I think I knew what was coming then & felt you knew though we tried to persuade ourselves differently. . .

> The excitement at such a time keeps one up in some strange way, but it seems to me as if one had no incentive to work or anything left. She was always there to praise one, & it was something to please her. Now there is no generation behind us, we are ourselves the old generation.

Nevertheless, with the positive nature of the 'sun disposition' she had inherited from her mother, Susan was revived by getting back to work: and to the preparations for the new edition of *The Living Chalice*, which she decided to dedicate to JBY. He was 'flattered beyond measure': and in return, because his mind was so full of her image, wrote at a single sitting the story that came into his mind after her letter arrived, and which he called 'The Last of her Sex'.

> It is a romantic sketch of you – & a true portrait, & at the same time a discourse on art & on life saying things that you would say – & that I learned from you – and I do justice to the rogue which is in you – you old enchantress.

He wrote to her as an intimate, a former lover: while she rejoined like a daughter writing to a sprightly father – perhaps reacting as if to the father whose friendship she had never known.

Susan may not have felt the need to involve herself too closely in the fight for women's suffrage: but during 1913 she allied herself with another cause for which she could employ her craft as a writer. Her writings already expressed her commitment to Plunkett's co-operative movement, both in continual work as assistant editor of the *Homestead*, as well as in the occasional article. Now her public spirit rose to support the labour movement during the heartbreaking months of the General Strike, which, from late August, brought Dublin to a standstill, and rocked the horizons of all generous-minded citizens.

Susan, with other writers and sympathisers, including Æ, assisted the hungry at Liberty Hall. 'To the Dublin masters', which appeared on October 4, is one of a number of ballad poems which appeared in the *Irish Worker* in defence of the strikers after the employers united in a retaliatory lock-out. In her verses Susan begged the 'Masters' to make peace with the workers before what she divined as a repetition of the French Revolution might come about. It is not one of her good poems, but her revulsion at the tactics of the 'Dublin Masters', combining with the constabulary against the workers, comes across strongly.

Later, writing in the half flippant manner she sometimes adopted when confiding in her new sister-in-law Bessie, whom she respected despite her lack of a formal education, she called it a 'great poem in that vile paper "The Irish Worker"'. She had sent it in about three weeks before it had been published. But she referred with admiration to Æ's letter 'To the Masters of Dublin' in *The Irish Times* of October 7, in which he had highlighted in superb language the same issues – which they must have discussed over and over again in the office – underlining the hideous conditions in which the families of the striking men lived. 'Like all aristocracies', wrote Æ to the employers,

> you tend to grow blind in long authority, and to be unaware that you and your class and its every action are being considered and judged day by day by those who have power to shake or overturn the whole social order and whose restlessness in poverty to-day is making our industrial civilization stir like a quaking bog.

Susan said to Bessie:

> It is awful the way the Masters are dragging out this strike, breaking the spirit of the workers. Dublin is in a most curious state now, no work to be seen anywhere. All building stopped. The papers are full of lies, anything not favorable to capitalism is suppressed. It is enough to make one a revolutionary!

She was correcting proofs of the new edition of *The Living Chalice*, which, she said, despite the additional poems, was still very small: though the new version of *Aids to the Immortality* would be bigger. She was also 'spinning out' words of wisdom for the *Irishwoman* every month, provided two more poems for that 'low-down paper' *The Irish Worker*: and another poem she had written on the Dublin tenements, to appear in the Christmas number of *The Lady of the House*, would be accompanied by her portrait. 'So you will see me in all my glory!', she told Bessie.

> The strike and the strife about it are still going on here. Jenny & I have attended various meetings about it & were present on the platform (the only place we could find a seat!) at the mass meeting of the Dublin Civic League. Only for the chivalry of these same strikers we would not have got in – the Antient Concert Rooms were crowded & even the street was full, but the workmen made a lane for us & insisted on getting us in though they couldn't get in themselves. Sympathy here is veering round day by day to the men, because the action of the Masters in refusing to meet them is so mad & so wholly unjustifiable. I have never seen Larkin yet, but had there been no Larkin all this would have happened, the time was ripe for it & really you would have admired those men, thousands of them so orderly and dignified, not a corner boy or a wastrel among them.

It is an awful state of things & if the Government doesn't take a high
hand with the Masters there will be a wild orgie of strikes at Xmas!

She added that the latest development in the situation was the project of forming a body of Irish Volunteers. There was such excitement in the air that George's
daughter, Elinor, had written verses which had been printed in the *Irish Worker*.[2]
'They didn't seem very well & are rather imitative of her Aunt, but she was
delighted!' said Susan drily. In her letter Susan asked after Johnny (who like
herself suffered from the Mitchell tendency to obesity), and how the 'thinning
process' was going.

We are going to do a 6 mile walk on Sunday with Mr. Norman. I suppose all that will be left of me will be patches of grease along the road,
where I have dissolved.

The second edition of *The Living Chalice* came out in December 1913, published by Maunsel, as was the new edition of *Aids to the Immortality* – both
handsome and neat, bound in blue cloth with vellum backs. *Aids to the Immortality of Certain Persons in Ireland Charitably Administered*, in its new form, is over
twice the size of the original small paperback – not necessarily to its advantage
artistically because the text is looser in shape, not so piquant, and many of the
political names and references with which it bristles have shrunk with the years,
some even to nothingness. Nevertheless it is still a delicious commentary on
the literary and political ethos of the period: and much more positive and outspoken than the earlier version. Susan was tempted to steal the sub-title of the
George Moore group of.satires as a title for the enlarged collection, to make the
new edition 'A Ballad History of Ireland', but decided against this.

Not wanting them to be over prominent, she split up the George Moore
satires, spreading them about the volume, and – though adding the amusing
'George Moore eats a grey mullet' and 'George Moore becomes the priest of
Aphrodite' – weakenened their collective power as a narrative of Moore's legendary exploits in literary Ireland. She was very conscious of Moore's own skill
as a satirist, and included her opinion of his volume *Ave*, taken directly from her
article in *The Irish Review*, as the greater part of her Preface or Author's Review. The preface itself is a parody of Moore's own style of analytical
reminiscence: and her continual preoccupation with Moore indicates that she
considered them as co-lampooners of the literary movement; and that therefore it was incumbent upon her to observe and create verbal cartoons of him in
all his 'distinguished sinfulness'.

Her flippant provocation in the preface, dangling the notion of whether
she is impartial in political satire or not, adds to the piquancy of her teasing. In

---

[2] 'Justice' by E.F. Mitchell. *Irish Worker*, November 15, 1913.

private life, she reflected her upbringing in certain religious and social preferences (and prejudices). She was fiery and impetuous in her political sympathies.
But in her published verses, she expresses the wider cynicism with which all of
literary Dublin was watching the limping attempts of Redmond and the British
Government to introduce a limited Home Rule Bill without alienating Carson.

Susan had studied the loyalist protest of 1912, *Against Home Rule: the Case
for the Union* – a volume presented to her by "An Ulster Volunteer" – in which
Carson, Balfour, Wyndham, and others, detailed the inflexible position held by
the Unionists of Northern Ireland. She understood their argument well, pen-
ning the delightful 'Ode to bluff' and 'The second Battle of the Boyne' with
detached humour.

The final confection of the book, entitled '1915', divines what may be the
political crisis to come within two years of the publication of her book:

> A janitor burst in the door, 'The Green is full,'said he,
> 'Of rebel Orange soldiers, they've taken Trinity;
> Carson and Londonderry are marching up the stair,
> And Campbell, he is coming' – he hummed a well-known air.
> Strode in Sir Edward Carson, his new sword by his side,
> To triumph with the cause for which he would, but hadn't – died;
> Strode in Lord Londonderry, a-boiling in his veins
> The blood of Castlereagh which did him just as well as brains;
> He, like another Cromwell, points to Redmond where he sat,
> Saying, 'Take away that bauble,' and they took John out of that,
> They gave John and the others 'single fares to Holyhead.'
> The Viceroy followed after, so weak about the knees,
> They lift him on the motor that scurries to the Quays;
> And Erne of Enniskillen shouted, holding up a rope,
> 'There's this for John Bull's viceroys or viceroys of the Pope:
> Send England to the devil, she left us in our need,
> No fostering Home Rule now, Separation is our creed,
> Raise the flag of Independence where long since it should have been,'
> And rebel Ulster's Orange flag floats over College Green.

(She was not to know, writing when she did, that her satirical prophecy of
insurrection would be fulfilled, but with a different cast of characters.)

Susan's farcical mood in *Aids* is changed to introspection in the introductory poem to the second edition of *The Living Chalice*. Absorbed with the agony
and ultimate reward of creativity, the style is reminiscent of Æ rather than of
herself. The aim of the poem is to analyse the spirit of struggle and inspiration
that informs all of her poetry, and so bind the book together: but the imagery
pales significantly in the company of the strikingly individual verses which follow.

There are thirteen new poems, which include 'The music of silence', Beethovian in its strength and resolution, as she speaks about her deafness, and the isolation and confusion it can cause, as well as the joy it permits in the shape of an inner music which is perfection. Her metre as always is carefully worked and lyrical. The language is slightly archaic, the mood personal and passionate.

> I cannot hear the trembling speech of grass,
> Nor the shy little voices of the wind,
> I cannot hear the happy talk doth pass
> Between my friends, nor in it meaning find.
> But I can hear earth's voice in thunder roar. . .

'The nursery of the heart' is a theological account of love, again personal in slant; 'Love in heaven' dwells on the tension between earthly and heavenly love, as do many of the poems; and in 'Carrick', rebelling against the sickness and strains of adulthood, she goes back, in simple rhyming couplets, to the love scene of her birth, to recall 'the young surprise of life' in County Leitrim –

> Our own window set so high
> To catch the wonder of the sky.

Apart from a tightening up of punctuation, the original poems stand as they were in the 1908 edition, intermingled with the new and slightly rearranged, culminating in poems from *Frankincense and Myrrh* (some renamed to underline their epiphanous message, 'The star in the east' left out for some reason). Thus the general theme of the volume, questioning obsessively the nature of love, finishes on a note of optimism.

Her poetry is always meditative, lingering on natural and supernatural allegiances. The beauty and playful rhythm of 'Immortality', which has always been the most popular of her poems, is buoyed by the individuality of her transcendental imagination:

> Age cannot reach me where the veils of God
>   Have shut me in,
> For me the myriad births of stars and suns
>   Do but begin,
> And here how fragrantly there blows to me
>   The holy breath,
> Sweet from the flowers and stars and hearts of men,
>   From life and death.

JBY, writing from New York, said, 'I have read your poems – some of them – again & again, but not often enough'; and wished she had been a man, or that the full emancipation of woman had come about, so that she could have spread her 'full & varied music over the whole of life.' He was glad she liked Katherine Tynan: but thought there was nothing of worth in Tynan's recent verse except what had been stolen from Susan – 'no doubt unconsciously', he added.

The following April, he wrote,

> Last Sunday in a splendid suite of rooms lined with thousands of books – all choice editions – & with quantities of pictures – Puvis de Chavannes, Æ, Monet, John B. Yeats, Jack B. Yeats, and all the best French modern artists, and quantities of Augustus Johns – amid all these surroundings sat all alone an old – no an elderly gentleman with a seraphic expression on his countenance – the said countenance wet with happy tears – & he read in a little book – & the book was your poems which he found lying on the table – the room was Quin's.

Her poetry was 'women's poetry', he said, adding that he meant poetry of the finest kind. Later, writing to Willy, he commented,

> In good poetry we look for the word, the line, the concrete allusion, & these . . . having found the something that haunts . . . Susan Mitchell is not a great poet, but how perfectly she answers this test . . .

'Of course,' he told Susan,

> you would laugh to see what an effort it cost to say you are not a great poet – I hope you will live to be very old – for then you will have time to write more poems & have time to see yourself acknowleged as an "important" poet. Don't tell the others . . . but Willie did say, "Yes she is the nearest approach they have to a true poet".

SEVENTEEN

'He still prances naked . . . before a prudish world'

GEORGE MOORE AS 'AN OVER RIPE GOOSEBERRY'

The two new volumes were as well received as the first editions had been. *The Lady of the House* in January 1914 described the *Living Chalice* poems as 'exquisite . . . spiritual, chaste, cultured, delightful. Russell Lowell tells his readers that "Freedom needs all her poets . . . ". Ireland shares this need, and is to be felicitated that in Susan Mitchell she has found a cultured singer and a devoted daughter'.

The second volume's title, the reviewer thought, gave little indication of 'the rare chaplets which have been woven, in a spirit of delightful drollery, for a widely diverse assortment of brows. Pagan Moore, Art Gallery Lane, Napoleon Redmond, Noah Carson launching his Ark, bold Sir Horace Plunkett on his good steed Co-Operation, and "T.W.", and Dillon of Ballaghadereen, ready to shoot "A.E.", J. B. Yeats, "W.B." – they are all there, with "Laughter holding both her sides"'.

Nevertheless, Susan's satire was regarded as less than comfortable in the current climate, because in April 1914 she could not get an Irish paper to take her next creation – a street-ballad purporting to be sung about Carson in the year 1916, and telling of his execution for rebelling against the British Empire with his Ulster Volunteers. With 'proud defiance', she wrote,

> . . . he died without a groan,
> And the first in Heaven to wring his hand were Mitchel and Wolfe Tone.

Through the intervention of Æ the ballad was published in the *New Statesman*.[1] Æ told its literary editor, 'Unfortunately all Irish papers are bitterly partisan & have no sense of humour in their politics'.

He had recently returned from London depressed. He found the size and

---

[1] 'Belfast Street Ballad: 1916', *New Statesman 3*, 2 May 1914, pp. 114-5.

crowds of London appalling – 'the more humanity crowds together the more inhuman does it seem': and he wished Ireland could get self-government, and 'be quit of all the big imperial rascalities which draw us about like a small boat tugged by a rope after a mammoth liner.' His ideal state would be about the size of County Sligo, he thought. Caught up in the sympathy for the unfortunate workers striking in Dublin, he began work on *The National Being*, in which he hoped to spell out an Irish labour policy in order to put some constructive ideas in their heads. Then Plunkett angered him by entering the political fray, and making a political speech at a co-operative meeting in Tipperary in May, which Æ saw as being in complete contravention of the movement's principles.

Susan for the moment was in the happier position of reading and reviewing poetry. 'I love it', she wrote to Seumas O'Sullivan about his new book of poems, *An Epilogue to "The Praise of Angus"*, 'Your jewels set each other off – they were never so delightfully strung before and I find new beauty each time I read. . . There is something in the placing of each poem that brings out its own peculiar beauty.'

And she compared 'the many & varied altars' at which the Irish poets worshipped Beauty. 'What a pungent incense Stephens gives her, and Lord Dunsany with his sonorous liturgy of praise & you singing your psalm up in the violet rays of light, among those things which are almost beyond sight'. 'Sing on', she said, 'and make us still more happy'. Another Irish poet she was reviewing was Emily Lawless – her latest collection, *The Inalienable Heritage*.

Jinny was giving lessons in modern literature to Hilda Pollexfen, cousin and care of Lily Yeats; and she made a name for herself in local circles for her story in the *Irish Review*, 'The Devout Murderer'. For some reason she fell out with the beloved Susan. It was Æ who had to patch things up. 'I understand', he wrote to Jinny,

> a very terrible ogre of a sister towered up above you like Behemoth[2] & denounced you because she lost a half sovereign of yours. Well, I simply wish to point out to you the doctrine of reactions held good there as always. After having blown herself up like a child's balloon she collapsed like an army airship, and a miserable deflated sister came in saying she was not fit to live because of her bad temper & how angelic you were & how always placid & always nice, & I soothed her back from the abnormal rage through the abject humility stage to normal vanity by means of a good meal of good coffee & ham. She is quite normal now & the oscillations have stopped.

He wrote assuring her not to be alarmed, as she set off on holiday, and added

---

[2] The monster described in *Job*, ch. 40, v. 15ff.

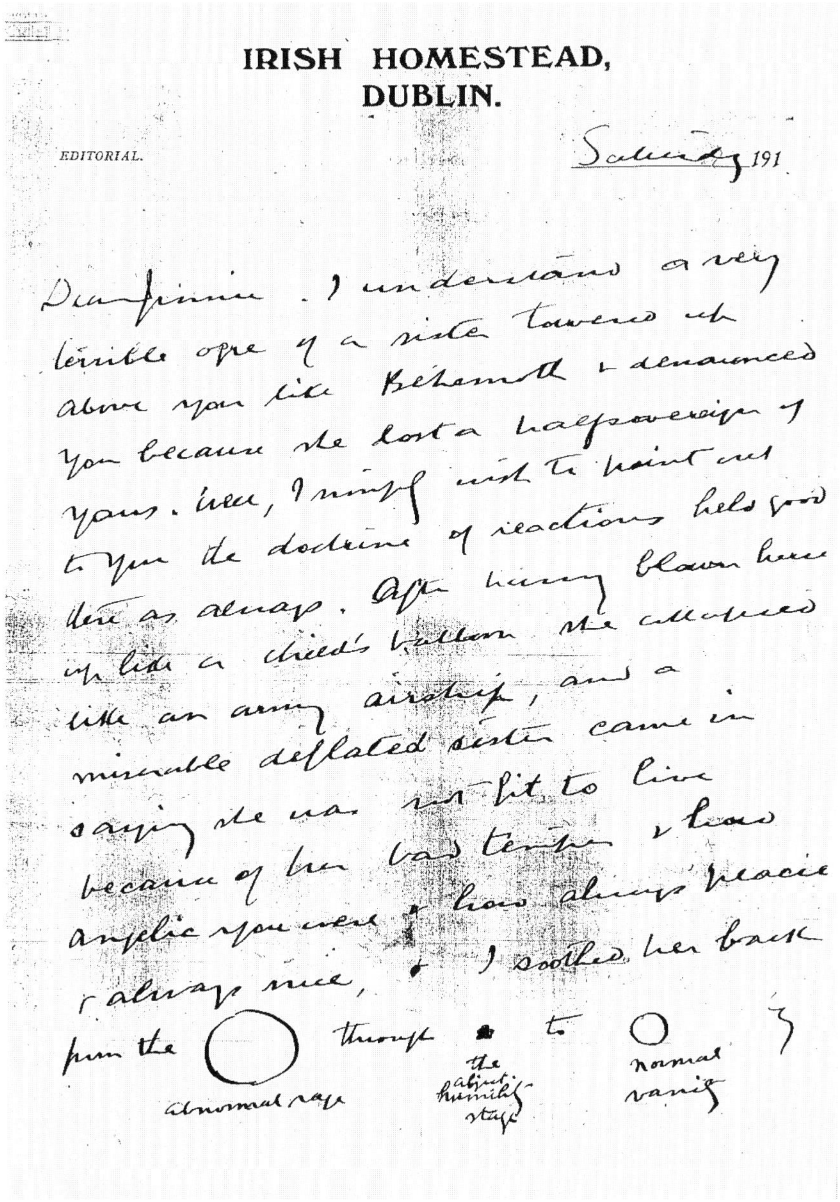

IRISH HOMESTEAD,
DUBLIN.

EDITORIAL. Saturday 191

Dear Jinnie. I understand a very
terrible ogre of a sister towered up
above you like Behemoth & denounced
you because she lost a halfsovereign of
yours. Well, I merely wish to point out
to you the doctrine of reactions held good
there as always. After having blown herself
up like a child's balloon she collapsed
like an army airship, and a
miserable deflated sister came in
saying she was not fit to live
because of her bad temper & how
angelic you were & how always placid
& always nice, & I soothed her back
from the ○ through • to ○ }

Letter from Æ to Jinny Mitchell, c.1914

the suggestion that she might base her next story on 'woman treated as a collapsible sister capable of infinite distention & wrinkling diminution into nothingness. Study Susan for your next study of a criminal, whose sheer affections led her to murder her relatives.'

He felt one had to be tactful with Susan. When she threw a small party for her friends, he confessed to Katherine Hinkson, that he was an individualist, who liked talking to one person at a time and disliked parties: 'but she would never forgive me if I turned traitor. So I will endure singing & other things I do not understand. Anyhow she is as good as gold & her party must be complete.'

Susan and Jinny's lives were, like Lily's, girt round with young relatives, because Bidz's daughter, Dora, came to live with them off and on for most of the War while she did her degree at Trinity. After Jimmy Brabazon's death in January 1915 there were the two younger daughters, still at school. 'It happened quite suddenly yesterday evening, as he was sitting in his chair after dinner,' Susan wrote to Johnny from the Bank of Ireland House in Dundalk. 'He had been complaining of a pain in his chest .. the Doctor said it was only indigestion, but it must have been heart, they think a clot'. It was decided then that Susan and Jinny would share a house at Prince Arthur Terrace in Rathmines with the nieces.

In May, she and Jinny had a weekend in Wicklow with the Bartons, who gave them 'great motor drives to Tara & Mellifont'; and in the summer, when George Moore felt it safe to return back to Ireland after his friends' initial raging at the poisons of *Vale* (the final volume of his satirical trilogy on literary Dublin), Susan attended a party, where Lily Yeats sat in 'an almost overpowering position' between Moore and Gogarty, as Lily told JBY in a letter: 'Gogarty brilliant, Moore slow and fumbling for his words. . . fat and white, not unlike an old sheep, his hands very fat and womanish. . .. He simmered with pleasure whenever the talk touched a book of his.'

Susan had reason to be interested in meeting Moore again, for she had been commissioned to write a book about him for George Roberts, to be included in the Maunsel Press's *Irishmen of To-day* series. Her aim was to strip him naked, and expose him to the world. 'At least as far as I know at present', she said to Seumas O'Sullivan, telling him, 'I cd always spare you half an hour or hours. . .' 'Moore is here', she continued, 'delivered into my hands & takes an interest in it. He is desperately afraid I won't make him bad enough – & fears I won't be frank. I will be just as frank as nature allows me, & will not violate my own nature . . . & so I told him'.

George Moore would be her own 'Hail and Farewell' to serious prose. It might be regarded as Susan's apologia as a writer, because the book is as much about herself as about George Moore. As her final original work, it unconsciously helps to fulfil a prognosis George Birmingham had made recently, when he suggested that during this second decade of the century Irish writers would turn from poetry and drama to a decade of prose. 'Persons are my medium', she had declared in the introduction to *Aids to the Immortality*: and now she had an opportunity for using a single – notorious – personality as material for her craft, with a skill that makes one wonder why she contributed no novel to the Irish renaissance. Her acknowledged admiration for Jane Austen, because of the propriety of her tales, is echoed in the elegance with which she pitches her own satire.

For ten years she had been inextricably connected in the Dublin literary mind with George Moore, because of the goodhumoured yet malicious darts she had aimed at him on its behalf, the verses gathered together in *Aids to the Immortality*. In the *Irish Review*, Grace Gifford pictured the relationship as 'Cupid and Psyche' in a delightful cartoon showing a bewinged George Moore skipping about with a bow and arrow, aiming a shaft at Susan, who sits with her typewriter set on a recherché writing table. Moore's vanity was touched by the idea that she was writing his portrait. He hated to be ignored, and she had always received his approval, being one of the few invited to his farewell dinner in 1911. She had sung a complimentary valedictory song that evening. She was one of the few to whom he had been merciful in his venomous trilogy of reminiscence, *Hail and Farewell*.

Susan had first met Moore when she lived in London – during a rehearsal of *The Countess Cathleen*, 'in some dark by-way. . .I was told that he was present, I cannot recall any form, only an irritation in the dusty atmosphere'. She had been fascinated by the idea of 'this man of wicked books', who 'had the rosy face and innocent yellow hair of young virtue, kindness was on his lips, though his eyes were not quite so kind. . .'

> George Moore seemed to me then to be a man of middle height with an egg-shaped face and head, light yellow hair in perpetual revolt against the brush, a stout nose with thick nostrils, grey-green eyes, remarkable eyes, a mouth inclined to pettishness, lips thick in the middle as if a bee had stung them. He had champagne shoulders and a somewhat thick, ungainly figure, but he moved about a room with a grace which is not of Dublin drawing-rooms. Afterwards, seeing George Moore in the street, I found he was the only man in Dublin who walked fashionably. The strange word suits him; perhaps he is the last man of fashion in these islands. He wore an opera hat. Nobody in Dublin wears an opera hat, and, when Moore put it like a crown upon his yellow head or crushed it fashionably under his arm, it acted on Dublin like an incantation. I remember my own instantaneous homage.

She added to her description certain epithets applied to him in contemporary Dublin: 'an over-ripe gooseberry', 'a great big intoxicated baby', 'a satyr', 'a boiled ghost', 'a gosling'. She compared his mannered ways unfavourably with the distinguished air of JBY. She had been amused to read in the opening

'Cupid and Psyche', Grace Gifford's cartoon in The Irish Review
September/November 1914

volume of *Hail and Farewell (Ave)* about his elaborate staging of his Irish career. 'It is not unusual for a man to see himself dramatically, but it is not given to every man to plan out a moving scenario for his life and then to make his actions fit it. I cannot help suspecting that Mr. Moore may have sketched out his "Ave, Salve and Vale" before ever he set foot in Dublin, and when he leaped upon the stage here all was prepared to his own order'.

Judging by the enjoyment with which Susan penned her 'intentionally personal book about a very personal writer', it would appear that she had been stalking him ever since she had first referred to him as that 'bundle of prettified manners'. Moore fascinated her for his variousness as much as he repelled her for his nastiness: and she had a portion of affection for him, seeing his intelligence and abrasiveness as a necessary tincture in literary Dublin. She dedicated the book to Æ and John Eglinton, who like her had escaped the whiplash of her subject's spite – and therefore wouldn't mind being associated with Moore.

In her text she was critical of the three books which had preceded her own in the *Irishmen of To-day* series.

> I cannot help feeling that Mr. Darrell Figgis, who so ostentatiously presents us with a clue to the labyrinth of "Æ", is lost in it himself and can never lead us out. Mr. Hone, one of the very few impartial Irish writers, is listless about Mr. Yeats, his book has no more blood in it than a balance sheet. There is blood in Mr. Ervine's "Carson"; he knows nothing about Sir Edward Carson, of course, but his teeth are firmly fixed in the calf of someone's leg, all the time, and he draws blood without a doubt.

The dismissive comments were made with her usual provocative humour. Lily told JBY that she herself thought Hone's book good and valuable – he had asked Yeats's sisters to correct the facts in proof – while she had heard that Ervine had acted cleverly by leaving Carson out altogether. Æ, she said by contrast, thought well of the Carson book, telling St. John Ervine that only an Ulsterman could have written it. However, Susan was writing, she added, of a man who was more characteristic of his nation than a Carson or Redmond. 'In my writing I am like the child who suffers the meat course, but saves his appetite for the pudding. Moore the Irishman, Moore as we knew him in Dublin, is my pudding': and she determined to adopt an original approach, demolishing him as deftly, and with a little more kindliness, than he had dealt with his fellow writers.

Chapter one considers 'the outer George Moore', and chapter two his poetry – 'Mr. Moore is not a poet'. Chapter three devotes itself to Mr. Moore's paintings, in two sentences: 'Nobody in Ireland has ever seen any of Mr. Moore's paintings except "Æ", to whom he once shyly showed a head, remarking that it had some "quality". "Æ" remained silent.'

Such is chapter three. Chapter four is on Mr. Moore as critic. And so on. She progressed through eighteen chapters, discussing the various aspects of Moore that interested her (such as Moore and his ideas about women, nationality and religion), and giving particular attention to his novels *The Untilled Field* and *The Lake*, to his three volumes of reminiscence, *Hail and Farewell (Ave, Salve* and *Vale)*, of course, and to *The Brook Kerith* – 'the most living to me of Mr. Moore's novels'.

Susan's is a quirky book, where the writer has felt at liberty to digress as she pleases and air her own opinions, and it is best enjoyed in the context for which it was written. In chapter eight, prying into Moore's flirtation with religion (he had made a hullabaloo about his conversion from Catholicism to the Church of Ireland, insisting on being confirmed by the Archbishop of Dublin), she declares strongly, 'I am not afraid to state that I think the silence as regards discussion of their religous ideals between Catholics and Protestants is the most powerful cause of the cleavage between the creeds in this country. It leads to the most absurd misconceptions of each other's beliefs'. (This has been true for the greater part of this century.) Earlier in the chapter, she analyses the relations of religion and political affiliation:

> On those who have effaced their identity in religious or party nomencla-ture the question as to who is the real Irishman must continually obtrude itself. Can it be decided by religion, politics, lineage or name? The weeklies are often very fierce; mostly Catholic and Nationalist, it seems to me they would have these terms interchangeable; to be Irish, they suggest one must be both. Hence the Nationalist and Catholic descendants of Cromwell's troopers with names unmistakably Saxon are accounted Irish, while such as I, a Protestant, having names stiff with Gaeldom in every generation of my family, have our claim to Ireland disallowed. Yet it is an old truism that for leaders Irish Nationality had Emmet, Tone, Fitzgerald, Mitchell [sic], Davis, Parnell, all Protestants.

Amidst all this, she does address herself seriously to assessing Moore's quality as a writer, and finds that in his books of criticism, *Impressions and Opinions* and *Modern Painting*, there is nobody quite like him, 'because very few people bring such a momentum of personality to bear upon their writing'. His art as a writer is genuine: and when writing about painting, he is even greater than in his criticism of literature – 'that one should smell the paint in these sentences is not wonderful'. 'He met Manet before he met Christ and . . .to Manet he has given all he knows of worship'.

'Mr. Moore's genuine love of art was the tie that bound him to many strange associates,' she wrote; 'it was the basis of his love for Shelley, his admi-ration of Yeats and "Æ". . . Indeed, so great is Mr. Moore's love for art that I believe if when he returned to Ireland he had found good stained glass in the Catholic churches, & altar pieces there by artists he respected, he would have become an ardent champion of the Catholic faith, & Protestantism would never have received an adherent so little to her mind, and whose hunger for art she also was totally unable to satisfy'.

As to his novels, his love and his sacrifice of himself for his art had had its reward. 'Three of his novels show us very clearly what this reward has been', wrote Susan, tartly. 'In "The Mummer's Wife" Mr. Moore obtained power, in

"Esther Waters" sureness, and in "Ave" [his initial and unexpected attack on the Dublin intelligentsia] he found a complete expression of a most vivid and original personality'. And she pursued this notion of *Hail and Farewell* as novel (rather than reminiscence) published in parts, allowing herself to expand with genuine admiration on the originality of its form.

Summing up Moore's career, she wrote:

> His Irish temperament saved him from what might easily have degenerated into a catalogue of details and the use of the observer's notebook. He gradually obtained mastery over his materials and his art became less a picture of life and more and more a manifestation of his own temperament. In "The Lake", written in 1905, for the first time he began to get a mastery of his style. . . .We begin more and more after this book to find happy turns of phrase such as that which delights us in "Ave" . . . "The Lake" was written in Ireland. It seems as if it was a true instinct that drew him to Ireland, his incessant labour for his own making was not in vain, his best work was done here.

Mitchell's book, which draws our attention as cleverly to George Moore the Irishman as to George Moore the writer, captures without flippancy, and from all aspects, Moore in his 'naked' reality, 'prancing' in bohemian fantasy before a slightly doubtful Dublin. 'Dublin . . . learned to like Mr.Moore more in his character of jester than of patriot; so pleasantly did he, like Bottom, put an ass's head upon him and gambol in our walks' was Susan's opinion: and she lamented that his impatience and perversity had not made him a more worthy interpreter of Irish life, as he could well have been, prophesying accurately that he would be remembered less by the creations of his imagination than for his malicious and witty account of his contemporaries.

Her book, like the introduction to the second edition of *Aids*, is in the tradition of Swift's sage and leisurely ridicule: though the exclusiveness of the subjectmatter has meant that, like the other volumes in the series, the wit – greatly enjoyed by her contemporaries – could only be ephemeral. Susan knew the introductory letter of *Gulliver's Travels* well, because the *Temple Classics* edition that Lily Yeats had given Jinny for Christmas in 1898 had found its way into her own library. However, unlike Swift, who detested 'that animal called man', she took a delicious delight in her victim, and part of the enjoyment of her book is owed to her genuine affection, and her respect for Moore, despite his absurdities. The veracity of her portrait is confirmed in Gogarty's briefer, and no less candid, picture in *As I was Going Down Sackville Street*.

Moore had been enthusiastic about Susan's book since the spring of 1915, when he had seen her article about him in the *Everyman*, 'a little masterpiece' he told her.

I haven't read anything as good this many a day. It is perfectly put together and written with much insight. You will probably do a little book
about me that will be read when my own writings are forgotten. But
have you settled with Roberts? If you haven't get on with the book at
once and don't try to cut it down, write all you have to say and at the
length that you feel. Any publisher will be glad of a book written like the
article.

'*But*', he added, '*write it at once*': 'I'm thinking of you and not for one moment
of myself.'

After the commission had been confirmed by Roberts, JBY described it as
'a funny job – God bless & help you'. But Susan quoted Moore's letter to him,
for his enjoyment. She told him that she was writing a good deal at present,
different things. This was in October 1915, when the War was well advanced.

I wrote a poem about the Point, but broke off in despair I had made it so
sad. I cannot leave it on that note, though it is a familiar note to me. . . I
could write terribly sad poems – but I feel I can't do it, & the saddest &
most poignant thing I ever saw I daren't write about.

But I feel alive when I'm writing – a pleasant thing it is. As to George
Moore – I will avenge Dublin on him. He interests me as a subject very
much, & I explain why in the book. I think it is because I have a natural
disposition to levity.

And she went on –

Maurice Moore [his brother] explains him very well by saying there was
nothing nasty in him but his mind, he is a most respectable elderly gentleman – & I believe it is a treat to see him planted firmly at the table
drinking his tea & eating bread & jam. Moreover as I said in a review of
him elsewhere – he never smears himself or wallows in his emotions as
do our friends the Bennets, the Wells & the Hardys. There is an austerity
in his warmest love-scenes that always makes me feel he himself was
absent, he was never a lover, our George, that is why he does not offend
women, say what he will about them! He is not a lover, but he is an
admirer, we like that best.

She wrote complimentarily about JBY's painting, because Lolly had sent in to
the office a portrait of herself that he had done when she lived with them in
1899, 'not finished as to the figure, it used to hang on the staircase at Dundrum.'

She had just seen the family. Willie looked 'masterful & fine in his grey suit
– he is talking ex cathedra & very animated. Lily looks much better, though the

George Moore by JB Yeats, 1905

asthma continues . . . Lolly . . . is getting better also, & was in a pleasant mood.'
Susan felt more cheerful about them than she had done for a long time.

With her letter, she sent some of Æ's editorials about the Germans. Like
JBY he thought the conflict was a spiritual one: and, if he were ten years younger,
even with his eyesight 'which wouldn't be much use for shooting!', and with
his ideals, nothing would restrain him from going to fight. Susan on the other
hand had only known one German well, who summed up for her the nation,
their strength and weakness: and there was a boundless element, she believed,
that had never really been roped in. The 'Prussianising' of Germany was nearly
over.

> Their efficiency does not impose on me at all. It isn't any more the real
> thing than convent school education is real education. I studied my Ger-
> man for 11 years & I think he was a type, materialism & militarism will
> not hold him long. . . You can't keep Goethe & Wagner & Beethoven
> with their noses to the grindstone for ever. We have an irresistable desire
> to teach him his place – a most natural desire. The men who come back
> from this war will teach us something.

'Anyway', she concluded, 'it is a great time to be alive, though it would be
more comfortable to be dead.'

EIGHTEEN

'With Patriotic Glow'

THE DUBLIN INSURRECTION

Susan wrote the last chapter of *George Moore* 'in a city that has been shattered by the big guns of modern warfare', commenting sadly, 'It is a heavy ending for a book begun with a light heart. With every twenty-five years of Irish life we expect a tragedy, with every fifty years it inevitably comes'. She had hated the Great War. Equally she hated the war in her own country.

In fact she was thoroughly depressed, wondering too, 'what effect upon our normal constitution here in Ireland had all the movement of that febrile time that we call the Irish literary revival. Has any intellectuality at all emerged out of it, any public opinion, any essentially national flavour in our life?' Earlier in the book her musings on the fact that Ireland is so full of people so busied in being Catholics, Protestants, Unionists and Nationalists, that they have no time to betray any Irish character, had been half in a mood of drollery.

Moore had been impatient, writing to her, 'You've been a year writing this book; and I hope it is nearly finished. Ask Æ to write to Macmillan New York about it': adding a postscript, 'There is no doubt in my mind that you have written a very good book,' and he repeated, ' — one that will very likely survive my writings'.

Susan was thinking not so much about Moore as about how to survive in the Dublin of that moment. It was Eastertime. Æ had been out of town spending a long weekend with Edward MacLysaght in Clare when Sinn Féin had taken over Dublin. The city was divorced from the country; and coming back, finding transport a difficulty after Ballybrophy, he had had to walk fourteen miles to get home. On 27 April, the day the leaders surrendered rather than turn the Rising into a bloody battle, Hanna Sheehy Skeffington's pacifist husband, editor of the idealistic *Irish Citizen*, was arrested. He was summarily executed the following morning, for no reason at all, by a mad British officer.

The office of the *Irish Homestead* had been set on fire during the shelling, and the paper did not appear again until 13 May. Sackville Street[1] was worse than the picture papers showed it, said Susan. 'We escaped all right, though in a pretty hot spot near Portobello Barracks,' she wrote hastily to Johnny in

---

[1] Now O'Connell Street.

Kanturk. 'We could hear nothing of the country'.
     She wrote later at greater length –

> It was an awful time & I still feel as if it was a nightmare from which one
> had awakened – only the ruins of Dublin prove it to be no dream. I will
> never want to hear a rifle shot again in my life.
>
> It was a curious thing that I never heard the bombardment at all, though
> Jinny & everyone says it was the most appalling noise for more than 2
> nights. My ears only catch high & sharp sounds like rifle shots. Rathmines
> had a good share of the war and the Rialto where Mark [her nephew]
> lives was a terrible spot. All his family retired to one top room & put a
> wardrobe across the window. The bullet marks on windows & walls
> were everywhere. No corner seemed safe from them.

She told him, 'All my books were burned as Maunsells was burned to the
ground, but worse still my agreement with them is *gone!*' Still they were bringing her new book out soon. 'Our publishers (Homestead) also was burned, but
our printers are all right. . . . There was no trouble in Sligo, but of course we
knew nothing of them for a fortnight.'
     There followed more complex horrors. Casement, whom she had known
through his association with Plunkett's movement, was arrested and charged
with high treason. Lily wrote to JBY on May 29 about a party at Commissioner
Bailey's house, where one of the late arrivals was General Maxwell, sent over to
quell the rebellion. Lily described him as 'the public executioner'.

> He came with Lady Fingall. . . about 20 to 11 o'clock. There was a
> silence and a gasp when he came in. If he had not been in uniform the
> shock would have been less. I felt myself looking at his boots for blood-
> stains. James Stephens turned a yellow green and looked as if he would
> be sick. Susan left at once'.

She didn't talk about it, but, despite her pacifism, Susan's sympathies were
totally with the condemned leaders. Her friendship for Constance Markievicz
now stood the test. Constance had been kept in solitary confinement at
Kilmainham until 4 May, the day Willy Pearse, Joseph Plunkett, Edward Daly
and the O'Hanrahan were executed. Constance and Maud Gonne's husband,
Major MacBride, were sentenced to death by being shot: though in her case,
and to her displeasure, the Court recommended mercy on account of her sex.
Major MacBride died the following day, and Constance was sent to Mountjoy,
convicted to penal servitude for life.
     Susan managed to obtain a permit to visit Constance, with Constance's
sister, Eva Gore-Booth, and her friend, Esther Roper, who both joined her at

Rathmines by taxi immediately after they had arrived in Dublin on the *Leinster*. 'It was such a heaven sent joy seeing you, it was a new life, a resurrection', Constance wrote to Eva afterwards, via Susan.

> Though I knew all the time that you'd try to see me even though I'd been fighting & you hate it all so and think killing so wrong. It was so dear of Esther to come all that long way too, Susan too, for I expect lots of people will think it very awful of her. Anyhow you are three dears & you brought sunshine to me & I long to hug you all.

She had a long list of instructions about Surrey House, which was very untidy, she said, as she had had no time to put it straight after the police raid. 'I feel rather as if I was superintending my own funeral from the grave.' She wanted her servant, Bridie Goff, who had been arrested with her, to get a month's wages at least: and she lamented for Mrs. Connolly, so devoted to her husband, who had small children.

> Anyhow its very economical living here & I'm half glad I'm not treated as a political offender as I should feel so greatly tempted to eat, smoke & dress at my own expense. In the mean time I live free, all my debts will be paid & I suppose after a time I will be allowed to write again or see a visitor. . . Try & get in touch with Mrs. Connolly, Mrs. Mallin & Bessie Lynch for me. I would be sorry for any of them to be hungry & I would be sorry too if they thought I had forgotten them for they were friends.

She told Eva not to worry about her at all – 'it's only a mean spirit that grudges paying the price. Everybody is quite kind & though this is not exactly a bed of roses still many rebels have much worse to bear.'

> The life is colourless, beds are hard, food peculiar, but you might say that of many a free person's life & when I think of what the Fenians suffered & of what the Poles suffered in the sixties I realise that I am extremely lucky.

It fell to Susan to deal with Con's affairs. Surrey House was deserted, her elegant home where patriots had congregated before 1916. One of Collins's men, Frank Kelly, remembered those days:

> We had tea in the kitchen; a long table with Madame cutting up slices of bread about an inch thick, and handing them around. The bread was eaten as quick as she could cut it. She had lovely furniture and splendid pictures. When we used to go into the sitting-room, someone would sit at the piano and there would be great singing and cheering and rough

amusements. She had lifted her lovely drawing-room carpet but had left her pictures on the walls and on the bare boards there was stamping of feet.

In one corner James Connolly would sit at the fire and take no part in the pranks of the juniors. I remember him one night. He sat at the fire, looking into it, hour after hour, and never saying a word. Then he got up and went home. That same night Collins was reciting at the top of his voice Emmet's Speech from the Dock. A few weeks after we were all in the thick of the fighting.[2]

The chaos of Surrey House at the height of its occupancy had come under frequent criticism: Surrey House empty was another matter as it became increasingly vulnerable. Pictures were missing. Eva told Susan of a canvas by Constance that a priest had traced. But she was concerned about the garden. There were some particularly precious plants behind the green house, which she could not identify – Con had been the gardener – but she felt they should not fall into the hands of some ignorant person and hoped Susan knew enough about gardening to rescue them.

Their brother, Joselyn, wrote from Sligo, sad that such a mess had been made of things, 'but I suppose this was inevitable'. Susan already knew him from the co-operative movement. He had played an important part in the organisation of creameries. He was eager that Madame's instructions should be carried out to the letter. She wanted to keep the hall in Camden Street for the locals, and the cottage where she had trained the boys: and was paying a wage to Bessie Lynch, who could not get work. 'Is this because she was mixed up in the trouble?' Sir Joselyn asked in November, when Susan was still sorting out Con's affairs, and suggested trying for assistance from the National Aid Fund.

Casi Markievicz, Eva learned through a doctor from Galicia, was flourishing in Kiev. He was painting and putting on a play: and was anxious to know the fate of the pictures he had left in Surrey House.

Preparations for the publication of *George Moore* had continued despite the Rising. Released in October by Dublin's Maunsel Press, and in New York by Dodd, Mead & Co., the book was received more enthusiastically than Susan could have imagined. The *Times Literary Supplement* liked the way the individual named in the title was the chief theme, which had not been the case in the previous books of the series, and the fact that she did not write in a spirit of 'solemn reverence' for the subject. The summing up was that, with an intimate and entertaining literary manner, she combined a good deal of shrewd criticism. 'If all studies of men and books were as entertaining as this the novelist would have a serious rival in the literary critic,' said the *Glasgow Herald*.

---

[2] S. O'Faoláin, *Constance Markievicz* (1934), pp. 209–10.

Many friends and admirers wrote to her. W. F. Bailey spent exactly three hours and a half reading *George Moore*. 'That is the time it takes by the clock and to me they were 3 1/2 very rapid hours. Within them I seemed to see all my friends of the past decade marching by clothed in their most characteristic attires'. He hoped she would add to it a *Salve*, but not a *Vale*. Crawford Hartnell, asking vainly for a contribution to the Christmas *Lady of the House* – 'I shall keep the last sheet open until 11-12th November, and you simply must come in' – told her that 'in these sad, dull grey days', he had '"put up" grateful thanks for "George Moore"'. Even Bernard Shaw approved, and remarked to his wife 'I say, that young woman *can* write': Charlotte passed this item of news on to Susan, to her pleasure.

Joseph Holloway found the book delicious, and wanted a trilogy on literary and Bohemian Dublin. Mrs. T. P. O'Connor thought it put paid to the argument that women could not be broad and dispassionate in their points of view. Even Joyce was moved by *George Moore* to include Susan Mitchell in *Finnegan's Wake* as 'Miry Mitchel'. A lesser writer, Paul Elgard, like Susan from the Shannon area but now in retirement in Guernsey, picked up the book and remembered 'the girl I knew at the Gaelic League's meetings and who sang so well at the concerts' many years before. 'I was fascinated by something in you I could not understand at the time. . .'. H. G. Wells wrote; and Colonel Moore, George's brother, called, full of delight with the book.

George Moore, however, was astounded. In addition, he was very angry. He had only just sent Susan a copy of a letter criticising Shorter's article on him in the *Sphere*, in which he had finished by saying to Shorter, 'No doubt you will be disappointed when you read these lines and you will say, 'why didn't I write this in the "Sphere". Now – despite all the liberties he had feigned to grant her – she had not taken him seriously as a subject at all. 'The injury that most rankled', wrote Joseph Hone in his *Life* of Moore – written with the comforting reassurance that the subject had gone to his grave – 'was Miss Mitchell's neglect of all that he had said on the subject of the instinctive and far-off origins of his Protestantism'.

> Æ thought the book very clever, and his steadfast defence of Miss Mitchell was the cause of some discord. There must be, Moore now thought, some malice in the shaggy friend, a benevolent malice, no doubt, but the discovery jarred with his conception of a model mystic, and very soon he became sure that Æ had instigated many of the offending passages.

Susan, for her part, among her varied activities, was once more trying to reconcile the many parts of herself with her own inherited instinctive Protestantism. She started going to church again. 'When material life is crumbling about us, what more natural than to seek in a spiritual life the stablility we long for?' she asked herself. However, her being was appalled by the emotional energy with

ing to us of their religion proceeds from the fear of our laughter and of being led away by our superior wisdom. Where the
first reason moves Protestants silence is right and just, Protestantism in Ireland has a bitter record and it does well to hold
its tongue; but to those who are neither poor nor unlearned why
offer the insult of our silence? My panacea as you may perceive
has at last been offered; I cannot escape the common fate of a
writer about Ireland. Free discussion is my potion. For
God's sake let us discuss everything. So only shall we approach
each other and learn respect for each other's point of view.
Everyone knows the value of discussion in elucidating ones own
cleverness and fixing one more firmly than ever in ones own
opinion, and I have no doubt that free discussions between the
religions In Ireland would be of more value to Catholicism here
than much motu proprio and many ne temere and decrees for these
it seems to me in another nation have paved the way to statutes 1
like to Praemunire.

Original typescript of George Moore. *Susan Mitchell recommends discussion between
members of different religious groups in Ireland*

which the congregation threw themselves into singing the national anthem. It
aroused many questions in her mind, with which she wrestled in an article as a
'Meditation on the Beatitudes'. It was published in the *Church of Ireland Gazette*
on 17 November 1916.

Reading through the passages of the Sermon on the Mount, she concluded
that 'the firm', the 'going concern', as she called the official Church, had com-
promised its lofty ethic, and, for the sake of temporal power, had itself become
a kingdom of this world. 'Is there a single martyr Bishop to go out and die in
Christendom to-day for the teaching Christ gave in the Sermon on the Mount?'
she questioned. She hit hard at the Church of Ireland, making no bones about
her nationalist sympathies.

> In our own country, nearest and dearest to our hearts, we have two or
> more Christian Churches. The one I know best has wagged its tail and
> barked approvingly at the heels of the State, and, carrying its flattery
> beyond even what the State desired from it, introduced into its mythol-

ogy a new deity, and its General Synod, with only one protesting voice, added to its public worship a hymn to the King of England, and a prayer for the confusion of his enemies, rendering to Caesar a little more than his due, and to God a little less than his.

Seeing the pitiful results of the miniscule insurgence at first hand, as well as grieving for the annihilation of so many young men further afield, some of whose bereaved parents stood beside her in church, she recoiled at the irony of singing out the triumphalist verses. The anthem blessed – at one and the same time – one of the main protagonists of the slaughtering War, and the state from which her own country had for years been endeavouring to obtain independence by peaceful means, and which had now answered protest with legalised violence. To her, the offending hymn appeared as an Ode to War, a Paean of Repressive Politics.

Warre B. Wells, editor of the *Church of Ireland Gazette*, had gladly published the article, though he did not agree with much of it, 'but sincerity will always find a welcome in the *Gazette*', he told her, 'and it will, I hope, disturb some complacencies'. He told her in strict editorial confidence that the qualities which she admired in his paper had loosed many nails of wrath upon his head. Sarah Purser writing to her about the same time quoted Mrs. Kettle who said that she wanted both England and Germany beaten. 'It seems as if being blessed is all peacemakers get', Sarah said to Susan.

The first reaction to Susan's article was a letter to the paper from R. W. Seaver, of St. John's, Malone Road, in Belfast, who approved 'such moral courage and independence of outlook in a lay member of our Church' but who got hold of the wrong end of the stick. 'Plainly . . . Mr. Seaver has entirely missed the point of my article, which was that the Christian Churches, as Churches, so far as I know, with the exception of the late Pope, made no protest whatever against the war,' Susan replied. 'I think lay Christendom expected such a protest. . . We asked for words from heaven, and we got recruiting posters on the churches'.

She was not attacking the individual priest, who had done 'heavenly deeds', 'in lives risked freely upon every front'. But she indicted official Christianity for not upholding the Sermon on the Mount, which appealed to the imaginative intellect of man. Again she blamed the Church of Ireland.

> In the spring of 1914, before we dreamed of war, I saw in Ulster a prelate of the Church of Ireland, lawn-sleeved, in full Canonicals, bless the banners of the Ulster Volunteers. Did he not indeed know that he gave the Church's Benediction to Civil War in Ireland?

There were other reactions to her article. Canon Price felt that poets lived in a world of their own, and that she should attend and support the Church more.

D.G. Allmann pointed out that 'the Beatitudes do not forbid war; they do not mention it'. The editor closed the debate by questioning the 'nerveless pacifism' of wealthy Quakers, who obeyed one precept but were inclined to ignore another. He recommended interpreting the Gospel according to circumstance – 'We are enjoined not merely to be as harmless as doves, but as wise as serpents'.

Clearly Susan's crusade had failed for the moment, though there must have been support for her from those who scented the imminence of renewed armed conflict in Ireland itself, and realised what was at the root of her protest. The *Gazette* might welcome Sir Edward Carson's inclusion in the triumvirate of the new War Council: but for Susan he was still like 'a decayed Pharaoh', 'impressive in an uninspiring way', Æ told fellow Northerner St. John Ervine.

Lily was in sympathy with Susan. In January on Twelfth Night, she saw her at the Cahills' housewarming in Merrion Square, where Cruise O'Brien did a splendid imitation of Willy. 'She looks well', Lily reported to JBY. 'Her success has been very good for her. She, so to speak, speaks out now and has confidence in herself'. Grant Richards, publishers, had been talking to her about a new book on the literary and artistic movement in Dublin.

But the War weighed heavily, and Lily was conscious that it was affecting JBY as well. Here in Dublin,

> Food goes on getting dearer and dearer and also worse and worse in quality. Tea tastes of nothing at all. Hot water poured over a very little hay at its best, generally just hot water. Somebody is making money.
>
> I wish they would close all the public houses and stop all drink – the boozers and tipplers are still boozers and still tipplers, while the wives and children are short of bare necessities of food. The rise in price of drink does not stop the chronic. He and she must get it and they do.

On 7 June 1917, Susan and Jinny moved temporarily to 1 Wesley Road, at a rent of £3 a month. Life was settling into a more normal shape: Susan's diary records visits to Frances Hogg, lunch with Lady Fingall, tea with Lady Ardilaun, supper now and again with the Yeatses, and her dealings with Constance's affairs, part of which was the weekly payment of the Countess's servant, Bessie Lynch, very often out of Susan's own pocket.

With their nieces they then settled into a roomy house, 25 Leinster Road.[3]

---

[3] Kathleen Brabazon's Memior relates, 'I ran the house with the help of our wonderful maid, Anne Kane: she cooked, polished, waited on the aunts and was the friend of the whole family . . . The aunts had a large sittingroom on the second floor, and here on the second Saturday of the month Aunt Susan was at home to all her circle of acquaintances: every shade of opinion met happily in that room, the only refreshment being tea and homemade cakes. In this house the aunts had a flat of their own and had their meals separately.

Susan started her own 'At Homes', and her Saturdays became a regular feature of Dublin literary life. All sorts of vibrant people might be met: Dr. Kathleen Lynn, fresh from jail and deportation for attending the Sinn Féin wounded during the Rising, Pádraic Colum back from a poetic airing in America, and later Frank O'Connor, in whose career Susan took a particular interest. Susan continued to air her opinions in public. She read a paper at the Wild Geese in February, for the National Literary Society in March, and to the Hermetic Society in April, when she was also at the annual meeting of the United Irishwomen. But she was still bothered about her position in the Church of her fathers. Her heart beat, in truth, for all the 'rebelly crew', as Constance Markievicz affectionately named her supporters.

Susan's ardent nationalism was echoed in the Arts Club, which had moved to 44 St. Stephen's Green, to rooms looking down on Dublin's oldest park. George O'Brien as a young barrister found there 'a new kind of nationalism unlike anything I had met before.'

> I found myself for the first time among people whom I found socially agreeable and who had nationalist convictions. I had always previously thought, I imagine, that the upper classes in Ireland were all unionists and that nationalism was confined to the lower and middle classes. But now I discovered that people whom I could admire for their social ease and upper class attitude were nationalists.[4]

Other members of this more privileged class to which he refers extended their nationalist ideals in the Irish Guild of the Church (Cumann Gaedhalach na hEaglaise), founded shortly before the outbreak of War. The original members of the Guild – about twenty of them – met in St. Ann's Vestry in Dublin in January 1914. They had the blessing of Douglas Hyde, about whose treatment in Moore's trilogy Susan had been most indignant. Sir Roger Casement, the Hon Mary Spring-Rice, and the Lord Chief Justice backed them too.

The opening proposal that a society be formed, 'confined to members of the Church of Ireland, to promote the objects of the Irish Revival among Irish Church People', was discussed with enthusiasm. Three principal aims were spelled out: to promote the use of the Irish language in Church services, especially in Irish-speaking districts; to collect suitable hymns from Irish sources; and to encourage the use of Irish and Irish music in the Church. Those present were also eager to express in some fashion the connection between the contemporary Church and the ancient Irish Church: and, when they met for the second time, they added as their prime objective the promotion of 'all that tends to preserve within the Church of Ireland the spirit of the ancient Celtic

---

[4] J. Meenan, *George O'Brien: a Biographical Memoir* (1980), p. 75.

Church; and to provide a bond of union for all members of the Church of Ireland inspired with Irish ideals'. At the inaugural meeting of the Guild in April 1914, the Bishop of Tuam was elected President.

Lil Duncan the Gaelic scholar, Lily Williams the artist, and Nelly O'Brien – sister of the painter Dermod O'Brien – were immediately involved. Personalities from very different backgrounds, like Ernest Blythe and Seán O'Casey, attended the communions in Irish at Christ Church, and were anxious to see a prayerbook in the Irish language. George Moore's brother, Colonel Moore, spoke to one of the first papers, that on 'Nationality and Religion' by Canon Vandeleur: and by July the Dean of St. Patrick's, who was one of the Vice-Presidents, and Miss Young were preparing an Irish hymnbook (published as *Duanaire Diadha* in 1916). By the following January, regular services in the Irish language were being conducted in the Lady Chapel of St. Patrick's Cathedral, including the St. Patrick's Day service. Among other events, which included a series of lectures on ancient Irish Church history by Professors MacAllister and Henry, there was a production of Douglas Hyde's nativity play by the members of the Guild.

Susan, preoccupied with the writing of *George Moore*, took little interest in the Guild at first. But a dispute arose after the tragic events of the Rising, which gradually persuaded her to take an active part in its proceedings.

On 13 June 1916, the Bishop of Tuam resigned from the Presidency, because he disagreed with a draft resolution, approved by the majority, deploring the recent rising in Dublin. Only months before on St. Patrick's Day, he had commended the Guild for its avoidance of politics, 'for we are determined to steer clear of the rocks on which in the past so many Irish efforts have been wrecked.' After much discussion at the annual general meeting, the Bishop was satisfied with an amended resolution, which accorded with establishment attitudes, and stressed the Guild's loyalty to the monarchy!

Emotions cooled down temporarily. But those at the roots of the Cumann were unhappy with the amended resolution. In her diary for 1917 Susan notes going to a liturgy practice of Cumann na hEaglise on 13 April. The following week she and her sister Jinny were elected as members of the Guild. With half a dozen others she read five minute papers at a meeting in November. An entry in her diary reminded her to 'Take notes of Killaloe's speech' – the Bishop of Killaloe was a Vice-President and happened to be Susan's former rector in Birr, Dr. Thomas Sterling Berry ('Ster dear' – whom she had liked so much).

She was prepared for action.Her reason for taking notes was based on the realisation that Bishop Berry, with the Bishops of Tuam and Limerick and three others, was growing increasingly suspicious of his fellow committee members, and feared that the Guild was growing over sympathetic towards the Republicans. The six called for a special meeting of the committee – at which none of them, in the event, was present – to give an assurance that all would abide by the resolution of loyalty passed at the annual general meeting in the summer of 1916. The members of the executive committee who did meet issued a statement indicating that they were opposed to any form of political expression by the Guild. To regard the 1916 resolution as binding on individual members would, they believed, be as injurious as imposing it as a condition for membership of the Church. They reasserted their loyalty to the Church of Ireland and to the principles expressed by the president of the Cumann on St. Patrick's Day 1916.

The statement failed to halt the slow creep of uneasiness. Then an almighty row occurred at the annual general meeting in 1918, when, after Dr. Berry had been elected President and taken the chair, Mr. Irvine rose to his feet with a proposal, 'That the following resolution declared passed at the annual general meeting of Cumann Gaedhalach na hEaglaise in June 1916 is hereby rescinded and that in rescinding this resolution it is distinctly understood that the Cumann expresses no opinion whatever in regard to the relations at present existing between the two nations Ireland and England'. Before putting the resolution to the meeting, the President explained that, if it were passed, he and the other Bishops would be compelled to resign, since by the nature of their office, they were obliged to affirm the Church of Ireland's loyalty to the Crown.

Irvine's proposal was passed by a majority, whereupon the President and many other members resigned and departed, shortly to form themselves as a new group, Comhluadar Gaedhalach na Fiadhnuise, the Irish Guild of Witness. The minutes continue: 'Miss Susan Mitchell was afterwards moved to the chair, and Professor Trench read an interesting lecture on the Galatian Celts.'

Susan was thus recognised as a figurehead of non-political nationalism in the Church of Ireland, and in Cumann Gaodhalach na hEaglaise, whose meetings removed for the time being to the studio of the artist, Lily Williams, in 18 Lower Pembroke Street.

NINETEEN

'The First Faint Hopes of Ireland's Future'

THE FIRST IRISH CONVENTION

Susan's struggles with her spiritual and political conscience passed by unknown to JBY in New York. He had his own struggles, for the moment alleviated by some lecturing and portrait commissions. He was pleased with four life-size portraits he did in Pittsburgh, 'that city of smoke'. The last two 'as regards the head were done in a single sitting,' he told her in a letter. 'The fourth I insisted on doing in my own way – & when it was finished it was pronounced that all were wonderful, but this last especially so'.

He continued to write regularly with his literary and philosophical ponderings, still remembering her as the lovely red-head with hazel eyes, whose wit had capped his at the turn of the century in London. Even with 'frosted chestnut hair', Paul Henry was entranced at the first exhibition of his Achill paintings by her 'tremulous, rapturous' smile, which no one could easily forget. For her niece, Kathleen, she was the centre of attention at any affair. 'Her hair was snow white on top but a rich red brown at the back, and when animated at a party she had a lovely colour, natural not artificial.' JBY could not rid himself of his image of Susan at the peak of her attraction and seemed to imagine that she was permanently thirty. 'Fifty years ago I heard of the Mitchell charm, or rather of your mother & all your aunts & of their sayings & songs. God Almighty must have said to himself, "these little people are passing & will soon be forgotten. I must bestir myself" – so you came into the light'. She was compared with all the charming women he admired in America. None rivalled her for the passion in which he believed she abounded, '& in which Miss Purser is deficient'!

> I remember so well the look with which you sang the line "I sent you late a rosy wreath". It was always the same look. There was always an imperceptible pause as if from a sudden reminiscence, & then you looked away from everybody as you sang the words. When you are 50 you will sing it still the same.

She sang, he remembered, oblivious of company, hearing only her own voice – 'rapt away in a cloud of song'.

For him Sarah Purser – who he chose to forget had made him famous in Dublin, but whose powerful personality he liked to admire from a distance – was the antithesis of Susan. Her image, like Susan's, continually obsessed him. 'American women are like Sarah Purser – her nephew whom I met in Pittsburgh said she would not succeed here. He is a fool – she would carry everything before her'. Susan, on the other hand, had she not been a woman, 'and under conventions that beset the woman' (he could see her laughing) – what love poems she could have written! Susan's poetry had an assurance and an inward tranquillity which was at the same time militant and triumphant.

> That's what I mean when I called you a passionate woman – when I read your poems yesterday, I at once saw you. I saw your eyelid quivering, & heard a break in your voice. I think passion is a sort of suffering tranquillity, & also a triumphant sorrow – triumph is the essence of your verse – not of joy but of suffering.

He received her book on George Moore at the end of October 1916. 'I don't know what to say, excepting that it is & will remain "*one of the immortals*", there is the lightening that merely glimmers & there is *forked lightening* – & both are there . . . you play with your subject, & then suddenly you strike. . .' (He was repeating the notion he had perpetuated of Susan since he had first known her, as a kitten with needle-sharp claws).

> God! how you must astonish the Pursers! They are critical & scornful & what is called "superior". All the same they understand – no real excellence escapes them. . . I would like to know what the Pursers think and say. . .

The portrait of Moore he found Shakespearian – 'a whimsical truth & all flushed out with glittering startlingness. Your portrait of Dublin also..' He objected to one statement only. 'Willie never forced his sisters to read any book – it would have been so *unlike* him. . .'

He wished he were at home to make a portrait of her for the next edition. When he heard from her, her letter 'made the cold black room . . . feel like summer when all the windows are open & it is not too hot.' 'What is the Mitchell charm? . . .Long ago Dowden[1] would tell me of your Aunt Mrs. St. Leger & how every young man who left Sligo & returned reported himself to her before he went to see his own people'[2] He considered that the book might

---

[1] His friend the poet and critic, Edward Dowden.
[2] For Susan's aunt, Bessie St. Leger, see *The Sligo-Leitrim World of Kate Cullen: a 19th century memoir revealed*, Woodfield P., 1997, pp. 79, 80, etc.

be owed partly to her red hair. 'I am convinced that all men who have had a demon, whereby to fascinate their friends' (he referred to Socrates, Sydney and others) 'have had red hair. . .I often take up your book, reading it is like a pleasant canter over the elastic sod, mounted on a mettlesome nag. . .That's what it is. There's a demon – red hair'.

JBY's own book, *Passages from the Letters of John Butler Yeats*, edited by Willie with Ezra Pound, was published at the end of April 1917, by Cuala, and was an instant success. JBY glowed when writing to Susan, because of Æ's review. 'Am I being dogmatic and pretentious?' he asked. 'It is all because of my book & Russell's criticism that I am such a vain old man'. He was already writing his autobiography, but had deviated to write a story 'which, entre nous, will be known as "a fabulous story of the birth of Susan Mitchell" – for the public it will be "A Wizard's Daughter" – It is clearly my mission to interpret you, & I accept it with pride'.

He had finished the story by mid-August, and sent her a copy, but his repeated enquiries throughout the following year suggest that Susan never received it. It is a Wildean fairy tale of necromancy and human wiles and sentimentality: and JBY assured her that the wizard's daughter, a fusion of two opposite captious personalities through magic, who became the Princess of Picardy, was an accurate likeness of herself. '*She is you* & I think it is a good portrait. You are perfectly capable of saying – "Bring that man before me alive or dead – & not caring a straw whether it were dead – & afterwards you would pardon him . . . and make him your slave'.

Clinching the link with Susan, he saw his character, after her somewhat pragmatic death, being reincarnated in many forms, until she reappeared 'in an obscure island on the western side of Europe. . . in the street of one of its little towns a woman with dark red hair turning gray and brown eyes between well shaped eyelids. She is the latest tenement of the soul of the beautiful Princess of Picardy'.

When he wrote later, 'labouring' with his memoirs, about which he was 'sometimes . . . hopeful, & sometimes very despondent', he would not admit that the red hair was in any way turning gray.

> No! you will never be old – that cannot happen – immortal youth of richness & fire are all yours . . . Always you are like a spring morning, that is why we like you & it is especially why old men like you, for they feel their strength coming back.

In one letter, JBY wrote of his disappointment with President Wilson, whom he found lazy and incompetent, unprepared for the War into which America was about to embark. Roosevelt should have got the post: and, as was his way, JBY sketched rapid portraits of both men. He wasn't thinking of politics in Ireland these days, being far more preoccupied with his autobiography and with a play, which had something of Susan in it.

Susan, in Dublin, was witnessing 'the first faint hopes of Ireland's future' (so described in her unpublished poem, 'A Song of the Convention') in the negotiations that Æ was making for a forum to resolve the increasingly delicate political situation as Sinn Féin gained popularity. With Colonel Maurice Moore and James Douglas, a Dublin Quaker, he sought a meeting with Lloyd George, out of which arose the short-lived Irish Convention.

The Convention appealed to Sir Horace Plunkett, with whom Susan over the past year had become increasingly at ease. (Despite his claim to be a 'cowardly Philistine', he enjoyed her 'too-little chatter in ink and print' and listening to her singing.) He saw the new forum as the first hopeful beginning of the end of the Irish question. 'There will be an overwhelming desire to make it succeed', he told the American papers. Through his intercession, Lloyd George ended internment, and in June 1917 released those imprisoned as a result of the Rising.

'I am sure your heart is full . . .knowing Madame as you did', wrote Katherine Purdon to Susan, who had recently returned from spending her annual holiday divided between Johnny in Kanturk and Katherine at Hotwell in Co. Meath. 'O if only the unhappy dissensions could be forgotten. Æ's words are beautiful, so informed by calm wisdom and a wide sympathy: ah yes! "let us pray" as you said in one of your last letters'.

The Convention met in Dublin in July, with Horace Plunkett as Chairman, and Æ and Edward MacLysaght among the invited delegates: and Susan, in lighter mood than she had been for some time, could raise her ballad voice once more in teasing satire, her intention simply 'To sing a song of the Convention' -

> Until within the walls of Trinity
> You've raised from zero to infinity
> The first faint hopes of Ireland's future,
> You never really know how cute you are.

She praised in jovial mood, her friend, Sir Horace, the Chairman –

> A subtle, versatile and rare man,
> Who mingles with ecstatic dreamery
> Sound views on butter-churn and creamery.

She picked out Shaw and Moles –

> Two simple kindred Ulster souls,
> Each guarding in his room a rifle,
> And swift to shoot at any trifle;

Each cherishing one common hope
About His Holiness, the Pope.

Other members of the Convention were Diarmuid Coffey – 'with accent British, but soul (like every Celt soul) skittish'; and Cruise O'Brien – 'The sweetest singer since Amphion!'

Despite the artlessness of the lines she composed for the entertainment of Dublin audiences, there is a darker note – with something of the surrealism of Merriman – in her notion of the auto da fé dream, 'planned by the merciless Mahaffy', Provost of Trinity College. Following these ominous lines comes the frivolous vision of the leader of the Irish party embracing the future leader of Sinn Féin –

Redmond
Addressing as "My dearest Edmund",
And clasping near and ever nearer
Against his bosom De Valera.'

Susan could not help having a chuckle at the expense of the clerical representatives.

Elsewhere the scene was not so placid.
With angry looks and accents acid,
With flashing eyes and crimsoned features,
(Like fearful prehistoric creatures
Who one another in the slime ate)
The Moderator and the Primate,
Were at it tooth and nail and tongue,
Were at it fist and boot and lung.
I gather that they disagreed
About the Athanasian Creed.

The Convention, despite the earnest efforts of many excellent-minded members, was doomed from the beginning. Sinn Féin would have nothing to do with it, and, though assured that there would be no coercion, the Ulster Unionists were un-cooperative. By December, Æ was convinced that the Government was concealing something sinister beneath its hesitations and vagueness. He felt, besides, that the Convention was truly representative only of Ulster, and that any agreement that might be reached would not be regarded as binding by the rest of the country, since all interests had not been taken into account.

Edward MacLysaght's resignation in January, for much the same reasons that had been troubling him, accelerated his misgivings. On 1 February, he wrote to Plunkett in disillusion, tendering his own resignation, and promising that his withdrawal would be quiet, he had no intention of agitating public feeling.

Susan was moved by the sensitivity of the situation to drop her satirical pen and enter the more serious arena of political commentary. Her article published in the April edition of *The Englishwoman* is reflective, and sets out to trace the animosity against the Parliamentary Party that had grown in Ireland over the past decade. Its leader, John Redmond, she had ridiculed in one of her strongest satirical compositions for his feeble attempts at obtaining Home Rule. The alienation of the party, she said, had started with Birrell's Council Bill in 1907, and had solidified during the Strike of 1913 when the party had done nothing to alleviate the suffering. 'The irreconcilable element always present in Irish life scented the political possibilities presented by Sinn Féin, which was then more a cultural and industrial than a political movement.'

> Protestant Ireland dressed as it has always been, somewhat out of date, in clothes of Reformation cut, began to sniff the fires of Smithfield, the Orange Lodges began slowly to kindle their spirituous and spasmodic Protestantism into something a little warmer, and then Mr. Lloyd George's Insurance Act came along, with its possibilities of development to another sectarian Society – the Ancient Order of Hibernians, and a general heating-up of the passionate elements in Irish life took place. This flared into flame in Ulster when the absentee landlords of Irish politics in Westminster had brought to fruition another Home Rule Act.

'Ireland needs Ulster and her diverse point of view', she admitted, adding, 'It is one of the strange ironies of history that it was in Ulster, the loud theorist of Unionism, the most successful blow of Separatism was first struck.'

Susan was convinced that the vast bulk of Irishmen who volunteered in 1914 – with the exception of a few nationalists who felt they were called to redress the wrongs of Belgium, and by their sacrifice assure Home Rule for their own country – did so in the enthusiasm of the moment, not realising 'what Nationalist Ireland has been realising ever since, that they were exploding in England's favour the powder that in a year or less would have been exploded against her'.

Edith Somerville disagreed entirely with this last, outlining her views in the following number of the same paper. From West Cork, she condemned the Gaelic League, which Susan had praised, and the National Schools, for traiterously fostering hatred among young children, who accepted Germany as their champion, and were now enrolling themselves under the banner of Sinn Féin (with their concept of 'Ourselves Alone'). The well-to-do farmer who responded in company to the patriotic 'race-conscious' songs enjoyed in his own home the security of the Union, she said, and the prospect of a ready market for his colts as Army mounts.

She did admire Æ and Horace Plunkett without reservation, and she felt it was a happy augury that Horace Plunkett, the instigator of Irish rural co-operation, had been Chairman of the Convention.

> Those who believe in the Convention believe equally in the principle for which it stands – Co-operation, political and agricultural alike. We, in the wider Ireland, have had enough of fighting, and class bitterness, and hating every one but Ourselves Alone. We are, on the whole, friendly, decent people; many of us have been asking for Home Rule for a long time; many of us have not. But we are burying our rusty old hatchets as deep as we can and putting our trust in the results of the Convention.

Edith Somerville's article appeared in *The Englishwoman* in May, after the Convention had made a statement recommending that Home Rule should be introduced. Her form of liberal Unionism was common among Irish upper class Protestants with an army background, whether from the country or the city.

It was more practical perhaps than Susan's idealistic nationalism, which hurdled religious barriers, and aimed to accomodate all opinions. But Susan on the other hand spoke from the practical experience of working with non-political, non-sectarian co-operation in Plunkett's IAOS (Irish Agricultural Organisation Society).

Whatever their differences, however, the irreconcilable aims of the various factions both Catholic and Protestant would continue to be a stumbling block. In the event, despite the reasonableness of the Convention's recommendation, the political situation was so tense that the Government ignored its decision. Sir Horace wrote to Susan wearily in June, 'I am trying to forget that there was a Convention or is a War. As Æ says, "Does anything matter?"'

Susan had been watching the development of another aspect of politics with interest. Two of her friends, Stephen Gwynn and Helen Chenevix, were prominent in the Irish Catholic Women's Suffrage Association and the Irishwomen's Reform League, who demanded that the women of Ireland be included in any settlement of the Irish question. Edith Somerville, too, in her role as President of the Munster Women's Franchise League – and announcing herself as 'a Southerner, and a Unionist, in the sense of possessing a most sincere desire to see Ireland united' – had written to the *Irish Citizen* on 26 May 1917, suggesting that women of every shade of political opinion be taken into the Irish Convention, to provide a lubricating element.

Such pleas had passed unheard by those in power, whose recommendation that women of 35 be granted the franchise was received with scorn: and when the vote was granted to women over 30, suffragists would have to continue agitating because, not only were they not being treated as the equals of men, but there was no question in the new Act of women standing for Parliament.

An impassioned article in the *Irish Citizen* in March 1917, entitled 'The Temple of the Spirit', is a reminder of the intensity and idealism with which Irish protagonists for equal suffrage worked, their motto – as has already been stressed – being 'For Men and Women Equally the Rights of Citizenship; From Men and Women Equally the Duties of Citizenship'. The article describes the huge responsibility that lay with women of the day. Women would bear an extra responsibility when war ended, because men had had their sensibilities deadened by war.

Carson, who was the most powerful figure in the cabinet next to the Prime Minister, was opposed to a second reading of the Franchise Bill because he believed that with the present register (and the stormy situation in the South), the Unionists would be in the majority in the next Parliament: while Redmond's supporters, who were totally unpopular, thought they might be able to save their seats and salaries by thwarting the suffrage. But the suffragists had an able supporter and spokesman in Tim Healy, who was urging the Suffrage Association to arouse public opinion against a dissolution of the Bill, and to leave all questions of detail aside until it had passed into law, because of its importance for Ireland.

There was a new outbreak of arrests of political suspects in the autumn of 1917; and Alice Milligan – whom Æ had described to Susan as 'the wild tram-dwelling sheeogue of the North' – was among those who marched with Constance Markievicz to Mountjoy Prison and Drumcondra Canal banks to sing and cheer the Republican prisoners. She wrote to Susan Mitchell a few days later comparing her move to Bath – where she had gone to drink hot water in the pump room for her rheumatism – with Susan's summer move to Wesley Road. 'I witnessed your efforts to fit your delightful old furniture & pictures into a small house, & now in contrast I am busy trying to fit very ordinary & inadequate things into a delightful Georgian old house in Bath & to give it an old world air. It is as interesting as mounting a play. Your "ancestors" would be in place here . . . & your self!'

She thought there were 'gleams of light' in Bath, though the general atmosphere seemed 'Military, Gouty & Church of England'; and she longed for news of Ireland. 'Strange to say in the horrible coaly midland monotonous towns the people are co-operators & reverence A.E.' Her brother, riding in a tram, had heard a fair middleaged lady who had crossed recently from Dublin talking about how badly the Government were acting, and what fine people the Sinn Féiners were. She asked Susan to send her a copy of the *Irish Times* (the Unionist paper), to keep her in touch. Susan, reacting to the sheeogue much as Æ did, sent the *Freeman* and the *Independent*: and marked the envelope of Alice's letter firmly 'did *not* write'.

There were 'gleams of light' for Susan in Dublin – to relieve the overwhelming social and political tension. With Lily she went to the Abbey in December to see Gogarty's new play. The theatre was so full that they had to sit under the balcony, Susan in an extra chair, squeezed in beside the stalls. They saw Lady Gregory, but decided that her mood was uncertain so did not speak to her.

Jinny, still emulative of Susan and continuing her efforts at short story writing, had completed a reminiscence about a part of Sligo that has since disappeared. 'Swans in Duck Street', a dreamy imagining of a faery presence of Celtic glory in Duck Street, which ran northwards out of Sligo, and where poor children ran barefoot with the birds through muddy pools, appeared in the 1917 Christmas issue of *Ár n-Éire*. Susan herself was writing little, other than the odd satire: but sent a contribution to the Christmas *Lady of the House* called 'Out of the dust'. Based on the painting, *A Dublin Pavement Artist*, by Jack B. Yeats, it reiterates the social concern of her earlier poetry with sincerity, but little originality.

Her most forceful contribution in support of the Franchise League was to read a paper on January 29, 1918, on 'Going to School', in which she discussed the defects of the Irish national character arising from a false and alien system of education. Her general reticence and hesitation to enter actively into the fight for franchise reform – apart from any political reservations she may have had – was typical of her personality. As a writer it was her pattern to stand apart and make any comment in her humorous satires. As a woman with a volatile temper it was prudent to refrain from entering the fray. 'She is . . . most good hearted . . . though with stronger political prejudices than I have', wrote Æ to St. John Ervine about this time. 'Her kind heart always modifies her extreme hand & I do not believe she would hurt a Unionist fly'.

The introduction of a bill imposing conscription on Ireland in April 1918, though, did much to intensify moderate as well as extreme nationalist feelings. Everybody viewed this move as detrimental, the latest imperialist horror. Esther Roper's brother, who was visiting Dublin to see the state of affairs at first hand, told her that he had seen people of every kind, from Æ to James Stephens to Sinn Féin women, preparing lint and other materials which would be needed for Red Cross work if force was used. Sarah Cecilia Harrison, the portrait painter, and Patricia Lynch – who had become involved in the suffrage movement as a young reporter in London – were both writing to the papers: and a mass meeting of women was held at the Round Room of the Mansion House on 27 April, presided over by Madame Markievicz, with Nelly O'Brien of Cumann Gaedhalach na hEaglaise heading the Protestant protest against conscription alongside Roman Catholic opponents of the bill.

Susan missed the meeting as she was on leave. Æ was glad she felt rested. 'To see the weather is good', he wrote. He told her he had been moved by the talk about conscripting Ireland to write a poem about 'Spiritual Wickedness in High Places'.

He used poetic language as he wrote in dismay to the *Manchester Guardian*, protesting that English people had never understood the subjective life of Ireland because they were content merely to dominate it. Ireland in her imagination had never accepted the Union, never developed a psychic tie corresponding to the physical fact. With passions roused he declared, 'What power, they wonder, except one inspired by spiritual wickedness would weave this last evil for a land subdued, force it to warfare to uphold a power it hates, that has broken it, that has killed its noblest children, overthrown its laws, taken the sceptre.' A month later, on 9 June, St. Colmcille's Day, which had been chosen as Lá na mBan or Women's Day, the women of Dublin went to the City Hall to sign an anti-conscription pledge. Afterwards the Catholics went to pray at the Carmelite Church in Whitefriars Street, and the Protestants to Christ Church – whose doors were closed – to kneel outside in silent prayer. Demonstrations all over the country were carried out peaceably. Conscription never came into force.

About the same time Mrs. O'Delany wrote to Susan with a report of Maud Gonne MacBride's prison experience.

> Seagán [Seán MacBride] saw his mother for twenty minutes in the prison, in the presence of two female warders, who the moment she spoke of anything outside the question of his education, as for instance, to ask after Iseult, or hint at the bad conditions of the prison life, threatened to put an end to the interview and take her son away. Nevertheless, this much is evident that Mrs. Gonne MacBride is in a tiny dark stuffy cell, no air, little light, food very bad: eighteen hours out of twenty-four shut up in the cell and only allowed to see Countess Markievicz and Mrs. Clark one hour a day in, I understand, the exercise yard.

She might see her son once a week, and was allowed three letters a week, but no ink or paper, no books or painting materials to relieve the monotony, and was in very poor health.

Dark as life was, there were still moments of enjoyment. To the amusement of her colleagues, Susan wrote an edifying leader in the *Irish Homestead* on the first of June. Attending meetings of the United Irishwomen, whose President was her friend, Lady Fingall, she had learned a great deal about dairying, and could speak with authority on the Report of the Butter Control which had just been published. Count Plunket – cousin of Sir Horace – wrote from London approving the style of her 'less overweighed with forboding pen'.

A high point was the publication in July of *Secret Springs of Dublin Song*, a volume of verse and lampoons for which she was invited to write the preface. The contributions were anonymous: but it was well known that Gogarty had composed 'To Carson, Swimmer of Sandycove', 'A Lament for George Moore' and the comical 'Pilgrimage to Plunkett House', which poked fun at Æ's dual role as poet and organiser of farmers. Seumas O'Sullivan was the author of 'Ambition in Cuffe Street': and he and Gogarty had collaborated on the George Moore 'Inexpressive Nuptial Song', which consists entirely of asterisks, commas and full stops. Kathleen Goodfellow, Æ and Dunsany, also contributed to what is lightsome, frothy, local, but often academic, humour.

Lily Yeats was brightening the dark times with her parties at Gurteen Dhas, one of which was in honour of G. K. Chesterton. Susan, Lily told JBY, was 'one of the successes of the evening' as always: and she described how the party ended with a circle of people four deep surrounding Chesterton and Æ who were deep in debate with one another.

Susan sent another poem to JBY for approval in October. He liked it. 'But I like you best', he told her, 'when by a sort of random chance, a slipping aside, you touch upon the little things of life – the minutiae – it was Homer's way, & it is often yours. . . & a line of yours has often moved me to sudden tears'.

TWENTY

'The First Fruits of the Gun'

PEACE MORYA

Kate's prayer for her children was answered in Susan's imperturbable sense of humour throughout the troubled times. With her 'sun disposition', she infected those around her with a light-hearted cynicism by writing and singing a series of bantering ballads about the political impasse. 'Irish Convention Number Two. A.D. 1920: No Mistake This Time' was printed in the Christmas *Lady of the House* in December 1918.

> Lloyd George, the Taffy Premier,
>   By his Welsh gods he swore
> Since the great English nation
>   Could not rule Ireland more,
> That he a new Convention
>   Of Irishmen would call:
> For, though he'd rather take his ease,
> He'd Wilson and the world to please,
>   And daren't risk a fall.
>
> From Ireland – east, west, north and south,
>   The Hibs came running fast;
> And Unionists came haltingly.
>   And Ulstermen came last.
> Shame on the coward Orangeman
>   Who lingers in his home
> When weak-kneed Southern Protestants
>   May sell the pass to Rome. . .
>
> And Ireland is United,
>   As all the pictures show –
> John Dillon and Sir Edward,
>   How lovingly they go:
> While Colonel Wallace arm-in-arm
>   With Devlin doth appear -

> I wonder what strange policy
>   Joe whispers in his ear.
> Orange and Hib. methinks I hear,
>   As Chief with Chief hobnobs –
> A vast amalgamated plot
>   To collar all the jobs!

The word pictures conjure up similar vignettes of political conniving captured on television today. Susan's wasn't the only disarming doggerel in the 'come-all-ye' style to be published at the time; yet she was alone in the shrewdness of her sharp political comment, and the elegance and ruthless wit with which it was delivered. She describes how the imaginary Convention elects a chairman.

> "We want the mildest-mannered man,
>   To save a faction fight."

> At that a modest murmur rose
>   Each felt within his breast
> Himself best suited for the job,
>   But for the second best
> Once more they plumped for Plunkett –
>   The politicians bawl
> Most loudly for a man who has
>   No politics at all.

The rest of the ballad dissolves into happy burlesque, describing a unanimity which, alas! was not to become reality.

> "Come on," said brave Horatius,
>   "Strike while the iron's hot –
> The House is there, the Members here –
>   Let's take it on the spot."
> Mahaffy lisped remonstrance, but
>   His eloquence ran dry
> When all the Lords, uprising, stuck
>   Their elbows in his eye.

> And now they leave the College,
>   They roll across the Green;
> When Devlin knocked the sentry down
>   Sinn Féin flocked to the scene;
> And when above the surges
>   Horatius did appear,

The crowd sent forth a rapturous cry,
Ee'n De Valera, standing by,
  Could scarce forbear to cheer.

They cast the money-changers out
  And kept the cash inside
To start an Irish Treasury
  With money well supplied.
And then the Metropolitans
  Took oaths of fealty;
They'd seen the giant safe unlocked,
And all to swear allegiance flocked
  To him that held the key.

And Éamonn De Valera said:
  "Come on, my Volunteers,
And be the standing army for
  The Commons and the Peers".
And Carson said, "I've wired the boys
  From Lurgan and Coleraine,
And arms and men from Ulster
  Are coming by the train.

At the same time as composing ballads, Susan was launching into a career as literary critic, as a result of her Moore book. A special article in *The Shamrock and Irish Emerald*, a small weekly paper to which Corkery, Boyd and Katherine Purdon contributed, allowed her to set out her own views about Irish literature. Writing about the 'Ireland of the hunting-stable novelists', she spoke highly of the roistering Irishman created by Lover and Lever, and continued by 'those brilliant collaborateurs Somerville and Ross'. This character had such a general acceptance with the English public that they believed they were reading about the genuine article.

While she enjoyed the humour of these novelists, she said, 'Their unreal hilarity arouses in me at times a passion of resentment.' Her quarrel with the hunting-stable novelists was that they were depicting the Irish when they were tied by economic circumstances to the Big House, playing like court jester to those who paid the piper: but now that the true Irish nature had recovered its vitality and versatility this image was a severe handicap, and misleading. The hunting-stable novelists had 'whipped-up all life into a froth, piling it lightly over the tragic and the dark in Ireland, obscuring reality and, with the most amiable intentions, inflicting a lasting hurt upon the character of their country.'

She was still wrestling with her own ambiguous feelings about the Church. The Cumann Gaedhealach had been meeting regularly at Lily Williams's studio, and making as one of its annual social events a picnic to Lily's cottage at Ticknock, in the Dublin hills. One of the most influential members was Nelly O'Brien (Neilí Ní Bhriain), sister of the painter Dermod O'Brien. She herself was an artist, an enthusiast for the Gaelic League. As a granddaughter of the patriot, William Smith O'Brien, she longed to see the Church of Ireland acknowledging its spiritual roots in the Celtic Church of St. Patrick, in communion with other Irish Christians drawn from all of the modern divisions.

Susan's sentiments were similar: and it was probably at her suggestion, while still the reluctant Chairman, that the Cumann decided at its meeting in January 1919 to ask Douglas Hyde to be its President (it was Hyde who later recalled in her obituary that the Gaelic League group Nelly started, 'The Branch of the Five Provinces', was nicknamed in Dublin, 'The Branch of the Five Protestants'). Nelly had another job for Susan. At the same meeting, a motion was passed to proceed with the preparation of the Cumann's proposed paper, *An tEaglaiseach Gaedhealach* (*The Gaelic Churchman*): and Susan was asked to be editor – Nelly would gather together the material.

The Gaelic Churchman was a regular channel through which the Cumann could bring pressure on bishops and the National Board of Education, among others, to use Irish more consistently. That Susan ever consented to be editor is

Sketch of Douglas Hyde by JB Yeats, 1895

unlikely: but, moved by the horror of the guerrilla tactics resorted to by the desperate republicans (now making the Royal Irish Constabulary their particular target), she contributed to the first issue an impassioned appeal to the Church to do something about the situation.

'What is the Church of Ireland going to do about Sinn Féin?' she headed her open letter.

> Let us out with it, nor wrap it up more closely with timidities as that the Church is a non-political body., when we know well that every one of our churches at every service reeks with politics. Prayers and hymns are charged with them, the sermon rams them home.

In the past, the Church of Ireland had identified itself with one political party, and it still did so. But, Susan declared, the young life of Protestant Ireland was growing sick of the alliance. Modern youth, she said, saw the growing life and ideals of Ireland in Sinn Féin.

> I have lived all my life in Ireland, I was a persistent churchgoer, even to daily services for many years, and I make a modest claim to know my church and my country, and I believe firmly that Ireland has very little use for us as a Church any more.

Her idealistic article could have little effect, since the *Gaelic Churchman* boasted only one hundred subscribers. As Nelly O'Brien commented caustically in the May issue, the Church liked to call herself a National Church, yet repudiated any of the distinctive marks of nationality, such as language, literature and national history. Nelly had heard a clergyman being criticised for admitting two prominent members of Sinn Féin to Holy Communion: and in general there were fears that the Cumann's claim that the Church of Ireland was autonomous – instead of being in some way tied to the English Church – was a sign of sympathy with rebellion. Yet, despite the fact that Irish speakers had been driven from church to church, and were now denied their monthly communion in St. Patrick's Cathedral, she insisted that many clergy were secretly sympathetic. The attendance at matins in Irish in St. Andrew's Church on St. Patrick's Day was witness to the numbers of people who wanted to worship in their native tongue.

In October 1919, Susan began to contribute to a new publication. She was not the only person who had been feeling impatient with the *status quo*. Plunkett was frustrated in the economic plans of his organisation after Sinn Féin had obtained a majority in the recent elections, and set up its own Dáil in Dublin; while the depleted Irish Parliamentary Party at Westminster, having lost all credibility at home, threatened any chance of stable government. He decided to introduce what he hoped would be a new political force, the Irish Dominion

League. By obtaining dominion status, with an independent government, he thought, Ireland would avoid any possibility of partition. To this end he founded the *Irish Statesman* in June, with, as its editor, Warre B. Wells, who had been sympathetic to Susan on the *Church of Ireland Gazette*.

What he hoped would become an organ for political preparation became, rather, the mouthpiece for writers who had been trying to educate public opinion for years – Æ, George Birmingham, Stephen Gwynn, Erskine Childers, Bernard Shaw – with Cruise O'Brien and George O'Brien on the staff, who treated the whole venture rather irreverently. But Susan wrote critiques regularly in its pages, about books by authors as diverse as Birmingham, Maeterlinck and John Butler Yeats, whose *Further Letters*, selected by Lennox Robinson, she reviewed the following May. The *Statesman* survived fifty-two issues, by which time, with Ireland in militant chaos, the Dominion League had no possibility of a future.

Susan's first reviews for the *Irish Statesman*, in October and November, were of *Tales that were Told* by Seumas Mac Manus, and *Cork's Own Town* and *Songs of the Island Queen* – both dealing with ballads. Reading them may have aroused the reminiscing mood in which she wrote 'An Irish Country Town', for the 1919 Christmas *Lady of the House*. 'I see no reason at all why the country towns in Ireland should not all be re-lit with the glow that bathes my memory of two or three of them. Two of these little towns [Carrick and Birr] wear, to my memory, an aspect of perpetual summer, trees in leaf, and long, sunny, idle summer days. The third whose memories I would now recall has a graver air. I have known it in summer, but I remember it better in mild autumn and winter and wet spring.'

This was Sligo, which she had first visited as a very small girl to see Aunt Shepperd. She remembered little, other than Paddy Burns, who presided at Sligo station, who had once given her a red toy harp with golden strings.

Her mind conjured up the perfumes of 'one little town in Midland Ireland . . . sweet in my memory with sun-warmed air and the aromatic scent of honeycomb' [Birr]. 'Another, a sea village [Sligo], blows to memory airs austere with wild thyme. Another town memory comes to me with the sociable smell of smouldering turf' [Carrick-on-Shannon]. And she understood how, if unexpected perfumes could start her rebuilding these small towns in her imagination, 'sound stored in memory' could alert the creator in Mr. Yeats to build the Isle of Innisfree. Her article was illustrated with a painting of a Western town by Jack B. Yeats.

Susan was thinking of the Yeatses a great deal about this time. Her lecture on John Butler Yeats to the National Literary Society in Ely Place in December, attended by all the Yeats clan except Willy and George who were out of town, was esteemed an enormous success. Susan had written it all out by hand, and delivered it sitting, quoting liberally from JBY's letters to her. Besides outlining his career, and giving homage to his ever ready ideas, she now had the

One of JB Yeats's self-portrait sketches, c.1920

opportunity of offering her own opinion on him! and, she declared, 'His philosophy divined from his writing appears to me to be a negation of his philosophy expressed in paint'.

> His philosophy is that of a fighter but the war he wages is in his own nature where faith in life, in humanity, in heaven & all futures is perpetually upspringing in a soil unchangeably fertile, in spite of the efforts of his intellect to sterilize it.

She offered an explanation for JBY's perpetual virility of mind.

> People talk of Ireland's past and we are continually reminded that we are an ancient people with an ancient culture. Implicit in that culture is the faith in an Irish heaven – a land of the Ever-Living – of Immortal Youth. To the unsealing of the Fountain of Youth is due the intellectual renaissance that has changed the face of Ireland in our time, and it is not surprising that contact with that which is Ever-Living in our ancient story has kept young & green and fresh the spirits of those who are in a sense the channels by which the stream has reached us'.

Everybody was pleased with Susan's talk. She wrote in reply to Lily's appreciation, 'I could see your eye gleaming at me . . . & it was a great moral support. . . The audience was delightful, and I think the personal way I treated the subject just suited so friendly an audience. My intellect (suppose it to exist!) owes such a lot to your father and you all. You brought a kind of renaissance to me, and I felt a pride in telling of it'. There were those who thought Susan should write a book about JBY. 'Some day I must do the book,' she said, 'I wonder could I.'

Apart from her moments of literary elation, and the pleasure of the theatre tickets Lily sent her and Jinny with her letter, Susan had her mind on more sombre matters. The Cumann Gaedhealach, roused no doubt by her article, had been calling at the December meeting for a resolution to be passed, directing the attention of the Archbishop of Dublin to the serious state of the country, and the lack of any effort on the part of the Church of Ireland to exert some influence for peace and goodwill. Lolly wrote to JBY about the many 'Jeremias' there were around her: and JBY sent to Susan a drawing showing 'The Future of Ireland, nebulous and threatening, summoned before them by certain Jeremias who live in Dublin' (Susan and Æ are among the Jeremiahs, confronting the ghostly Future of Ireland).

But the truth was that even in Plunkett House, the supposed embodiment of good will, the atmosphere had become taut with distrust and disagreement. Or so George O'Brien thought. Just as Susan was conscious of the cleft between the Protestants, who were set in their ways, and their younger

co-religionists, who were attracted by Sinn Féin, he drew a distinction between the older generations of the co-operative movement, and those whom
Sir Horace had recruited more recently who were eager to implement new
ideas. He himself had been brought into Plunkett House by Father Finlay and
R.A. Anderson as an economist, to study post-War problems.

'The interesting population with which (it) was inhabited was outwardly
very united and friendly. There was an afternoon tea party every day in
(Anderson's) room at which everybody – with the exception of Æ and Susan
Mitchell – attended. But I think there must have been a considerable amount of
silent strain and tension. Plunkett House was in many ways like a Court in
which Sir Horace was King. Courts as a rule contain courtiers and favourites,
and Plunkett House was no different from other courts in this respect. Some of
the members of the IAOS staff must have regarded us as interlopers. Especially
among the different generations of typists, there must have been a good deal of
jealousy. There were court intrigues with petticoat influences in the background'.

Shortly after the Treaty, Constance Markievicz commented on the inter-
nal clashes of the period within Sinn Féin.[1] Bulmer Hobson, who had introduced
her originally to Helena Molony and the women insurgents of Inghine na
hÉireann, had plotted, she said, against Griffith, which had caused the rift between them: and he had intrigued against herself as much as against Griffith.
She had never grown close to Griffith, who knew nothing of the Gaelic past or
its vision, but clung to an ideal of a resurrection of Grattan's Parliament.

For her, James Connolly, whose background was both Fenian and Social-
ist, and who demonstrated that faith in a Gaelic ideal was the real motivating
power, was the great thinker. Her admiration for him does much to explain the
fervent nature of her own republicanism. She also admired Plunkett. No one
was interested in politics in her family, according to her account: but her brother's part in establishing Horace Plunkett's creameries had convinced her that
Sir Horace's 'non-political' movement was the greatest political movement of
the time, and would restore to the country the ideals of a Gaelic state.

If there were dissensions everywhere else, life seems to have continued in
comparative harmony upstairs in Plunkett House, within the four walls of the
Irish Homestead office. Æ's murals would have transported visitors into another
world, with their sidhe figures, their strange birds and animals amid miraculous
landscapes, listening to the harp strings of beautiful minstrels. Diarmuid Coffey,
who had been editor of *Better Business* until he fell out with Plunkett for refus-
ing to rise to a toast for the Queen, with his artist wife Sadhbh Trinseach found
his way up to 'Anti-Susan' (as Susan was known with her household of attractive young nieces) to exchange bantering ballads.

---

[1] 'Memories' and 'Memories (2)', *Éire*, August 18, 25, 1923.

January 1920 saw a new poem by Susan, 'The Arrows of Light', in the *Irish Statesman*. She contributed a beautiful valedictory poem, 'The Adventure', to the compilation of Irish writings and art, *The Book of St. Ultan*, edited by Katherine MacCormack. Another task in 1920 was writing the introduction to *An Egyptian in Ireland* by Ibrahim Rashad, who had come to Ireland to study economics and the co-operative organisation; and while Æ was away sketching in Donegal during the summer, she was correcting the proofs of a new volume of fairy tales by Katherine Purdon, who was not at all well. Katherine died in July, appointing Susan as literary executor. Susan mourned the intimate human quality of her writing, 'that drew the reader to her as a friend'. 'Her work is rooted in life, and it will not quickly fade'.

The condition of Irish life continued to be bleak. Sporadic guerrilla warfare which had followed the proscription of the Dáil the previous autumn was increasing so much so that a curfew was eventually imposed. On the active front, the great travesty of the year was the attack in April on Plunkett's peaceable creameries by the auxiliaries and the dreaded Black and Tans, sent in by the Government to quell the revolutionaries. Presumably they thought the creameries concealed arms. Sir Hamer Greenwood, Chief Secretary for Ireland, at first denied any involvement on the part of his troops, though it was widely recognised that they were responsible: and the bombs and burnings continued for a year. When the British authorities were celebrating their official Peace Day in July of 1920 by a huge display of military force in Dublin, the Irishwomen's Franchise League, who were at last near to attaining their own objective, but retained their interest in political and social matters, displayed from their windows a large white flag, bearing in black letters the words, 'Peace Morya!' ['Peace how are ya!']

Writing to her father in November 1920, Lily spoke of the 'state of barbarism' that prevailed, reprisals on each side, 'the Military with their machinery and regiments being able to kill and destroy the most, — on Sinn Féin's side it is all an insult to the memory of men like MacSwiney. I don't think he would have approved the shooting of men in their beds'. The curfew began at 10 p.m., theatre performances at 6.30. 'Firing is constant in the streets and there is much drinking among the soldiers and Black and Tans. I suppose like the war it will end someday, and we will again be discussing burning questions like foot and mouth disease and the sanding of the train tracks.'

Lloyd George's unfortunate remark at the London Guildhall at the beginning of November – 'There are troublesome nations still existing', sparked off Susan to new satire. The fate of the creameries had distressed Æ and Sir Horace immeasurably. She launched into her counter-attack without quibble, opening the verses – which went into the Christmas issue of the *Lady of the House* – with her usual ingenuous charm.

The Coalition and Lloyd George

Were walking hand in hand,
They wept, for still upon the map
        Was printed Erin's land.
"If that were only blotted out,"
        They said: "It would be grand".

"If tanks and planes and armoured cars
        Rolled over it a year,
Do you suppose," Sir Hamar said,
        "That we could wipe it clear?"

Susan reproduced a clear image of each of the personalities involved. Lloyd George was still talking and talking about Home Rule, and would introduce a fresh bill before Christmas.

"We'll talk it off the map", said George.
        "I've talked with all my might
Ever since my crude Limehouse days,
        And now most wrongs seem right.
It takes some practice, but the House
Provides that every night.

"Henceforth the name of Ireland's writ
        In" – "Butter," Carson said;
"Let us wipe out the creameries,
        "Soon will the land be dead;
For I always hated Plunkett
        And thought him off his head."
"If nothing's hurt but butter
        I can't fulfil my star,
I am a warrior and I lead
        The battle from afar;
I'm out for blood," said Churchill;
        "Let loose my dogs of war!"

The Premier and Sir Hamar
        Talked by the mile or so,
And then they hit upon a plan
        Conveniently low!
Even Bonar Law was faintly pleased
        And thought the thing would go. . .

And Winston's pups, unleashed, around

TROUBLESOME NATIONS

"THERE ARE TROUBLESOME NATIONS STILL EXISTING."— Lloyd George, *Guildhall, 9th November, 1920*

By SUSAN L. MITCHELL, *Author of "Aids to Immortality of Certain Persons in Ireland"; "George Moore," etc.*

1
The Coalition and Lloyd George
  Were walking hand in hand,
They wept, for still upon the map
  Was printed Erin's land.
" If that were only blotted out,"
  They said: " It would be grand."

2
" If tanks and planes and armoured cars
  Rolled over it a year,
Do you suppose," Sir Hamar said,
  " That we could wipe it clear?"
Remembering Llewellyn, George
  Exuded one more tear.

3
(But supplemental tears for Wales
  Are quickly wiped away.
Wales ate her conqueror's bread and knew
  Which side the butter lay.
If Tonypandys grumble, well,
  It's too late in the day.)

4
" Would it were Mespot.," Churchill cried,
  " And then we'd get some show,
For Christendom can't hear the shell
  That lays the Arab low ;
We aim it from the Holy Land,
  But this they must not know."

9
" I want to please you all," said George,
  " And end the matter quick;
With Carson *über alles*
  We'll make Sir Horace sick ;
Winston shall loose his pups " (my word,
  He spread the butter thick!).

10
" And you, our Hamar and our Law,
  On you we will rely;
Whatever's charged against us
  Yours not to reason why,
But stand up in the Commons
  And lie and lie and lie."

11
And Winston's pups, unleashed, around
  The lonely places ran,
And Irish dairies fell before
  The rush of Black and Tan;
And England won great victories
  O'er many a creamery can.

12
Thousands of seasoned warriors,
  With bomb and petrol, too,
Attacked the legioned cheeses,
  And milk that was not new,
And lactic acid microbes
  To Kingdom Come they blew.

'Troublesome Nations' (detail) in Christmas Lady of the House, *1920*

> The lonely places ran,
> And Irish dairies fell before
> The rush of Black and Tan;
> And England won great victories
> O'er many a creamery can. . .
>
> "I weep the creameries," Hamar cried,
> "I deeply sympathise."
> (With tears and sobs he'd sorted out
> Those of the largest size),
> Holding his pocket-handkerchief
> Before his streaming lies. . .

Susan would be as caustic about the incendiaries during the Civil War. She was a dedicated republican, but she abhorred mindless violence.

The extreme emotion of her political views conflicted with those of even her closest friends, Æ and Lily. Lily told JBY,

> Susan is a Sinn Féiner and she and I always quarrel because of it, so we don't talk politics. I don't think she is a true S. F., because I don't think she really believes that the police are shooting each other dead to oblige the English government. A real S. F. believes this.

Politics had spoiled Susan's evenings, which went on regardless of the troubles. Lily herself had given up being at home every Monday, and now concentrated on the first Monday in the month. 'Lunatics go simply to meet other lunatics and talk politics to each other', wrote Lily. She felt Susan was having other difficulties.

> Susan is rather weary and dispirited and hates getting elderly and losing her good looks. I tell her when I have shop doors swung in my face and my toes walked on by flappers, I just say in my heart, "Never mind. I was just as young as you yesterday, and a great deal better looking."

The two women looked at each other keenly when they met. 'Being almost the same age, each is a looking glass to the other. I know a lot more about clothes so have the pull there. She has the pull in brains'.

In the meantime, Susan was excited about the move, with Jinny, to a new flat at 77 Rathmines Road in December. Her nieces, finished at Trinity, were breaking up the home in Leinster Road, though Dora – after a stay in Paris, when Æ was able to procure through her tubes of paint which he could not get at home – returned to live with her for some while.

In late December, George's son, who was a clerk in a Roscommon bank,

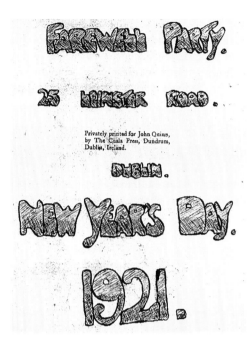

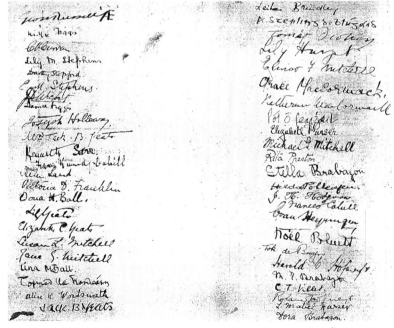

Invitation card to Susan Mitchell's Farewell Party, 25 Leinster Road, New Year's
Day 1921, on Cuala Card. Details of signatures of some of those present

was held up by six of the auxiliary police, who operated like the Black and Tans, only wearing a different uniform. Susan told the story of how they held revolvers to the heads of the manager and the clerks, took over a thousand pounds, and left telling them not to attempt to move for two hours. The manager escaped and went to the police, who, knowing the culprits, went to the nearest public house, and found them with all the money, except for sixteen pounds: and the matter was hushed up, the hope being that the public would think it was the work of Sinn Féin. The manager and clerks had since received threatening letters with skulls and cross bones on them. 'Such is life these times under English civilisation', was Lily's comment.

In February 1921, JBY wrote to Susan from New York to tell her that one of her poems was to be included in an American anthology of importance, and to apologise that his article on her poetry had had to be delayed as her book was on loan to a friend. A few months before he had been delighted with her review of his *Further Letters* in the *Irish Statesman*.

He told her he did not believe in the mystics' heaven – 'because to expect me to enjoy it is to assault my human nature – & yet I did not know that this is the foundation of all my thinking till I read your paragraph . . . it had a sort of roguery of insight in it . . . Yes, I do love this life'. However he was increasingly conscious of time catching up. He told her that his object was to get home in time to do three portraits, of herself and Lily and Lolly. 'This done, I shall say Nunc Dimittis. . .

> I have a firm belief that we are part & parcel of some great machinery which is working smoothly & with no waste. – Somewhere – somewhere – Keats & Shelley & thousands of others – are still alive – & to doubt it is to be an atheist. . .

Susan was now reviewing regularly for the *Freeman's Journal* and, in her assessment of the latest novels, could also express her views on the current situation in Ireland. She felt that George Birmingham had it in him to write a really fine Irish novel, a revelation of the Protestant Irish heart.

> The Protestant religion has never been persecuted in Ireland, so that the Irish Protestant's national feelings have never been quickened by the spur of persecution. The Catholic patriot had a nation behind him. The Protestant, often as racially Irish as his Catholic brother, has had his environment dead against him, an environment representing power, wealth, social success. Here is a subject for a powerful novel, and yet the Irish novelist has always feared to touch it. . . Why cannot George Birmingham give us the big things in Protestant psychology?

Edith Somerville felt Susan's criticism of her new book, *An Enthusiast*, was able and candid. Susan had thought her very brave to write a domestic novel when passion and emotion in Ireland were at such a fever-heat: but her book reflected 'gallantly' an attempt to come to terms with the new aspect of Irish life which had made her so bewildered and uneasy. Nevertheless, it was only in the basest of her characters, Susan suggested, that Miss Somerville showed her wonted genius for characterisation. He was sketched 'with a power that corrodes the page. . .'

Edith Somerville told her that, while she found the review detached and refreshing, 'it seems to me that you review *me* more than the book! You say I haven't been able to hide my personal point of view – I wish *I* knew what it was! My sympathies are horribly on both sides – *all* sides I might say (except the extremists of the Black North) & I would give a good deal to be able to shut my eyes & charge, like a bull at a gate, one way or the other!

> However . . . this letter is only to thank you for a most fair & candid, & (may I say?) exceedingly well-written review. I hope (& feel sure) that we shall meet again some day, & fight things out comfortably! I should like to try & persuade you that *all* the "Park walls of the old Ascendancy" don't grow fungi!

JBY saw Susan's 'clever' review of George Moore's *Abelard and Héloïse* in the September issue of the *Dial*. 'I find Moore in it,' she wrote, 'Moore who is himself the best work of art he ever created. He does not really get a fling in the text. What is the use of his spancelling himself with the love story of Abelard and Héloïse, a thing he cannot remotely understand, for Moore has had too many love adventures in the imagination to have had any in the flesh'.

'It was a pleasant shock to see your familiar name suddenly among these unknown people in the Dial– who deal so largely in the nebulous,' JBY wrote to her. 'You are not that – you put your finger on the very centre'. He told her, 'I shall soon be home – this worry of leaving my friends here & of bidding a farewell is depressing me. I wish it was over & done. . .' He had just been reading '"The Rainbow", by a man called Laurence. This man is by all accounts a man of genius': and he again expressed his longing to leave New York. 'I do not think I could hate any place as I do N. York – its straight & dusty slovenly streets. – "oh for a crooked street", sighed somebody – who was it that wrote "the crooked halls of pleasure"?'

> When we meet you must shut your bodily eyes & close & open wide . . . find me younger than ever. Behind the perishing mortal is a something that endures & an invincible hopefulness.

Æ commented about Susan's frequent letters from 'Old J.B.Y.' about this time that JBY was working off arrears of correspondence before he came back. 'He knows', he jotted on one envelope that arrived in Plunkett House, 'once he is here, he won't be able to write & can only talk. Three letters in two days is very heavy traffic for Translatlantic Liners'!

However, at the same time as JBY was showering Susan with mail, he told Lily he had changed his mind about coming back. She was indignant, thought he was starving himself with a diet of crumbs and hot water. 'We are expecting you', she told him, 'and Susan is coming with us to meet you, and Clare Marsh (his special favourite) suggested coming in her motor'.

As he delayed and delayed, however, Susan was taken ill and went into the Portobello Hospital for a serious operation for gallstones and appendicitis. The operation went well. JBY wrote to her sympathetically. Lily sent her five beautiful roses from Gurteen Dhas, with the dew still on them.

Afterwards she stayed at Killeen Castle, at Dunsany, in Meath, while the terms for the Treaty were being thrashed out in London. 'We had a lovely drive down here – trees the most delicious autumn reds & roads carpeted with crimson leaves', she wrote to Jinny, from the pillowed luxury of a cooked breakfast in bed, and bath prepared for her, resorting to pencil half-way through her letter as the pen ran dry.

> Lady Fingall brought me to my room, next hers. It is a huge room with three church windows & a lovely view of demesne. A big bed – a Prince Albert! fourpost cut down with chintz hangings & a satin eiderdown. A lovely wood fire in grate, easy chair & sofa.

> We went down to tea & met Lord F. & the grandchild, a dear little girl of one & a half. A doctor came in after tea, a man called Murnane, young & pleasant, he stayed to dinner & told me a lot about De Valera's telegram & how the Pope's wire to George had been engineered. He stayed talking a long time after dinner. . .

> I sat before my fire a long time . . . Lord F. is so like Aunt Shepperd & you that I feel quite at home!

TWENTY ONE

'Everything Good and Bad has Boiled up'

LIVING THROUGH CIVIL WAR

Susan was back to work in December, and writing a review of Brinsley Macnamara's new novel for the *Freeman's Journal*, when after lengthy negotiations the Treaty was hastily signed. Macnamara, she felt, came 'very near to being a poet'. But his manner reminded her of a Dublin street song –

Then I took up a hatchet and gave Connolly a fall,
And I cut him up in pieces, which appeared the worst of all.

'A Poet and a Poet's Wife'. Susan Mitchell in conversation with George Yeats, Gurteen Dhas, Dundrum, 18 September 1921

She hadn't lost her kitten's claws, despite the operation and the ravages of the years. But she was now so deaf that people had to shout to make themselves heard. Her output as a writer was small. She considered herself a slow worker; and most of her work had to be done at night, or at the weekends – with Saturday a half day.

According to Æ, even when white-haired she was 'no older within than when she was the beautiful girl earlier friends than I remember'. JBY had been writing appreciatively throughout the autumn of 1921 from New York, sketching her in his letters as the angel of judgement facing George Moore, or as a colleen snuggling up to St. Peter. He compared her prose with her poetry:

> There is in [your prose] a freedom – no – a sense of power – as if you had all the phrases & all the thoughts at once within easy call – & the sentences & phrases are painting. . ... There is a thing called *spontaneity* . . .in your *littlest* poetry – it is the self – the unimpeded unspoiled self.

He himself was much too busy to believe himself old – 'I am in the grip of what I may call an "energy" – that is my desire to leave complete a magnum opus . . . a . . . full length life size portrait of myself – on which I have been at work for years. That done I shall be a free man. . .'

Months before, Crawford Hartnell, who edited *The Christmas Lady of the House* – the Home Journal of Ulster – from Dublin, had written to Susan approvingly about her poem 'Troublesome Nations'. 'If we had an Irish Charivari the verses might have suggested a cartoon subject – Ananias surrendering the champion belt to Hamar, the bolt being appropriately hasped with a lyre'. He had heard about the verses from all parts of the country, and they appeared to have caused much amusement. He wanted more in the coming issue.

The events of the next year were to provide grist for her mill. 'The first fruits of the gun' – the compromising terms of the Treaty into which Lloyd George had hurried the Irish delegates in London without reference to their colleagues at home – caused a split in the Dáil because of a strong opposition to partition and general fears about its outcome. Michael Collins who headed the provisional government formed in the middle of January was prepared to accept the Treaty. In reaction, De Valera resigned from the Presidency[1] to organise a new opposition republican party. By April, his irregular army occupied the centre of the Irish judiciary – the Four Courts, in Dublin – and, too impatient to await the outcome of the national election in June, he destroyed the Customs House in May.

> Well they robbed for poor old Ireland,
> Food and drink and money too.

---

[1] To be replaced by Arthur Griffith.

> 'Twas the Golden Age for playboys
> In the Spring of "22"...

was Æ's summing up of events, in the three quatrains of his satire, 'The Rising of the Wind' (based on the traditional political ballad, 'The Rising of the Moon'). It was most probably composed with the collusion of Susan in the office, at one of the two large desks which 'rose like rocks out of a sea of newspapers and literary litter,' as one visitor to Plunkett House described what she saw. 'The walls were covered with brown paper, which was painted with strange figures with many-coloured wings'.[2]

Susan saw one election meeting – 'at Findlater's clock, addressed by French-Mullen. Johnny & I skirted round there to look at them but it was a very small crowd of idlers & of course we couldn't hear any speech. Johnny thought F. M. was a man. She would be proud...', she told Jinny, who was staying with Victoria in Bundoran. The election favoured the pro-Treaty parties, who were little inclined to negotiate with the extremists, and so civil war was provoked at the end of June. The republicans, forced out of the Four Courts by pro-Treaty troops, blew up the building before they left.

In her JBY lecture of two years before, Susan had spoken indulgently about 'our aggravating brother, Ulster . . . the spoilt child of the Irish family, possessing the sneaking affection of those members his contrariness most annoys'. Now with her nicest nastiness, she extolled 'The Irish Bombardier', representative of the dedicated republicans whose cause she had so energetically defended in the past, adopting the melody of the patriotic poem, 'By Memory Inspired', for the satirical song she sang:

> By high ideals fired,
> And with all thinking tired,
> The bursting bomb I love to dwell upon;
> And with patriotic glow
> I decide what's next to go,
> Here's the memory of the Custom House that's gone, boys, gone,
> Here's the glory of the city that is gone.
>
> In December Twenty-one
> Came the first fruits of the gun,
> But the Treaty I don't care to dwell upon.
> I know it isn't bad,
> And that's what makes me mad,
> For I want to see the bombing carried on, boys, on,
> I want to see the bombing carried on...

[2] See also p. 86.

Despite all her genuine anguish for 'the Heaven that was Ireland' that was gone, referred to in the poem, after this Susan's idealistic notion of the restored Gaelic state vanishes from her writings. She was planning for the ideal home that she and Jinny hoped would be theirs. Cousin Pierce Finucane (who looked 'like the knave of hearts' according to Lily Yeats) had died two years before, without heirs, and leaving no will. '26 next of kin appeared, but Susan says the lawyers have reduced them to 12 by finding the rest illegitimate', Lily told JBY at the time. '"Speaks well for the morals of our family", says Susan'.

Now Kate's family memoir, which Susan produced, in the manuscript exercise books filled by her daughters and herself, came in useful. Labelled outside, 'To be read by friends but not by relations', the lawyers found it not only useful but amusing. The Mitchells and their American cousins all received a share of the bequest: and Susan and Jinny were putting theirs into a house – though in June 1922 Susan, writing to Jinny, wondered could they afford it. It might be better to go to a nice boarding-house.

There was a crisis in the *Irish Homestead* in October, to which farmers and co-operators responded gallantly. 'The Homestead has more than turned the corner, in fact it has nearly got round 2 corners', Susan rejoiced to Elsie, Augustine Henry's wife, who had a mystic bent and also shared her love of classical myth and poetry. 'We asked for water (£1000) & they gave us wine (£1430) & the argosies still float in or, should I say, sail in, all canvases spread'. A more serious matter was her niece Kitsy's operation for an abscess of the antrum. 'I was strained in my very soul with anxiety', said Susan. Kitsy, Victoria's daughter, a pretty girl with a burst of auburn-gold locks, according to Æ's portrait in Sligo Museum, was a brilliant musician; but like Susan would be plagued with tubercular problems for her whole life, and Susan naturally took an interest in her.

On 6 December 1922, Susan wrote to Victoria, thanking her for her cake, and listing among birthday presents she had received a Liberty necklace from Æ 'of some queer silver & blue colours, very pretty'. 'Today', she told her sister, 'the Free State began & I went round to see the opening of the House, but there was only one onlooker at first & then he was added to by about 7 or 8, & nothing of pageantry was to be seen, except that the rather dirty flag on Leinster House was replaced by a new & striking one, the orange part being very rich in colour'.

Æ had refused to be a senator, even though many had pleaded with him, but he said he had no gifts for public life, and was more useful as a writer. 'However people feel they can trust him & in some ways it's a pity he won't sit, but he would hate to give up his independence'. She marvelled about the appointment of Tim Healy as Governor-General. 'I don't think they could bear the idea of a lord and anyway Lord Granard isn't much good except socially. I met her once at a luncheon party & she brought me home in her car. She was a most strange unreal being – powdered & painted out of all humanity'.

And Susan added, 'Isn't it funny to think of Tim Healy. I wonder if he has outlived the odium that attached to him so long for his treatment of Parnell.[3] He is a very clever & witty man & personally I like him as he always praised my books!'

Dublin, she said, was in a state of disruption, with great searchings by the soldiers – 'trams held up & people held up at every street corner. Tonight on leaving the office I found the Square nearly in darkness & soldiers armed to the teeth on the footpaths & across the Merrion Street end of the Square. They say there are a couple of companies up from Cork, but everyone is moving about & shopping as usual.' Writing to Bessy at the end of January, she told of the fearful night before, when there was an explosion in Leinster Road. Merrion Square was so dangerous after dark.

The troubles accelerated. The following week, she and Jinny (who, she said, was doing all the running, and living up to the family name for Aunt Shepperd, 'Janie-go-for-it') were enjoying the bitter February weather of Sligo – 'the hotel being like a story of the old coaching days, with roaring fires & rich food'. She told her niece Marjorie, who had gone to South Africa to join her sisters, that everything in Ireland was going up in flames:

> . . . the last fortnight with increased fury, & even the houses of those Unionist landlords not in politics have gone. Annagassau, Mr. Russell's in Louth, is the last, following on Clermont, & Moore Hall. We are all quite mad here, & though there are rumours of peace, I don't know what we'd do with it if we had it, we are all so demoralised.

> Horace Plunkett's beautiful Kilteragh is gone, a reward for his life of service to Ireland, & poor Gerald Heard nearly burnt in his bed. It has all got beyond comment now & we have all forgotten what the war is about.

The day before, the Pathé office in Dublin had been set on fire, so there were no news films in last night's pictures (Susan and Jinny were in the habit of going to the cinema about twice a week at this time). The next target had been paupers: Nenagh workhouse had been burnt down after the inmates were turned out. 'Leap Castle is gone & I suppose all its ghosts. . ..If you have anything to do with lawmakers in S.A. discourage the use of petrol & paraffin & guns.'

Æ thought that fifty of his paintings must have gone up in the conflagrations. Thirty-two of the best had been in the collection at Kilteragh, where the dining-room Lady Fingall remembered in *Seventy Years Young* had 'its table of boundless hospitality set beneath Æ's fairy sands and seas': and, in the hall, 'Æ's magic' had looked down on the musical evenings, and Lord Shaftesbury singing his songs from Ulster glens.

---

[3] Tim Healy was Parnell's secretary and instrumental in his downfall.

The people of Dublin were living 'from day to day, hoping the war will soon be over, & with the heart-sickness consequent on hope deferred', Susan told John Quinn. The burning of Plunkett's house was an 'ugly manifestation of Irish character. . . Everything good & bad. . . has boiled up. We are under no illusions now; our vanity is punctured; we have seen our ugly faces in the glass.' She defended the war only as 'the undoing of 700 years of idiotic government', which could not fail to be terrifying. 'But there is something sweet & lovable in the Irish character still to be manifested & to build up life here.'

Recovering her sense of humour, she could tell the story of the two ladies in Lincoln Place, carrying large paper parcels containing rifles & ammunitions. The soldiers examined them and arrested them. One 'raised ructions' in jail, complained of overcrowding, but was all right now, in a comfortable room with a nice fire and only one companion.

She and Jinny had got the Finucane money at last. 'It petered down to £281 + 19/9 each, not to be sneezed at though not all we had once expected. We don't know whether to eat it or keep it, at the moment it is on deposit. . .I couldn't think of anything I wanted to buy but a vest, afterwards I took heart & bought a petunia red velour-faced cloth at Brown's Sale & made a very chic coat frock to match my hat, it cost 5/10d! but there is still something left of the £281. 19. 9.' She added, 'I suppose the splendours of S. A. will eclipse all our little mole hills here, personally if I went to Africa at all, I would rather be in the neighbourhood of that dear & extravagant Tutankhamen who had such a re-fined taste in furniture'.

Her exasperated 'It has all got beyond comment now' to Marjorie, is re-flected in the equivocal froth of her contribution to William G. Fitz-Gerald's collection of essays, *The Voice of Ireland*. 'The Petticoat in Politics' muses in satirical fashion on the role of women in public life from the earliest times to Susan's own day. She discusses Queens Maeve and Macha, and the loves of Deirdre and Grania. As in all of her satire, she managed to find a reason for sticking bodkins into George Moore, into 'George Bernard Bricriu' [Shaw] (Bricriu being the legendary troublemaker) 'so uncanny in his insight into femi-nine character', and into Lord Carson, the Ulster Bricriu.

Political men talk longwindedly, she remarked. Women move rather than talk towards their goal. 'Processions innumerable mark their way. . . It is their symbolism; and perhaps that is why, when I think of the Cumann na mBan – our latest Irish feminine politicals – I can see nothing but feet.' Faithful to her instinct that it was the the role of Man to be articulate on Woman's behalf – that his task was 'to reveal her to herself' – Susan reaffirmed in her article that wom-anliness is the loveliest quality of woman. 'As sex equals or sex antagonists, men and women are ridiculous.' This did not mean that they could not work natu-rally and usefully together, on an equal footing.

Men playing alone at their moss-grown games of politics have made a mess of human society. The entrance there, not of two or three, but of two of three hundred women partners, might take the game into wider fields and fresher airs, broadening the humanity of Government. . . they might find in it a clue to the wider understanding of each other's nature. Thus should woman move graciously to her place in Irish politics; for only when the petticoat goes out of politics can the Woman come in.

The ceasefire at the end of April, when Ireland 'north and south, settled down in weary but welcome peace', 'quiet only from exhaustion', was nevertheless, it has been remarked, the beginning of a longer period of general tranquillity than the country had known since the first half of the eighteenth century.[4] Plunkett, who had been working successfully to interest powerful Irish-Americans such as John Quinn and Cornelius Sullivan in his project, at last persuaded Æ to edit the revived *Irish Statesman*. He agreed to give Æ complete control over the publication, and to allow some of the important features of the *Irish Homestead* to be maintained.

Æ heard that the enterprise was to go ahead when he was painting in Glengariffe, in County Cork. Two good days had allowed him 'sun baths'. 'Also bathed in my blue turquoise pond', he told Susan. He asked her to think of any ideas which might help to keep the paper living and readable, and to note down the names of writers she thought might be suitable.

Susan herself was reluctant to take a holiday, though he wanted her to go and be back fit for the new journal. 'Take your holidays, my dear, & enjoy them', Æ urged. 'If I want you specially I will call with trumpet voice. The old I.S. has to be wound up. The new I.S. to be registered. After that the circular of the Homestead to shareholders has to go out & a special meeting called & resolution passed. I dont think all this will be done in a couple of weeks or three or four'.

He had already been getting promises of articles from Larchet – on music – Lady Gregory, and others. There was a prospective freedom about the new editorship, without prior obligations to agriculture or co-operation: and when it emerged the *Statesman* was to be the authorative voice on politics, economics and social matters for educated Ireland, preserving the hermetic spirit of the *Homestead* which was incorporated in it. 'I want a weekly literary letter', Æ planned, 'not done by one person but by four or five in rotation. Say you, one week, myself a second, Robinson a third, Stephens a fourth, to keep at peak . . .'

Æ was finding the summer too hot for his liking, but he hoped the weather would keep hot and fine for Susan's sake. 'Get brown – take sun baths if you can.' It needed another letter to convince her that she could take her full holi-

---

[4] See J. C. Beckett, *The Making of Modern Ireland, 1603-1923* (1981), pp. 460-1.

day. The office was quiet, Æ insisted. 'I have stray visitors, an American professor of literature & his feminine belongings looking on a live poet with awe and
admiration'. He thought a shower of rain was coming to make the heavy air less
'smouldery', so that they could breathe.

The second *Irish Statesman* came into being on Saturday September 15,
1923. In her review of *Mors et Vita*, by Shan F. Bullock – which had an introduction by Æ – Susan was in full form. 'Poetry', she stated, 'the most exalted
language known to man, would seem to be the speech most native to him, for
when pressed back to the bed rock of his nature in extremity of joy or grief, it
springs to his lips.' Generally, however, it was not poetry she chose to review
but drama, and fiction, many of the novels slight, though she treated them, for
all her ambiguous manner and elusive irony, with kindness.

She felt free to discuss anything. 'Overcrowding in fiction', the Abbey
Theatre, 'Irrelevancies'. A girl in a Dublin street with a cloud of 'dim hair'
motivated her article, 'Back to the poets' – who used to write about women's
hair. In her first contribution to Æ's 'Literature and Life' series, she discussed
'The "I" in literature'.

We have become 'accustomed to a literature over-run with naked souls,
and where the "I's" of every writer elbow personal reserve off the footpath', she
claimed. She herself was no exception.

> A friend whose literary tastes I admired cautioned me in my early youth
> against beginning a letter with the singular personal pronoun, & she her-
> self achieved, in a report sent to a local newspaper on some trifling social
> event in our countryside, a style as lofty and remote as an editorial in the
> Daily Telegraph. I often sighed for this aloofness, but could never attain
> it, for the personal ever delighted me.

And 'the personal', which JBY had admired in her poetry, entered into her
criticism. Reviewing *Doomsland* by Shane Leslie, she compared Leslie with
George Moore. 'Mr. Moore dipped his pen in vitriol, when he wrote of Ire-
land. Mr. Leslie essays the same but his vitriol is merely sour milk'. Seeing *First
Aid* by George Shiels reminded her that 'Dublin has really keen affection for
Ulster'.

While Susan reviewed novels and plays, Harry Norman devoted himself to
his original love, music: and Jinny also contributed some articles. In some ways,
the paper seemed to be in the hands of the same literary clique which had
grown up in the early years of the century, with James Stephens, WB, and
Gogarty drawing in younger writers like Frank O'Connor, Liam O'Flaherty,
F.R. Higgins, and Austin Clarke to publish there; the tendency being to look
inwards to the paper, rather than looking out to what was written elsewhere.
But, since the cream of contemporary Irish writing was gathered within the
Statesman's pages, this was only natural, and the standard of writing was high,

articles were varied, and verse generally good. Writers like Simone Téry, commenting on French literature, were also involved.

Life seemed to return to a normal rhythm once again, despite the rumbling of political volcanoes, such as the Republican fast in the autumn of 1923. In October, Susan and Jinny bought the lease of the house they named 'Halcyon Cottage', at 3a Rathgar Avenue, a few doors away from Æ, (halcyon meaning 'peacefulness' and 'calm', the still centre in a stormy ocean where the sea bird may build its nest.) The small villa, with which Susan became permanently identified, but which she dwelt in for less than three years, cost them £875: and was quite obviously theirs. The drawing-room, with its wooden beams and pilasters, and the arch surrounding its door, looked over a small garden, and became the scene of some of Dublin's best loved parties.

Johnny and Bessie moved about the same time, and Susan sympathised 'because of our own move so lately made & though we had first rate men & so short a distance to go it took from 9.30 in the morning to 9.30 at night & the fearful rain made it an experience I wouldn't like to repeat'. Jinny was digging up the garden, and was delighted to have space for her plants. The cook, Sophie, had had flu almost ever since she had come, and 'it makes her very ferocious'.

She was relieved that the hunger strike was over – 'it was a horrid shame to put prisoners to such a test, of course it broke down': and she spoke of the

Susan Mitchell's house, Halcyon, drawn by Mike Carroll, 1981

Portrait study of Susan Mitchell (Lafayette, Dublin) with her autograph

Walcot cousins. Sara had died of heart disease. 'George & I took a carriage & met the funeral at Kingsbridge. She was buried with her father and mother in Mount Jerome'.

The *Statesman* was doing well, and the circulation was well above what they had anticipated, with American subscribers abounding. Besides writing reviews and articles for it, Susan continued to review regularly in the *Freeman*: and she had been sent to Lafayette to have her photograph taken to accompany her new poem in the *Christmas Lady of the House*.

This latest poem was a light and carefree satirical paean, aroused by remarks made at a Gaelic Society meeting in Trinity College condemning 'Pseudo-Gaelicism' as 'a form of Jingoism produced by local peculiarities of history'. All of the innocent and enjoyable trimmings of the Gaelic Revival had been swept aside – saffron kilts and cloaks, uilleann pipes, dancing ('no native writer made any allusion to dancing'), Gaelic football, and the national colour green – as having nothing to do with genuine Gaelic culture. 'The nearest approach to an Irish national colour was royal blue'.

Susan's eyes narrowed, she unsheathed her claws. It was in the nature of – not quite – an attack on herself and so many of her fellow writers and visionaries, imagining a cultural Ireland that, in the event, was never to be. Then, purring, she pounced forward with 'The Wail of the Pseudo-Gael'.

> Put by my kilt of saffron,
> My fibula put by.
> Rest thee, my tibia, too, no more
> In Rinnce Fada on the floor
> Shalt thou in courage high
> With suppler tibias vie?
>
> . . .And when at Gaelic tea-fights
> We passed the sweet tea-cake,
> Adding "mavourneen deelish,"
> And noises strange did make,
> Dear Erin, for thy sake,
>
> We thought that in our mission
> Were Rahilly and Hyde
> And Bergin, the precisian. –
> They hold us in derision,
> The men who were our pride,
> The men for whom we lied!

To Halcyon Cottage, where Susan sang her political lampoons in her memorable way, the gifted young now gathered: the three Reddin brothers, Nora Ringwood (her cousin), and other students, Fitzroy Pyle (another cousin), Michael Hermann Franklin (Victoria's son), Muriel Gahan. There were her own contemporaries – Helen Laird with her husband Con Curran, the Yeats sisters, Douglas Hyde, Edmund Curtis, Osborn Bergin, James Stephens, Pádraic Colum: and there were passing visitors, as well as steady admirers, such as Bethel Solomons and his wife and Tom MacGreevy. Bethel Solomons wrote later, in *One Doctor in his Time*:

> Susan Mitchell had a warm place in the hearts of us all. She came up to my shoulder, had hay-coloured hair, a bright complexion, sparkling eyes, a great sense of humour, a body filled with kindliness and a head full of

brains. She and her sister gave parties in their house in Terenure and
although the conversation was good, singing and music were more in
the vogue. . .

And he added, that, when he married, she and Æ gave him a picture. 'He [Æ]
is giving the picture and I the frame', said Susan.

Others present at the evening *At Homes* remember dancing the Lancers, a
sort of quadrille or square dance; or Susan's soft mezzo soprano rendering of
'The Rising of the Moon'; Susan sitting on the floor, singing , 'I know my love
by his way of walking', with Yeats, Æ and the company standing in a mesmer-
ised circle around her. She sang her controversial 'Belfast Street Ballad, 1916' to
the jaunty, galloping rhythm of 'O Limerick is beautiful as everybody knows' -

> Twas in the year nineteen fifteen bold Carson's blood did flow,
> The last of Ireland's rebel sons, the pride of Sandy Row,
> Successor to John Mitchel and true brother to Wolfe Tone'.

All that was inspirational in life was not gone. In a very different mood, she
appreciated the 'unusual beauty' of *At the Hawk's Well*, performed in W.B.
Yeats's own drawing-room. Susan was completely carried away by what she
described as 'a terrible army to set in motion against mere drawing-room folk,
only the initiate of beauty could meet it undismayed.'

> The idea in the Noh plays seems to be opposite to all that is desirable in
> realistic drama. Action is slowed . . . life moves in shadows. . . Everything
> that took place on that small stage in Mr. Yeats's drawing-room seemed
> slowed, as the pulse might be slowed by a powerful drug . . .

> The stage was in the middle of the company, yet it seemed remote, the
> beautiful verse was recited close to our ears, but it came to them as a far
> away chant, and yet with this studied suggestion of remoteness I have
> never felt anything more intimate and vivid than the effect on the imagi-
> nation. . . The poignant music of the flute echoing the verse in the
> hearers' soul, the thin tapping to whose rhythm the players entered, the
> angular gliding movements of the players, the necromantic dance of the
> hawk, I am powerless to express the emotions they raised, because while
> the sense of beauty is solaced, the intellect seems partially narcotised by a
> play of this kind'.

WB's original and ingenious staging of his drama had at last won her over.

TWENTY TWO

'Death my Gentle Nurse'

SUSAN'S LAST DAYS

W e in Ireland now are relaxed placid, after the high tension of those years . . . One shudders going back in memory to those days when the gun and the bomb were never silent, because memory brings us what we hardly realised during the tumult and the fighting, the hideous physical suffering and terror that followed in the wake of that revolt that we believed to be necessary to our existence as a nation.

This was how Susan summed up the peaceful atmosphere of Dublin in *The Irish Statesman* at the beginning of May 1925. She herself was 'relaxed placid' in these first years of Plunkett's new paper, where she had a standing as a leading journalist and commentator, and her intellect and her imagination could flourish.

She had developed her style with its mild irony – slightly bantering but always kind – to be very readable, while at the same time elegant and literary. Speaking about a now forgotten novel, she remarked; 'The tale is rich in romantic titles for men and places, and if there is nothing rare or original about it, sometimes one is thankful for the expected'. *Spring Song* by Liam O'Flaherty evoked a simulated shocked admiration for his daring. 'He has gone exultingly to the task of stripping us of some of our most cherished attributes. His passion for scraping off what one might call the ornamental stucco of character is so burning that one feels very little more would make him flay us alive and deprive us of even the decency of skin!'

It was while she was in Portrush on holiday in July 1924 that she became ill once more. She wrote on her return home to Victoria and Harry, congratulating them on their silver wedding anniversary. (She remembered the 'white over pink – ("very trying colour")' she had worn as chief bridesmaid, and told how, at Pierce Finucane's auction she had nearly indulged in crested forks for them only to be restrained by Jinny who said that Victoria hated silver.) Jinny had been 'so worried' at Portrush. 'The vagaries of my [diseased] throat & eye . . . kept her awake two nights'. They had intended going to Kilrush, to see Johnny's new house, but she felt so bad that she had written putting the visit off till September.

All the same, they had had a lovely fortnight. 'Sea Bank is a delightful hotel & Mylius as agreeably Scoto-Germanic as ever . . . in our courteous farewells, which included the handshake & the tip, wished to be remembered to you all. "And you thought I didn't remember you", he said to me with that playful glance & smile. He certainly greeted me as an old friend when we appeared at dinner, so I suppose he had some memory of my noble contours. I managed to slip away without going to the Causeway – something of a feat, I think. . .'

And she added: 'I still find reading very trying to my eye, but it looks nearly normal again & the purple patch underneath is fading out. I am not looking forward to the operation in August that Dr. Graham says he will do so nicely. He put in a probe before I went away & the corner of the eye is sore yet, the probe went right through the tear duct & came out in my nose, it was the sorest thing I ever felt.' Her old friend and admirer, Dr. Robert Woods, 'would have been so angelic & powerful a personality' she would not have realised he was hurting her. 'But Dr. Graham, though very nice, has not Woods's charm!'

Despite being indisposed in August – when she held court in her bedroom with elegant propriety, and Æ was a regular visitor on Sunday mornings – she was fired by an editorial note in the *Statesman* in early August to write a satirical poem in reply. Æ spoke of 'the epidemic of tall silk hats which have broken out on the top of many Irish heads. It was perhaps a way they took in the hope of convincing our visitors that this was a civilised country. He called the hat the 'Mark of the unaesthetic Beast': and enquired why Ireland could not invent a hat of her own.

Susan's ode 'To a tall silk hat' – written on the spur of the moment, and not very distinguished – challenged the hat as the dusty 'herald of mortality', a clothing for funerals. Now transported into a society that had no need for it, 'with thee on his pate, Some little man grew great'.

> Thy cylinder contains
> The cold remains
> Of brains.
> Thou hast brought down
> The mighty to thy crown.

The verses, printed in the *Statesman* on 16 August, provoked one witty rejoinder, by 'Trimalchio': and they were reprinted in the *Madras Mail* a month later, by which time Susan was back to serious reviewing of novels and drama.

Novels, she said, she judged by her knowledge of humanity. She was getting more interesting material now, the latest work of Compton MacKenzie, Rose Macaulay, Forrest Reid, Joseph Conrad, and George Birmingham. In October 1924, she contributed 'A meditation on Charlotte Yonge' to the 'Literature and Life' series – this was one of her last essays of this kind, except for that on Shaw's *St. Joan* the following year, after seeing the recent performance in Dublin. 'With a high-spiritedness unabated', she observed, 'he seems to snatch Joan out of the very teeth of Catholic canonisation and dump her un-asked into a Protestant hagiography'.

Reviewing plays regularly brought out the 'personal' in her. Joseph Holloway, the theatrophile, meeting her and Jinny at performances, sent them Christmas greetings on postcards decorated with pen-drawn caricatures of the dramatic personalities they all saw. In January 1925, at Ernest Toller's *Masses and Man*, and a play by Gribble, 'the intolerable chill of the Abbey Theatre made [the plays] . . . a mortification of the flesh. If our plays must have the character of sermons – and I rejoice in this character – why not heat the pews?', Susan asked in her critique.

She reviewed plays by Dorothy Maccardle, Lennox Robinson and August Strindberg. This last, *The Spook Sonata*, bravely tackled by the Dublin Drama League in April 1925 ('one cannot praise too highly the players' realisation of the strangely muffled parts assigned to them', said Susan) made its impression on Dublin, and the artist Margaret Clarke based her painting of 1927, *Strindbergian*, on it[1] . Susan Mitchell had her own views. 'A play may be anything and every-thing nowadays except a play as the old fashion had it,' she wrote. 'As the externalisation of life, romance and realism in high tragedy or high comedy kisses hands to us and fades away, a new dramatic love comes to us, an internali-sation of life, the drama driven inwards. . . It is desperately uncomfortable, this hair shirt of misgiving under the theatre dress clothes that once we donned without a thought'.

Iphigenia in Taurus, by Euripides, was more to her taste, also performed by the Drama League, but in Lennox Robinson's back garden in Dalkey, on the coast south of Dublin, 'the setting of Killiney Bay. . . a drop scene of rare beauty, and few of the audience could have escaped an enchantment that seemed to recreate for the eye the life out of which these plays were born. On such a day in such a scene the apparition on earth of divine beings seemed not incon-gruous . . .'

As for modern novelists, she had reservations about Sinclair Lewis and Virginia Woolf. Sinclair Lewis's *Martin Arrowsmith*, which 'might have been the perfect type of the scientific novel to come' made her exclaim, 'The nov-elists are out-specialising the specialists!' 'It is extremely clever – and alas! so very tedious. . .' 'I like Virginia Woolf's beautiful book [*Mrs. Dalloway*], but I am not going to read it again. I have not the nerve. . .

> When I emerged from it, battered with its tumult, I thanked whatever
> God had isolated us human beings from each other, locking each into

---

[1] Exhibited in *Irish Women Artists from the eighteenth century to the present day*, National Gallery of Ireland, 1987, no. 101.

the opaque case of his body, and then placing a very stiff handle on the door of communication between the formless and the articulate in us – allowing only such thoughts as had garbed themselves in coherence to turn that handle and come downstairs to the reception rooms. . . Virginia Woolf's method is that of Joyce, but *Ulysses* was a moral thunderstorm, with a universal world war and the noise of all its engines of destruction shocking through it: Mrs Woolf has not an ounce of the moralist in her.

Contemporary novelists were being drawn to exploring a chaotic world, because it dragged them out of the clichés of narrative. 'It calls for an unusual sensitiveness to words', she concluded.

Halcyon might suggest happiness and prosperity, but Halcyon Cottage, Susan found, was not a haven for health. She spent most of February 1925 in bed, and after that all of May. The sudden death of Nelly O'Brien – 'a brave soul' – in late Spring saddened her considerably. On June 3, she wrote to her niece, Dora, who had gone out to her sister Stella's wedding in South Africa and stayed on – 'I have come to life again after more than a month of general decay'. All reviewing had ceased. She had a kind of bronchial cold, which kept developing, in bed, into a kind of flu.

> When the bronch. was over I could hardly get my heart to go on beating. However Dr. Maguire soon started it with injections (hypodermic) of strychina every day & I'm all right again now, after a delicious idle week at Roundwood.

She often stayed with Kathleen Fitzpatrick, the writer, and her brother, at Roundwood Park in Wicklow; occasionally in Donegal with their sister, the Hon. Mrs. Phillimore, whose book on St. Paul Æ had described as 'jewels set in mud'. Dr. Frank Purser's wife, Mabel, was a close friend in the Hermetic Society. Once, at Roundwood, she and Susan were seen lying on their backs with their bare feet placed against the trunk of a tree – they said, feeling the pulse of nature.

Susan told Dora about Whit Monday at Roundwood, with the Pursers, and her niece Kitsy.

> The Strolling Players did *Alcestis* in Father Butler's garden. Frank [Purser] drove Jenny & me down with his party & Kitsy went with the gang in a Furey Charabanc. We all picknicked out of our fingers in the Roundwood dining room (as the weather threatened) . . . The weather grew beautiful & we lounged round in baking sun.

> The play was charming. Elizabeth as Alcestis was wonderful, I wept freely. Alex Stewart was a splendid Admetus – & Kitsy was really exquisite as

Apollo, dressed in Pierce Finucane's shimmering watered silk, bare legs far above the knee (Philip Little [the poet], 2 priests & a Capuchin Friar bore it without a quiver) & a fillet of hay, a golden bow & quiver. She really was more an Angus Oge . . .

Susan's last task before going on holiday with Jinny in August 1925 – the Sea Bank in Portrush was full, so they went to Belfast – was reviewing in the *Irish Statesman* the Cuala Press printing of WB's lecture, delivered to the Royal Swedish Academy. She described it gracefully. The book was charmingly produced,' she said, 'a courteous acknowledgement of the courtesy accorded the poet by the country that gave him the Nobel Prize. It is gossip, distinguished gossip, stamped with the elaborate pattern of Mr. Yeats' style. It has the simplicity and formalism that distinguish a prose that always inveigles the reader . . . One feels in these impressions of Sweden a happy, untroubled mood in Mr. Yeats. . .'

Back in Dublin at the *Statesman*, she had further comments to make on the sexes – 'what do the sexes really know of each other, though each to the other for thousands of years has been subject of unremitting study?' She saw George Shiels' play, *Professor Tim*. 'One's intelligence not being needed in the play one was at liberty to concentrate on the actors, and their individual gifts in every case made themselves felt'. The appeal of Ibsen's *The Doll's House* was profound, 'because for most of us life is spent in one kind or other of a Doll's House'.

True to her departed friend, Katherine Purdon, of the 'tall, wavering figure', 'whose light movements retained in elder years the grace of girlhood', she had been trying to get *The Folk of Furry Farm* reissued, after its success ten years before: and this was done by the Talbot Press in the autumn. In her introduction, Susan compared Purdon with other Anglo-Irish writers and claimed that none conveyed the same sense of respect for her characters as she did. She understood the peasants' pride. She particularly understood the people of Meath, her own county, 'those dwellers on fat lands', often criticised for their sloth and idleness. Katherine could reproduce their vivid and homely speech so genuinely. She had known her since the *Homestead* office was in Lincoln Place, when she had come in timidly to visit Harry Norman, who was editor at the time. The bright figure 'vivified the dull little room. . . The kind eyes, of so warm a blue as to be almost purple . . . invited friendship.'

But life went on. Susan had taken to the bicycle again, only able to wave the hand in greeting as she passed her friends. 'The traffic has speeded up frightfully in the last 2 years & my eyebrows are in my hair most of the time.'

There were parties. The Yeats sisters had only 'very select' company, 'the richest cream of Dublin culture'.

The men (not Æ or Con Curran) wore evening clothes. WB was very late owing to his not being able to find his dress trousers. He thought as he could not then wear dress clothes he had better steal in late & be lost in a crowd. Which he did & loomed up darkly at about 10 o'c, keeping his back to the room & otherwise concealing himself. Which, as he was one of the tallest men present, the other being Æ, was somewhat difficult.

She and Jinny had a sparkling Hallowe'en party, with a play as entertainment, and niece Kitsy handling the violin 'with dash'. They had become 'desperately giddy' at Halcyon, with great Sunday suppers – 'cold corn beef . . . & any strays that like to come in', such as Edmund Curtis, who was giving them a party in Trinity – 'isn't he sporting?' – and various students. At their dance, there were about thirty in the Sir Roger, 'while Kitsy sat on the piano & played the fiddle for it & for foxtrots. . . Now that we see it can be done we'll try again with real music'. She had asked the Yeatses to send her 'Christmas Nursery Song', published by the Cuala Press and for which Beatrice Elvery did a delicious drawing, out to the nieces in South Africa.

Michael J. MacManus, who came from Carrick-on-Shannon like Susan, had taken an interest in her satirical ballads for years, and had recently published

Susan Mitchell's niece, Kitsy Franklin (left), playing chamber music with her family in Sligo, c.1920, Victoria and her husband Harry to right

a book of Irish parodies, *The Green Jackdaw*. He told her of a visit to Carrick Regatta in August, which had left him sad. 'Somehow the old spirit of reckless good-humour was missing, and missing too the faces of nearly all those who – whatever their faults – used to make it what it was, the Kingstons, the Beresford Whites, the King-Harmans, the Lloyds and the rest. The old Georgian mansions look greyer than ever, silent and shuttered – or blackened ruins. The old gentry are indeed as rare on the banks of the Shannon as the 'Times' long ago gleefully prophesied the Celts would be. And I'm not at all sure that the change is for the better. After all, these were not the English that we fought to eradicate: they had real roots in the soil and their disappearance has made an appreciable difference to the sum of things Irish. In their place we have got – God help us! – the Free State!'.

During December 1925, Susan was frequently at the Abbey. She saw *The Dance of Death*, by Strindberg, and *Major Barbara*, by Shaw, which 'swoops hither and thither like a bewitched aeroplane, but it never fails to place its bomb where it will do most damage'. *The Throwbacks* by Gerald Macnamara – 'as tickling to the palette as devilled bones' – and Lynn Doyle's *The Lilac Ribbon*, performed by the Ulster Players at Christmas, were the last plays she was to review.

Her eye was inflamed again, and at the beginning of January it was operated on, painfully but successfully. But, Jinny said, it took a great deal out of her, and she was very weak. Horace Plunkett, himself ill, wrote to her in consternation towards the middle of the month, 'longing' to hear that she was convalescing. When Lily Yeats saw her, she looked 'alarmingly white and pink'. She described it as 'a sort of breakdown.' The inflamed eye poisoned her so that her lungs were affected and became congested. Then rheumatism affected her heart. Yet no one was quite sure of the cause, or why she would not improve.

An invitation to dinner at the Vice-Regal Lodge lay on the hall table at Halcyon disregarded. Dr. Frank Purser, called in, packed Susan off to Elphis Nursing-Home for a change, but congestion and general debility persisted and she began to wander. 'She could be a great loss to many,' wrote Lily to her niece Ruth, 'among them me. I can't think of it. Her fine rich nature is a comfort and a joy'. Æ was so upset that he could not write long letters, manuscripts were piling up in his copy boxes, and angry authors were crying out. He had to drive his pen to get an article written.

Jinny was at the nursing-home from morning till night as Susan weakened. Then to everyone's stunned astonishment, she left the Dublin literary scene as suddenly as she had arrived. At 7.05 on the evening of March 4, 1926, she died.

'Susan Mitchell – who I am sure was a wise woman – always maintained that in what seem our most negative & doldrummy times we were growing the most of our wisdom,' wrote Mabel Purser to her daughter some time later. 'I never shall forget the smile on dear Susan's face when she was dying. She had sent a message to me to come (I had gone thinking perhaps she & Jeanie would rather be alone). When I came she gave me one bright cheerful smile, as much as to say, "Believe me all is well", & she closed her beautiful eyes & died'.

'All my heart lies buried with you, All my thoughts go onward with you', wrote Jinny, for whom life would never be the same again. All of literary and scholarly Dublin were at the funeral in Mount Jerome Cemetery, Co-operative colleagues, members of the Arts Club, all the Yeatses, the Pursers, Lord Dunsany, the Countess of Fingall, Douglas Hyde, and many others.

The *Irish Times* described Susan's 'piquant wit, which never lost her a friend. . . in the best tradition of the pre-Victorian humorists, without the over-pungent irony which sometimes distinguished our Irish satirists', her 'warm political convictions' which 'she never allowed. . .to warp her judgement of people, which was sagacious and acute.' 'Apart from her gifts as a writer, Miss Mitchell was a lover of her friends, of her country and of human kind'.

There were tributes in the *Irish Sketch*, in *Irish Truth*, *The United Irishwomen* and elsewhere. Katherine Tynan, in the London *Times*, wrote of her 'large, soft beauty'. 'One is glad she was spared old age. She had had for long a deafness which gave her a still look, as though she heard inwardly. To a creature like her, age and helplessness would have been a wrong and an indignity'. In *The Gaelic Churchman*, Harry Norman recalled how she had said to him, 'I have no principles, no principles, only people'.

Perhaps the most touching tribute came from Æ, who was momentarily lost and bewildered. He had lost 'the kindest & most unselfish of friends'. He made her poetry the theme of the *Irish Statesman* 'Literature and Life' article – the series they had initiated together – at the end of March. 'I think Susan Mitchell had the genius for life', he wrote, 'and she never neglected that exquisite gift in order that she might make herself better as a writer than as a woman, though I am certain that if she had turned her genius for life into letters there are few women of her time who could have written more brilliantly . . .

> I found in her one of those rare natures whose spirituality turns them to the world, taking it with out-stretched hands and laughter as if they knew what precious ores were in its dross and they had the instant alchemy by which the ore was revealed.

Recalling the intrinsic sadness that mingled with her infinite fun, he continued, 'the soul of Susan Mitchell reminded me .. of one of those laughing children who peer between the legs of the angels in a Donatello relief, or anon one of the tall grave angels themselves, by suddenly growing up to the height of some high argument, the next moment as suddenly slipping away to be again the frolic spirit. I do not think of any I have known who has left more endearing memories of themselves among their friends than this kindest of women'.

She is buried with the two women who raised her after her family was forced to split up, Aunt Wegg and Aunt Margaret Mitchell, near the Laburnum

Walk in Mount Jerome, in the grave next to her Mitchell cousins of Birr days. The Portland headstone, with its simple decoration of oak leaves, is inscribed with a couplet from her poem, 'Love in heaven':

> Only in clay the root of love can grow,
> Only in heaven the flower of love can blow.

Mourn not, though sorrowful and dark thou art,
Thy Sun Withdrawn.
Hail from the watching hilltops of the heart
The tender Dawn.
For Thee our soil and sorrow we forget
O Undefiled!
For still the hope of all the world is set
Upon a Child.

Cuala Press   Susan L. Mitchell.

Susan Mitchell's poem, 'Mourn Not', illustrated on a Cuala Card by Jack B. Yeats

Susan Mitchell's Writings

Aids to the Immortality of Certain Persons in Ireland, charitably administered.
[Cover illustration by Beatrice Glenavy.] Dublin, New Nation Press,
1908. Enlarged edition. Dublin, Maunsel, 1913.

The Living Chalice and Other Poems (Tower Press Books – Second Series – 6).
Dublin, Maunsel, 1908. New edition. Dublin, Maunsel, 1913.

Frankincense and Myrrh. [Frontispiece by Jack B. Yeats.] Dublin, Cuala Press,
1912.

George Moore (Irishmen of To-day).Dublin, Maunsel, 1916. New York,
Dodd, Mead, 1916. Dublin, Talbot Press, n.d.

POEMS PUBLISHED IN PERIODICALS

'The army of the voice' (unsigned). [Illustrated by Pamela Colman Smith.] *A
Celtic Christmas*, 1902, p. 25.

'Homeless'. *A Celtic Christmas*, 1903, p. 7.

'The living chalice'. *A Celtic Christmas*, 1903, p. 21.

'The voice of one' (unsigned). *A Celtic Christmas*, 1903, p. 22.

'Love's mendicant', 'The living chalice', 'The lonely', 'Amergin', 'The army
of the voice'. *New Songs* edited by Æ, 1904.

'If you like a stir' (unsigned) in 'A Celtic Renaissance Birthday Book,
Thursday 5 [January]'. *A Celtic Christmas*, 1904, p. 15.

'The Greenlands'. *A Celtic Christmas*, 1904, p. 17.

'Ballads of the Year 1905' (being selections from an unpublished Irish comic
opera)' (unsigned). *A Celtic Christmas*, 1905, pp. 8-9.

'Ireland'. [Illustrated by Æ] *A Celtic Christmas*, 1905, p. 19.

'The dark way'. *A Celtic Christmas*, 1905, p. 26.

'A dream'. [Illustrated by Æ] *A Celtic Christmas*, 1906, p. 5.

'The blushes of Ireland'. *Dublin Evening Mail*, February 9, 1907.

'Is it this you call Home Rule' (signed 'M.R.'). *Sinn Féin*, May 18, 1907, p.
2.

'A prayer'. *Shanachie,* Autumn 1907, p. 156.

'Oh, no! we never mention it' (signed 'S'). In *The Abbey Row, Not Edited by
W. B. Yeats.* Dublin, 1907, pp. 10, 12.

'Immortality'. *A Celtic Christmas*, 1907, p. 10.

'Christmas'. *A Celtic Christmas*, 1908, p. 9.

'The house of Life'. *Bean na hÉireann*, January 1909, p. 12.

'The ballad of Dermody and Hynes'. *Bean na hÉireann*, February 1909, p. 11.

'To the Women of Ireland.' *Bean na hÉireann*, April 1910, p. 18. Specially
    written for the tenth anniversary of Inghinidhe na hÉireann.

'The burden of the doorkeeper'. *A Celtic Christmas*, 1909, p. v.

'The music of the silence'. *A Celtic Christmas,* 1910, p. 1047.

'Leaguers and Peelers; or the Apple Cart (a dramatic saga of the Dark Ages in
    Two Acts edited by Susan Mitchell)'. *Irish Review*, October 1911, pp.
    390-406.

'Light of lights'. *Irish Review*, July 1912, pp. 246-7.

'To the Dublin Masters'. *Irish Worker*, October 4, 1913, p. 4.

'To the "Villas of Genteel Dastards"'. *Irish Worker*, November 1, 1913, p. 3.

'The Dublin tenements'. *Lady of the House*, Christmas 1913, p. 29.

'Belfast street ballad; 1916'. *New Statesman*, May 2, 1914, pp. 114-5.

'The Christmas tree'. 'The sorrowful birth'. *Lady of the House*, Christmas
    1915.

'Out of the dust'. [With a reproduction of *A Dublin Pavement Artist* by Jack
    B. Yeats.] *Lady of the House*, Christmas 1917, p. 11.

'Sligo Bay'. *Studies*, September 1918, p. 445.

'Irish Convention Number Two. A.D. 1920: No mistake this time'. *Lady of
    the House*, Christmas 1918, p. 21.

'Troublesome nations'. *Lady of the House*, Christmas 1920, p. 9.

'The arrows of light'. *Irish Statesman,* January 24, 1920, p. 84.

'The Irish bombardier'. *Lady of the House*, Christmas 1922, p. 12.

'The wail of the Pseudo-Gael'. *Lady of the House*, Christmas 1923, p. 4.

'To a tall silk hat'. *Irish Statesman*, August 16, 1924, p. 725.

'The ball-room revisited'. *Irish Statesman*, August 30, 1924, p. 797.

'The bleat of the children'. *Irish Statesman*, December 6, 1924, p. 406.

CUALA CARDS

[Susan Mitchell's verses published as greeting cards are listed in the Cuala
    Press lists, whose reference numbers are given here.]

'The star in the east' (18). [Illustrated by Jack B. Yeats]. (As 'To these high
    lands' in Cuala Christmas Card list (69).)

'The crib' (20). [Illustrated by Jack B. Yeats.] (As 'Day closes' in Cuala
    Christmas Card list (12).)

'The nursery song' (44). [Illustrated by Beatrice Glenavy.] (As 'A nursery
    song for Christmas Eve' in Cuala Christmas Card list (126).)

'Glencree' (58). [Illustrated by Dorothy Blackham.]

Cuala Christmas Cards

'Day closes' (12). [Illustrated by Jack B. Yeats.]
'The star is risen' (13). [Illustrated by Jack B. Yeats.]
'Mourn not' (16). [Illustrated by Jack B. Yeats.]
'The dove' (60). [Illustrated by Jack B. Yeats.]
'Christmas' (60).
'Bid old days' (67). [Illustrated by Beatrice Glenavy.]
'Red-berried holly' (68). [Illustrated by Beatrice Glenavy.]
'To these high lands' (69). [Illustrated by Jack B. Yeats.]
'Who can bring' (120). [Illustrated by Mary Cottenham Yeats.]
'Time' (122). [Illustrated by Jack B. Yeats.]
'A nursery song for Christmas Eve' (126). [Illustrated by Beatrice Glenavy.]
'Milestone track' (127). [Illustrated by E. C. Yeats.]

Select list of Articles by Susan L. Mitchell

[She also reviewed books for the *Irish Times* from about 1909-12, for the *Irish Review*, *Irish Homestead*, *Gaelic Churchman*, *Irish Statesman* and *Freeman's Journal* at various times.]

'Dramatic rivalry'. *Sinn Féin*, May 8, 1909, p. 1.

'Agricultural co-operation in Ireland. Lessons for South African farmers'. *The State*, May 1912, pp. 395-401.

'A meditation on the Beatitudes'. *Church of Ireland Gazette*, November 17, 1916, pp. 813-4.

'Ireland'. *The Englishwoman*, April 1918, pp. 3-10.

'The Ireland of the hunting-stable novelists'. *Shamrock and Irish Emerald* (new series), March 22, 1919, p. 17.

'What is the Church of Ireland going to do about Sinn Féin.' *Gaelic Churchman*, March 1919, p. 10.

'The clerical snob.' *Gaelic Churchman*, June 1919, pp. 1-2.

'An Irish Country Town'. *Lady of the House*, Christmas 1919, pp. 17-18.

'The Petticoat in Politics'. *The Voice of Ireland*, London 1923 (rev. ed. 1924), ed. W. FitzGerald, pp. 176-8 (pp. 164-6).

References

MANUSCRIPT SOURCES

SLM personal papers, out of which this memoir rose, are now in the Manuscript Collection, Trinity College, Dublin. Other manuscript collections consulted are:

Holograph copy of talk on John Butler Yeats, December 1919. Sligo County Library.

SLM to Seumas O'Sullivan. Trinity College, Dublin, Manuscript Collection.

SLM to Horace Plunkett, Plunkett Foundation for Co-operative Studies, Oxford. Plunkett Collection.

Diarmuid Coffey papers.

Bethel Solomons papers.

Armagh Notebook. Armagh Museum.

Outline pedigree of the Mitchells of King's County.

Kathleen Brabazon, Unpublished memoir, c. 1970.

Papers of the late Dora McGuinness.

Lily Yeats to JBY; G.W. Russell letters; Augustine Henry letters. National Library of Ireland, Manuscript Collection.

JBY letters to Rosa Butt. Manuscript Collection, Bodleian Library, Oxford.

Cuala Archive. TCD Early Printed Books Collection.

Cumann Gaedhealach na hEaglaise Archive. Representative Church Body Library, Dublin.

PERSONAL RECOLLECTIONS

Michael Franklin, nephew, younger son of Victoria Diana Franklin (née Mitchell).

Dora McGuinness, niece, daughter of Bidz Brabazon (née Mitchell).

Stella Latham, niece, daughter of Bidz Brabazon.

William Fitzroy Pyle, cousin.

Dr. E. L. Fitzpatrick, niece of Sarah Purser.

Muriel Gahan, Irish Countrywomen's Association.

Published Sources

M. Guckian, 'Susan Mitchell', *Carrick-on-Shannon Remembered: Aspects of History - Print & Pictorial*, 1998.

R. M. Kain, *Susan L. Mitchell* (Bucknell University Press - Irish Writers Series), 1972.

H. Pyle, 'External things and images: the portraits of Susan Mitchell, poet', *The Irish Arts Review Yearbook* 1991-2.

G.W. Russell (Æ), 'The poetry of Susan Mitchell'. *Irish Statesman*, March 27, 1926.

R. Skelton, 'Aide to Immortality: the satirical writings of Susan L. Mitchell', in *The World of W. B. Yeats*, ed. R. Skelton and A. Saddlemyer, 1965.

Other Relevant Publications

Books

J. C. Beckett, *The Making of Modern Ireland, 1603-1923*, 1981.

R. F. Foster, *Modern Ireland 1600–1972*, 1988.

W. J. McCormack, *Ascendancy and Tradition in Anglo-Irish Literary History from 1789-1939*, 1985.

A. O'Connor, *Concord Lodge, 854, Carrick-on-Shannon 1797-1897*, 1897. [A paper read at the dedication of Parke Memorial Masonic Hall at the Grand Lodge of North Connacht held at Carrick 1897 and printed by Concord Lodge 854.]

Poems of John Greenleaf Whittier with a note, biographical and critical by Eva Hope. London, n.d.

B. M. Malabari, *India in 1897*, 1898.

J.B.Yeats: Letters to his Son W.B. Yeats and Others 1869-1922, ed. J. Hone 1946.

J.B. Yeats, *Letters from Bedford Park: A Selection from the Correspondence (1890-901) of John Butler Yeats*. Edited by W.M. Murphy, 1972.

W.M. Murphy, *Prodigal Father, the Life of John Butler Yeats 1839-1922*, 1978.

T. West, *Horace Plunkett: Co-operation and Politics*, 1986.

W. M. Clyde, *A.E.*, 1935.

W. K. Magee, *A Memoir of Æ,* 1937.

Russell, G.W. (Æ), *New Songs: a Lyric Selection*, 1904.

Russell, G.W. (Æ), *Co-operation and Nationality*, 1912.

H. Summerfield, *That Myriad-Minded Man: Æ*, 1975.

Letters from Æ (George William Russell) edited by Alan Denson, 1961.

B. L. Reid, *The man from New York*, 1968.

Thomas Bodkin, *Hugh Lane and his pictures,* 1956.

J. Hone, *Life of George Moore*, l936.

Seumas O'Sullivan, *Essays and recollections*, 1944.

P. Boylan, *All cultivated people, a history of the United Arts Club*, Dublin, 1988.

J. Meenan, *George O'Brien: a Biographical Memoir*, 1980.

Seventy Years Young: Memoirs of Elizabeth, Countess of Fingall told to Pamela Hinkson, 1937.

The United Irishwomen, their place, work and ideals, 1911.

J. Van Voris, *Constance de Markievicz: In the Cause of Ireland*, 1967.

Prison Letters of Constance Markievicz, ed. Esther Roper, 1934.

Seán O Faoláin, *Constance Markievicz*, 1934.

R. C. Owens, *Smashing Times: a history of the Irishwomen's Suffrage Movement 1889-1922*, 1984.

R. Giltrap, *An Ghaeilge in Eaglais na hEireann*, 1990.

K. Tynan, *Memories*, 1924.

Articles

Constance Marckiewicz, 'Memories', *Éire*, August 18, 25, 1923.

'Unheard music: in memory of Thomas Goodwin Keller' by H.F. Norman, *Dublin Magazine* 17 no. 3.

Sheila Pim, 'Dun Emer – an unrecorded chapter in the life of Augustine Henry', *Moorea* vol. 3, 1984.

'Æ's Merrion Square murals and other paintings' by J. White in *The Arts in Ireland*, 1, no. 3, 1973.

Periodicals

Celtic Christmas.
Dublin Magazine.
Dublin Evening Mail.
Freeman's Journal.
Gaelic Churchman.
Irish Citizen.
Irish Homestead.
Irish Review.
Irish Statesman.
Irish Times.
Irish Worker.
King's County Chronicle.
Ladies Pictorial.
Lady of the House.
Sligo Champion.
Sligo Independent.
Sligo Star.

Sources of Chapter Titles and Illustrations

CHAPTER TITLES

Chapter titles have been taken from the poetry and prose of Susan L. Mitchell, as follows:

Introduction   Armagh Notebook.
Chapter 1   'Carrick'
Chapter 2   *George Moore*
Chapter 3   'The Greenlands'
Chapter 4   'George Moore Comes to Ireland'
Chapter 5   'The Heart's Low Door'
Chapter 6   'Carrick'
Chapter 7   'The Ark of the Covenant'
Chapter 8   'The Neglected Altar'
Chapter 9   'The Roads of the Heart'
Chapter 10   Holograph Talk on JB. Yeats, 1919.
Chapter 11   'Lines on a Threatened Imperial University'.
Chapter 12   'Down by Sligo'.
Chapter 13   'Author's Review' in *Aids to the Immortality* (2nd ed., 1913).
Chapter 14   'Author's Review' in *Aids to the Immortality* (2nd ed., 1913).
Chapter 15   'The Irish Bombardier'.
Chapter 16   'George Moore Joins the Irish Church'.
Chapter 17   'Author's Review' in *Aids to the Immortality* (2nd ed., 1913).
Chapter 18   'The Irish Bombardier'.
Chapter 19   'A Song of the Convention'.
Chapter 20   'The Irish Bombardier'.
Chapter 21   Letter to John Quinn, 1923.
Chapter 22   'The Greenlands'.

ILLUSTRATIONS

Reproductions on the following pages are by courtesy of:

Armagh County Museum 87, 88; Bord Fáilte Éireann (Brian Lynch) 31; Hugh Lane Municipal Gallery of Modem Art, Dublin 78; Midland Tribune Ltd., Birr 21; National Gallery of Ireland, 61, 68, 95, 100, 111, 114, 122, 139, 165, 192, 195; Sligo County Library and Museum, 39, 43, 66, 132; Trinity College Library, Manuscript Room, 23, 47.

All other illustrations are by courtesy of private owners.

Index

John Hamilton of Donegal, 1800-1884

THIS RECKLESSLY GENEROUS LANDLORD

Dermot James

Following the quite remarkable success of *The Wicklow World of Elizabeth Smith* (which was reprinted less than two months after publication), Dermot James has produced an even more ambitious work on the life of another benevolent landlord – arguably the most generous of all – John Hamilton of Donegal.

SOME REVIEWS

Dermot James has performed a worthy task in bringing this unique character to life in an intriguing book. Hamilton may have been untypical of his class, but that untypicality makes his life and labour so much more instructive.

The Irish Times

This book is a very interesting read . . . very well researched, a very valuable and unusual history of the times.

Gay Byrne, RTE Radio

It portrays John Hamilton as a man who won the respect and affection of his tenants. During the Famine only one of his tenants died of starvation and very few had recourse to the poor house or relief works.

The Impartial Reporter, Enniskillen

Dermot James has reconstructed the life of this county Donegal landlord in a readable and well-structured book which presents a man whose life simply does not fit the alien stereotype image.

The Church of Ireland Gazette

A full scale study of a very untypical landlord. . . . A thorough and very readable book.

Books Ireland

Price £10.95   ISBN 0-9528453-4-2

Published by The Woodfield Press,
17 Jamestown Square, Inchicore, Dublin 8.

ALSO PUBLISHED BY

The Woodfield Press

The Wicklow World of Elizabeth Smith (1840–1850)
edited by Dermot James and Séamas Ó Maitiú

The Sligo-Leitrim World of Kate Cullen (1832–1913)
revealed by Hilary Pyle

Ballyknockan: A Wicklow Stonecutters' Village
Séamas Ó Maitiú and Barry O'Reilly

The Tellicherry Five: The Transportation of Michael Dwyer and the Wicklow Rebels
Kieran Sheedy

John Hamilton of Donegal 1800–1884: This Recklessly Generous Landlord
Dermot James